HEAD OFF STRESS

Beyond the bottom line

D. E. Harding was no blinkered specialist. While a partner in a flourishing architectural practice, he taught comparative religion for Cambridge University. While a wartime major, he developed a unique means to spiritual enlightenment. He described his field as the meeting-place of psychology, physical science, philosophy and religion. His published works include a whodunnit, a philosophical treatise that took eight years to write, books on religion and the arts of living and dying and articles in the Transactional Analysis Journal, Architectural Review, Middle Way and the Saturday Evening Post. Ann Bancroft's 20th Century Mystics and Sages has a chapter on Harding as 'the man without a head' – a reputation which the Incredible String Band helped to establish with their Douglas Harding Song. Harding invented unique experiments for testing his hypothesis that we are not what we look like, and travelled the world sharing 'the headless way' – the way of *seeing* Who you really are. Harding died in 2007 at the age of 97.

D. E. Harding

HEAD OFF STRESS

Beyond the Bottom Line

With illustrations by the author

THE SHOLLOND TRUST

To Norm Taylor, who made me write this book

Published by The Shollond Trust
87B Cazenove Road
London N16 6BB
England
headexchange@gn.apc.org
www.headless.org

The Shollond Trust is a UK charity, reg. no 1059551

First published by Arkana 1990

Printed in the United Kingdom by Lightning Source UK Ltd, Milton Keynes

ISBN 978-0-9554512-0-1

CONTENTS

PREFACE   ix

PART ONE
BASIC PRINCIPLES   1
 1 Your Role and My Role   3
 2 The Basis   5
 3 First-aid Treatment for Stress   13

PART TWO
THE PRINCIPLES APPLIED TO EVERYDAY LIFE   19
 4 Eye Stress   21
 5 Facial Stress   26
 6 Body Stress   35
 7 Stress in Personal and Social Relationships   54
 8 Stress and the Pace of Modern Life   67
 9 Getting Rich Without Stress   83
10 How to Get Your Heart's Desire   98
11 Stress and the Human Predicament   112
12 Beyond the Stress World   125

PART THREE
STRESS AND LIFE'S STAGES   133
13 Childhood and Adolescence   135
14 Adulthood   152
    (i) Introduction   152
   (ii) Depression   156
  (iii) Indecision   174
  (iv) Failure   181
   (v) Loneliness   189
  (vi) Boredom   201
 (vii) Guilt   210
(viii) Sexual problems   218
  (ix) Life is difficult   226

(x) Conclusion – three ways of coping   239

15 Old Age   251
16 Death   259
17 The Beyond   277

PART FOUR
THE PRACTICE   297
18 The Practice   299

APPENDIX: The Prince, the Tadpole and the Frog   307
BIBLIOGRAPHY   323

TABLE OF EXPERIMENTS

1	Pointing	8
2	Finger pressing	9
3	Disappearing stress	14
4	Spectacles	22
5	Your two faces	26
6	Special inside information	35
7	General inside information	36
8	Down, in and through	41
9	An in-the-body experience?	44
10	In the bag	54
11	What moves?	70
12	The third person in orbit around the First Person	75
13	Motion builds	76
14	Cash in hand	84
15	Distance no object	86
16	Choosing what is	105
17	Trying on your safety-helmet, Part 1	114
18	Trying on your safety-helmet, Part 2	115
19	One world, inside-outside	130
20	Another bow before the evidence	158
21	The well of loneliness	196
22	Yet another bow before the evidence	266
23	The face of the world	289
24	360° vision	293

PREFACE

Dear Reader,

This is a wide open book. It makes its point from the start: so that if, on the first reading, you find yourself held up half way, you will nevertheless have got the point and missed nothing essential. In fact it is possible to get the gist of the message without opening the book at all, just from the cover.

It's like a swimming pool. Venturing in the shallow end, you can enjoy splashing about there; or go in waist-deep and swim a few strokes; or further in and swim strongly; or all the way to the deep end where you can swim underwater, or dive in from the highest board, without ever touching bottom. But the water – the hydro-therapeutic effect of it – is the same from end to end and from top to bottom. So don't worry if you find yourself happy only in the shallow end to start with: stay there as long as suits you, before venturing deeper.

Why (you may ask) if it's all made clear at the beginning, should I bother to write the last chapters, or you bother to read them? Because they are about how to apply and to live the discoveries made in the earlier ones. The anti-stress work advocated in this book is so simple and so easy that you can't do it wrong, and it's so searching that the therapy starts right away; but it is not so easy to keep up. See how you go, and remember that the ingrained habits of the stressful life aren't erased overnight. There's work to do – the most enjoyable I know – but it's indispensable.

That's why I must add: if you are held up half way through this book – say, at the end of Part Two – don't leave out Part Four at the end of the book, which is about daily practice. Following that practice will help you go back and tackle Part Three – unstressfully.

Douglas Harding
NACTON
Suffolk
England

PART ONE
BASIC PRINCIPLES

There is nothing like looking, if you want to find something.
J. R. R. Tolkien (Thorin speaking, *The Hobbit*)

The ignorant reject what they see but not what they think.
The wise reject what they think but not what they see.

Huang-po

Sit down before the fact as a little child, and be prepared to give up every preconceived notion; follow humbly wherever and to whatever abyss Nature leads, or you shall learn nothing.
T. H. Huxley

The aspects of things that are most important for us are hidden because of their simplicity and familiarity.

Ludwig Wittgenstein

1

YOUR ROLE AND MY ROLE

Long ago, the secret of transport turned out to be the simplest of all inventions – the *wheel*. Later on, the secret of mathematics turned out to be the simplest of all ideas – *zero*. In much the same way, the secret of the stress-free life turns out to be the simplest of all experiences – simple to point out, simple to get, simple to share, simple to renew. As, in the course of the next few pages, you will find out for yourself.

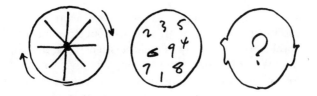

Your job will be to observe three rules:

The first is that you *carry out the tests*, the easy experiments I'm going to ask you to do. If you just read about them nothing will happen and you will be wasting your time.

The second is that you *go by what you find*, that you take seriously the results of the experiments. This means ignoring, at least for the duration of each test, things you have been brought up to believe, and looking for yourself. It means starting from scratch and trusting your own findings. It means being prepared for the discovery that you are more fortunate than you had ever dreamed of. I shall tell you exactly how to carry out the experiments. But they are all about you, and the ultimate authority on you is – Y O U. Just do what I ask, take heart and be open to yourself, and you can't go wrong.

3

The third rule is that you *realize your gains*, and make use of them. This means drawing on the anti-stress capital that is yours from the start. If you just let it lie there in the bank and refuse to write cheques on it, so to speak, you will go on living the life of a pauper – and one who is all the more stressful because, deep down, he knows that his poverty is self-inflicted. In plain language, take advantage of your discoveries, and be kind to yourself.

Please do your best to observe these three rules. For my part, I will show you how to get rid of stress, by a method that has five features:

It takes no time to learn.

At once you see what to do, and how to do it.

You can't do it wrong.

The switch-over to no stress is instant.

Afterwards, if you think you have lost the knack, you are wrong. It has lost you: your attention has been diverted.

To dump stress – what a prospect! But even before we start on the job this raises the question: 'If a life without stress means a life without problems, a perfectly peaceful existence – is this what I really want? Won't I be bored stiff (or bored flabby?) with nothing left to stretch me? In fact, won't I just be exchanging the stress of the troubled life I live now for the worse stress of unrelieved dullness and ennui?'

This book takes care of and resolves the contradiction between our desire on the one hand for a peaceful life and our desire on the other hand for excitement and adventure. In addition to its main guarantee of instant access to the Land of No Stress, is the assurance that you will miss none of the challenges, the thrills and the spills of the Land of Stress.

Does it all sound incredible, much too good to be true, and as yet mere vague generalities? I agree. So let's get down to business right away, and you'll see what I mean.

2

THE BASIS

NO THING, NO STRESS

Stress is a system of forces applied to a thing, plus its reactions to
them. For instance, this book is being pressed on all over by the
atmosphere, and in places by your fingers. It is also being pulled
downwards by gravity. It is under stress.

Everything on Earth is stressed. That includes liquids and gases,
no less than solids. The air we breathe and the water we drink are
under heavy pressure. Things in outer space are not exempt either.
The fact is that every body comprising the Universe is constantly
subject to the influence of every other body: as if each made its
living by playing sparring partner to the others. All are caught up
in an immense spider-web from which there's no escape.

What hope, then, of your breaking free? Why, the only reason you are able to sit upright reading this, and not collapse into a heap, is because your muscles are strenuously pulling against your bones.

Two escape routes lie open to you. The first is to become so small, so empty, so exclusive that there's nothing to you, nothing to be got at, nothing to act upon or react. The second is the opposite of this. It is to become so big, so full, so inclusive that there remains nothing outside you to get at you, nothing to pressurize you or to influence you at all, nothing left for you to react to.

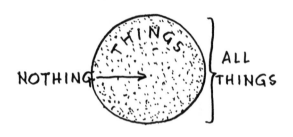

Let's put it differently. Particular things are stressed. If you were no thing you would be stress-free. Conversely, if you were all things you would, again, be stress-free. And if, by great good luck, you were both – if you were at once no thing and all things – why then you would be doubly stress-free, free beyond all doubt. This way, you would avoid being one of those unlucky intermediate things – things which are neither empty enough nor full enough to be free from stress. You would avoid falling between the two stools of total emptiness and total fullness, by sitting firmly on both stools at the same time. As nothing *and* everything you would be sitting pretty. You would be safe as well as comfortable. You would already have arrived at our goal. You would already be established in the promised Land of No Stress, no matter how long it took you to feel at home and to get acclimatized.

Well, I say you *are* sitting pretty, you *are* as lucky as that!

No: I'm not asking you to believe a word of this, but only to open yourself to the possibility that you are so fortunate. My business is to set up the tests that will enable you to make up your own mind on this most vital of issues. Your business is to go by what these experiments show you.

DISTANCE IS THE MAKING OF YOU

Ever since you appeared on the human scene, that scene has been bombarding you with the message that you are solid, opaque, coloured and shaped: which means you are some*thing*, which means that you are subject to stress.

Of course that's the way people see you. And of course they are right – from their position over there. And you are right to take up their viewpoint and, using your imagination, 'see' yourself as they see you – from (for example) two metres away. But that's not the end of the story. Viewed from a much greater distance, say 200 metres away, you look quite different: you are a blob in the landscape. Again, seen with the help of a microscope from a much smaller distance, say a centimetre away, you are another sort of blob in another sort of landscape. These views of you – near, middle distance and far – are just three of your appearances, which are infinite in number and variety. They all belong to you – *all* of them, and not just a few carefully selected middle-distance ones of you as a human being.

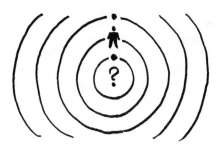

But there's one view of you which is quite special. Namely, how you look to yourself, not in imagination this time, but actually at a distance of zero inches, right where you are. This isn't one more of your countless regional *appearances* from different vantage points. It is what they are appearances of. It is the central *reality* that gives rise to them all. It is your inside story, revealed only to you. It is not what you *look like*. It is what you *are*.

And it is unique, absolutely different from anything you have ever come across. Don't take my word for it. See for yourself.

This brings us to our first experiment.

Please remember that it is no good going on unless you actually carry out this and the other experiments. However briefly, drop memory and imagination and belief and go by present evidence, by what's on show now. Be humble enough to look, and to take seriously what you find. Assume that what's presented has something important to tell you before you think your way round it and out of it, before you superimpose all sorts of ideas on it.

Experiment 1: Pointing

Point at the wall ahead . . . See how solid and opaque it is . . .

Now slowly bring your finger down till it is pointing at the floor . . . Still you are pointing at a something, a surface . . .

Next, bring your hand round and point to your feet . . . your legs . . . your trunk . . . your chest . . . Also somethings, also surfaces . . .

Finally, point to what is above your chest . . . to your neck . . . your face . . . your eyes . . . Or rather, to the place where people told you those things are to be found . . .

YOU ARE NOW POINTING AT NO SURFACE, AT NO THING AT ALL . . .

Check that it is featureless . . . colourless . . . transparent . . . boundless . . . Keep on pointing, seeing into emptiness . . . seeing how wide . . . how deep . . . how high . . . is this no-thing that is your side of that in-pointing finger . . .

And see how, just because it is so empty *of* everything, it is empty *for* everything. See how full it is of the whole colourful and changing scene – of the ceiling, the walls, the window and the view from it, the floor, those legs and that trunk and that pointing finger itself. See how the no thing that you are *is* all the things that are on show.

Have you ever been other than this NO-THING/ALL THINGS, this perfect union of stress-free exclusiveness and stress-free inclusiveness? Right now you can see that there is nothing inside you, that you have nothing of your own, on your side of that pointing finger, to be stressed, nothing to be got at. Equally you can see that this nothing, this emptiness of yours, has no limits upwards, or sideways, or downwards, no boundary beyond which an outsider could lurk, to bring pressure to bear on you. On both counts you are rid of stress forever because you – the real You that is no-thing/all-things – were never capable of it.

Congratulations!

Now I'm going to ask you to experience stress in a sample of those intermediate and particular things, and at the same time your freedom from that stress.

Experiment 2: Finger pressing

Hold out your hand and press your forefinger against your thumb as hard as you can . . .

Notice where the stress is, on present evidence – namely, in those things. And notice where the absence of stress is – namely, in yourself as the no-thing that is taking in those things, along with their shape and colour and opacity. Notice how *you* are no more

stressed by the stress in that hand than you are shaped by the shape of that hand, or coloured by the colour of that hand, or clouded by that hand's opacity. As empty for all things and their qualities and their stresses, you just can't help being different from all that. It is your essential nature to remain unaffected, as unstained and uninjured and unstressed as your T V screen is by all the murders and shootings and burnings that rage on it. As unsoiled as your mirror is by what it mirrors so faithfully and so unselectively.

In the following chapters we are going to apply this basic discovery to the problems of life, finding out exactly how to put it to use in those areas that until now have been experienced as stressful and distressful. We shall explore how important it is and how practical it is consciously to be no-thing/all-things; and how unpractical (as well as untruthful) to be just one of the countless things that fall between these two stools. In the course of this exploration the doubts and objections which are already occurring to you will be met, not so much by discussion, as by further experimenting.

Meanwhile, whenever you doubt your essential freedom from

all the ills that things are subject to, just attend to the one place in your universe where there is no occupant, which is thing-proof and therefore stress-proof. Cease overlooking this terribly neglected spot, this centre-point of your life, which on inspection instantly explodes into the universe, and all will come clear.

THREE CASES

To illustrate what the findings of this chapter mean in practice, let us conclude it by looking at three cases, three real people. The first is a Frenchman who, because he *things* himself so thoroughly, is uptight and awkward to the point of being ridiculous: or worse, a walking calamity. In a true sense he isn't a *real* person at all, but a living lie. The second is a Canadian girl who, living from the truth of her no-thingness, is beautifully at ease – a walking delight, you could say. The third is an American who discovers the unstressable no-thing right where he is, and turns out to be one of the more admirable presidents of the United States.

Jean-Paul Sartre, the celebrated French writer, is sitting in a café, fascinated by the behaviour of one of its waiters.

His movement is quick and forward, a little too precise, a little too rapid. He comes toward the customers with a step a little too quick. He bends forward a little too eagerly; his voice, his eyes, express an interest a little too solicitous for the order of the customer. Finally there he returns, trying to imitate in his walk the inflexible stiffness of some kind of automaton while carrying his tray with the recklessness of a tightrope-walker . . . All his behaviour seems to us a game. He applies himself to chaining his movements as if they were mechanisms; he gives himself the quickness and pitiless rapidity of things . . . He is playing at being *a waiter in a café*.

Let us take up the story. If, instead of playing at being *a waiter in a café*, he were to see that in his own immediate experience he is *the café itself*, along with all that is going on there (including those limbs of his, going about their own business), why, this phony and ineffectual waiter would turn into the opposite sort. If, instead of pretending to be a thing, he were to come off it and be no-thing: if he were to be himself for himself, he would be for others one of the best waiters in Paris instead of one of the worst. True to his reality, he would appear false to none.

He would resemble our second case – Karen, a Canadian girl who at the age of nine wrote this little poem:

> Have you ever felt like nobody –
> Just a tiny speck of air –
> With all those people around you
> And you are just not there?

Karen had the innocence and the courage to trust her own experience. She could have played the grown-ups' game and become a tense and shy little thing in a room full of bigger ones. Happy and fortunate Karen! Now herself an adult, I hope she hasn't altogether lost the sovereign art of vanishing into thin air, of unwinding into a no-thing-for-herself, of being, in short, a real person: that is, one who lets others take care of what she *looks like*, while she takes care of what she *is* – namely, unstressable capacity for them.

Our third instance is Woodrow Wilson, 28th President of the United States. He wrote:

> As a beauty I am not a star –
> There are others more handsome by far –
> But my face: I don't mind it,
> For I am behind it,
> It's the people in front get the jar!

It is not by chance that the man who came up with this wisest of limericks coped so bravely and creatively with the pressures of his job. He had a way through to the stress-free region behind the presidential façade and its tensions. The result for the people around him was not (we can be sure) so jarring as he playfully assumed.

FIRST-AID TREATMENT FOR STRESS

GO INTO THE TROUBLE

Life has a way of bouncing us, of knocking us off-centre and *catching us out, off-base*. Something unexpected and upsetting happens, and we suffer an acute attack of stress. It may be a bill for house repairs that is three times what we had expected, or some cruel remark dropped casually by a friend, or the death of a dear one. But we can also suffer stress for no apparent reason. Maybe we feel uptight, under pressure, depressed, put down or torn apart, without any idea why. This unaccounted-for stress can come up as a headache, or discomfort anywhere in the body.

At these times we need first-aid. This chapter is about such emergency measures, to be taken from time to time as needed – over and above the basic on-going anti-stress measures we are chiefly concerned with.

As in all first-aid, the initial and obvious thing to do is to remove the cause of the trouble, if at all possible. For instance, you can question that huge bill for house repairs, *going into it* in detail with the builder and (let's hope) 'disappearing' the items that won't survive scrutiny. Again, instead of avoiding your unkind friend, you can *approach* him and perhaps discover that there was nothing in his hurtful remark after all. It was by withdrawing from him that you made a mountain out of a molehill. As for that dear one of yours who died, maybe the time of mourning is over, and you are ready to realize that, though his temporary human appearance is no longer around, his Reality is just as available. The Aware no-thing that both of you really are is forever, and in seeing you are This you are perhaps nearer to him than ever before. In fact, you *are* him, in the place where bereavement and its stresses can never penetrate.

To an amazing extent our troubles, our stresses and distresses, are the result of keeping our distance, or actually running away from them. When we go up to them they vanish like a mirage.

This initial step in our first-aid treatment for stress establishes the direction of the whole treatment. The rule is the same throughout this book: *close in on the trouble. Get down to it: the road to freedom is down, in and through: not up, out and away.*

At this moment you may not be suffering from acute stress. But you can easily find some lurking body-tensions to try out our first-aid treatment on. Please now spend a minute or so locating an area of stress – however slight – some region that feels too tight, too much in evidence, achy, or actually painful . . . It may be in your neck . . . the region around your mouth or eyes . . . or just about anywhere in your body . . .

Right. You've picked your area of stress. Please stick to it through the experiment that's coming up. Above all, take your time and answer each question carefully, *on present evidence*, before going on to the next question. To succeed, you will need to spend at least five minutes doing:

Experiment 3: Disappearing stress

Exactly *where* in the room do you now find this tensed-up region, *on present evidence* . . .? How high off the floor does it appear to be . . .? How far down from the ceiling . . .? How distant from that wall ahead . . .?

Is it *one* volume, or split into two parts . . .? Or more . . .?

How *big* is it . . .? Try to locate its boundaries . . . sideways . . . upwards . . . downwards . . .

What is its *shape* . . .? Square . . .? Round . . .? Lens-shaped . . .?

What *colour* is it, if any . . .? Pinkish . . .? Greyish . . .?

Is it *fixed* . . .? Or moving around . . .?

Is it *pulsing* . . .? Or quite steady . . .?

If you've been carrying out this experiment conscientiously and spending some minutes over it, you are probably finding it harder and harder to discover any stress to look into. Most likely it has vanished altogether, at least for the moment.

Of course, having 'disappeared' the tension or pain, you may very easily 'reappear' it by thinking *about* it, which means retreating from it. You have to coincide with the trouble for it to go.

It is a fact that body tensions will not stand up to really close inspection – given enough time and attention. This is because they are attributes of your body, which (like everything else) vanishes as it is approached. It is *distance* that makes some-*thing* of you and your stresses, and the folding of that distance which makes no-*thing* of you and them.

Don't let life go on *catching you out, off-base, out to lunch*. Only come Home, only be the no-thing you are anyway, and all is taken care of. As there is calm at the eye of the cyclone, so there is relief from stress at the centre of life's tempest – and that's your permanent address. Imitate the beetle who escaped from the hungry tortoise by creeping into its shell. Making for the focal point of the danger was enough to dissolve it.

When I was very little my father had a magical method of 'making the pain go away'. One occasion stays vivid in my memory. I had fallen and hurt my leg. He held a penny (an old-time, large English penny) to the bruise. The magic worked. I homed-in on the reason for my crying – and lost it. The pain did indeed go away from me, as my father had promised it would, because I ceased going away from it.

All this applies equally to mental stress and negative emotions. They, too, thrive on avoidance, on distance. Dr Hans Selye, the noted stress expert, writes: 'It is well-established that the mere fact of knowing what hurts you has an inherent curative value.' You are hurt, or sad, or angry, or apprehensive? All right, *be* like that! Don't sidestep the hurt or pretend it isn't there. It *is* there. Go deeply into it. Really get to know what it is like. And find out what happens when it is not there, but *here.*

FIRST-AID MEASURES AND LONG-TERM TREATMENT

So it turns out that our first-aid treatment for stress is essentially the same as our basic and long-term treatment (which is, let's remind ourselves, ceasing to overlook the stress-free centre which anyway we're living from). The difference doesn't lie in the medicine's formula but in its use. The long-term treatment can (and should) go on throughout our everyday activities. So, far from preventing you from attending to the cooking and the baby, or dictating difficult letters, or driving safely, or chairing a meeting, it may be counted on to help those jobs along. Not so the first-aid treatment. Going up to and 'disappearing' your headache takes time and concentration on that alone, and will hold up work in the home or the office or anywhere else. There are occasions when it would be dangerous. It's for you to apply these two sorts of stress treatment as required – one every day and (ultimately) all day, the other in emergencies and particular trouble spots, with discretion.

I should add the warning that our first-aid treatment for stress is unlike ordinary first-aid inasmuch as results are hard or impossible to predict. The principle – that what we close in upon we abolish – admits of no exceptions. However, its application – notably the degree and length of our concentration – is another matter. We have every reason to try this treatment for all we are worth, no reason for regarding it as foolproof or a sure way of getting results at the level where we are seeking them. It can work miracles, but it can *seem* not to work at all.

The good news is that our first-aid treatment is rather more than mere first-aid, or just a makeshift way through a crisis. It *reinforces* the long-term treatment. Psychologists and experience tell us that the circumstances accompanying moments of great stress make a deep impression on us. As a boy of around seven I was once chased through town by a ferocious dog. Running away from trouble was, of course, only bringing it on: I should have stood my ground. I remember the scene well, the staring people and the houses streaking by – all of it registered for life because at that moment I was as stressed and distressed as I've ever been.

You can make positive use of this principle. By *welcoming* stressful occasions as urgent warnings to get back to your stress-free Home, you can build this helpful association between the dis-ease and its easing, between your stress and the unstressable core of you. To un-thing yourself when all's going well is good habit-forming practice. But un-thinging yourself when all's going badly is better still. Then the act of homing-in makes a deeper impression, and life in future is that much less likely to catch you out, or napping.

PART TWO

THE PRINCIPLES APPLIED TO EVERYDAY LIFE

Men have left their own country, their fathers and mothers, their households and kinsmen and families, and have journeyed from Hind to Sind, wearing boots of iron till they wore out to shreds, on the chance of meeting One having the fragrance of the other world. How many men have died of this sorrow, not succeeding in meeting such a One. As for you, you have met such a One here in your own house, and you turn your back on him.

Rumi

Forgetfulness of the Self is the source of all misery.

Ramana Maharshi

Most of our tensions and frustrations stem from the compulsive need to act the role of someone we are not.

Dr Hans Selye, *The Stress of Life*

PART TWO is about the day-by-day treatment of stress where it happens to crop up.

In it we work outwards from the stress in our eyes, our faces, and our bodies as a whole, through to our relationships with people, and to the world itself. The same principle of *DOWN-IN-THROUGH* holds at every level, but we shall find that its application varies a great deal and has many surprises for us.

4

EYE STRESS

THE TROUBLE WITH YOUR EYES

Everybody has unwanted muscular tensions from time to time. These tend to be very noticeable in your neck and face, and especially around your eyes. They are bad for you.

Dr Edmund Jackson, of the University of Chicago, claims that if you can only relax the muscles of your eyes you can forget all your troubles! He estimates that the tension around your eyes can account for as much as a quarter of the nervous energies burned up by your body. Encouraged and warned by these claims (without taking them for gospel truth), we shall in this chapter be finding out what to do about eye-strain and the damage it does to our life.

OPENING YOUR THIRD EYE

There is an ancient and much-to-be-desired experience, better known in the East than the West, called 'the Opening of the Third Eye'. This mysterious organ is situated, according to Eastern iconography, midway between the eyes and slightly above them.

Many imagine that this opening of your single or third eye is merely figurative, more to do with a change in what you're looking at than a change in what you're looking out of. They say it means you come suddenly (for whatever reason) to enjoy an enlightened or godlike or unified outlook on life. A few, taking the message all too literally, have (believe it or not!) had holes bored in their foreheads. But there are those who claim that the experience of looking out of one central eye at the world isn't figurative at all, but is as real as can be, and moreover that it holds the secret

of our well-being. One Near Eastern teacher linked having a single eye with the enjoyment of one's body as full of light, and with entering into life; and linked having two eyes with entering into hell. And for hell we may read the Land of Stress.

The turning point in the life of Ramakrishna, a famous Indian sage of a century ago, was when he was approached by a wandering holy man who took a splinter of glass and stuck it between the sage's eyes, and told him to concentrate on that. After a brief period of getting used to the turnabout, Ramakrishna's life became quite exceptionally spontaneous, lively yet relaxed and stress-free. So much so that he was one of the greatest of those who inspired the national renaissance of India in his time. I mention his contribution to history so that you will not be tempted to underrate what happened to him, or to dismiss what's about to happen to you. (But don't worry: the operation we perform here is a gentler, a less surgical means of opening your Eye – but one which is nevertheless just as effective.)

Experiment 4: Spectacles

How many eyes are you now looking out of, in your own experience?

If you have glasses, hold them out at arm's length. If you don't, simulate a pair with your fingers.

Now very slowly ... bring them forward, watching what's happening to them ... Put them on and lower your hands.

How many eyes did you *think* you were looking out of, at the start of the experiment? And now ...? How many do you *experience* looking out of?

See how perfectly those twin glasses are remodelled on the way in, to become a neatly framed monocle for the Single Eye.

Your Single or Third Eye is wide open. Congratulations! Did you ever look out of any other?

You can check how splendidly *wide-eyed* you are – how huge your Third Eye is – very easily indeed. Outline its extent and shape with your outstretched hands, held so widely apart that they almost vanish; and see how it's not so much an Eye as an open window – a huge, oval, glassless, *frameless* Opening on the world, a H O L E. Not a hole *in* something but simply a hole, edgeless and worldwide. (Imagine those absurd people trying to open *this* out with their electric drills!) And it's a hole that is doubly stress-free – visibly having nothing inside it to suffer stress, or outside it to impose stress.

Don't let people tell you what you are looking out of. They are in no position to say, wide of the mark by feet and yards. That celebrated and ancient Third Eye experience is perfectly real and perfectly obvious (once you get around to looking), and it works, and you can have it any time you like. Try it for eye-strain.

The stress and the strain we suffer, the energy we squander, trying to build things where no things can be! Trying, in this instance, to do as we're told and set up at the empty centre of our universe-of-things a pair of things to see it with – things that could only get in the way and block the view. Trying, indeed, to pretend that *things* could ever see anything. No wonder the faces of animals and babies, who make no such attempts at the impossible, are wide-eyed and serene and never screwed up in the slightest. They are all looking through their Single Eye without pretending otherwise. Or not so much *looking through* it as simply *being* it.

It's instructive to discover what young children make of their eyes. I'm thinking of those who are no longer infants and unconsciously single-eyed, and not yet adults and sure they are two-eyed. Some draw themselves with one eye. Others, growing up fast and taking their cue from the faces they see around, draw two. Johnny, at two years and three months, has other ideas. He asks his mother to draw a picture. She makes a circle for a face, and asks: what next? Johnny asks for a trunk to be added, then trousers, then feet, then hands. Next he wants eyes, so his mother draws two. But he insists on more and more until the whole face is covered with eyes. Only then does he declare the drawing finished.

For ages the wise, including the Near Eastern teacher I mentioned earlier, have been telling us that the really important lessons are to be learned from children. We can certainly take a hint from young Johnny. The continuing practice that this chapter aims at is being *all eyes* (as we say), which means consciously being so wide open to the scene that one *is* the scene. It's so easy and comfortable and natural to notice simultaneously what you're looking *at* and what you're looking *out of*; easy and comfortable and natural to live that saying of Meister Eckhart – 'We cannot see the visible except with the invisible.' After all, what could be more unnatural and unnecessary – if not plain crazy – than to interpose between you and the scene ahead a pair of ghostly and displaced eyeballs? (People over there – including the one over there in your mirror – have faces for keeping eyeballs in; here, you have nothing of the kind.) I know of no simpler, no more pleasurable, no more available yet unobtrusive way of coping with stress, than this well-tested Opening of the Third Eye. And the joke is this: while people may notice the new light in your eyes, and the unusual relaxation in the muscles around them, they've no clue to your secret – which is that, right where you are, you have shed those very things!

At the start of this chapter I quoted Dr Jackson's opinion that, if only you can relax the muscles of your eyes, you can forget all your troubles. Well, you now have a precise way of putting that very large claim to the test: a lifelong one.

Meanwhile, of this be sure: to end eye-stress, *look out of no eyes*. Right now you can see that what's taking in these printed words is no-thing, and it's perfectly relaxed.

5

FACIAL STRESS

YOUR ORIGINAL FACE

This chapter is about stress in your face–head–neck region. It's also about a very basic and effective kind of beauty treatment.

All things are stressed. Imagining yourself to be one of those things, you *take on* its stresses. But seeing that in fact you are empty for that thing, you *let go of* its stresses. Let's see what happens when that thing is your face.

Experiment 5: Your two faces

If you haven't got an oval or round hand-mirror an ordinary rectangular one will do. Hold out the mirror, find your face in it, and keep it there throughout the experiment.

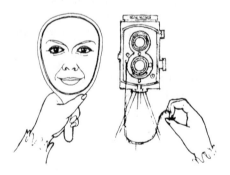

Dropping belief and imagination, see where that face presents itself . . . Notice the place where you keep it – at the *far* end of your arm . . .

This is where others, too, pick it up. This is where they hold their cameras to photograph it. And where you put your camera to make a self-portrait. It has never been much nearer to you than that, or much further away.

Moreover you can now see that that thing is not, and has never been, at the *near* end of your arm, mounted on *these* shoulders . . .

There, a metre or so away, is your human face, your acquired face, your appearance. It is a thing. *Here*, right here, is your non-human Face, your Original Face, your Reality. It is not a thing. See now how great the contrast is between them. See how spotlessly clear and unlined the complexion of this one is, how wide open and serene its expression, how relaxed: and – yes – how beautiful! And that little, closed-up face over there? Well, that's for the people around to cope with. It's they who are jarred.

This isn't a new-fangled and untested treatment you can't trust. On the contrary, it has a long and respectable history. A 1,000-year-old Buddhist text describes what you have just seen, on the *near* side of the glass in your mirror, as your 'bright and charming Original Face', and it would be surprising if, given time and attention, some of the brightness and charm didn't rub off on to that very different face on the *far* side of that glass. In fact, there is an ancient Indian text that assures us that it does so. It tells of a royal couple whose lifestyles were drifting apart. Unlike the queen, the king was so preoccupied with affairs (whether affairs of state or otherwise, we aren't told) that he had no time for Self-discovery. After some years together, the king suddenly awoke to the change that had been happening to the queen. 'Why are you so charming?' he asked. The reason, she told him, was that she had found her Self: she saw into her true Nature. The rest of the tale – how upset the king was, how he turned her out of the palace, how he realized, eventually, his own need to discover his true Identity, how he retired to the forest and found his guru there (who turned out to be the queen in disguise) – all this is delightful, but beside the point. Our point here is that, when the queen went on seeing exactly what you now see (I take it you sincerely carried out Experiment 5) – namely, her central and non-human Face – the effect on her peripheral and human face could not be hidden, even from her unobservant and preoccupied husband.

All that was long ago and far away. It was also about the *long-term* benefit of distinguishing between your two faces and putting each where it belongs. Let us now look at a recent story of a very different sort: one that is as much concerned with first-aid as with long-term results, but nevertheless carries the same message.

Eighteen years old, good-looking and intelligent, Marjory was one of the young ladies at an expensive finishing-school where I'd been invited to conduct a workshop, in the course of which we carried out most of the foregoing experiments. The next day she came to me, in great distress. She had been too troubled, too uptight, to attend to what was going on in that workshop. In fact, for months she had felt suicidal. Life, she said, wasn't worth living, and the main reason was that she was so 'unattractive'. Her face – her nose in particular – was 'horrible'. She hoped I could help, but very much doubted it.

It was no good telling Marjory that her nose was far less snub than she imagined, and that she was rather above average in looks. She just didn't believe me. And it was no good suggesting that she study a selection of the many excellent handbooks on stress-reduction, or seek psychiatric treatment, or go in for meditation or relaxation exercises. She was desperate, and summary measures were called for. Nothing less than an instant face-lift would do. I simply showed her where she kept that 'horrible' thing. I made clear to her how at that moment that thing was *my* business, my problem (or privilege), and not her business. It was enough. Enough, at that moment, to transfigure her face by relieving its stresses ... Later, I learned that her teachers were astonished at the change in her. Since then, my infrequent contacts with Marjory confirm that the face-lift held. There had been nothing wrong with her appearance except its *location*.

NO GOING BACK

Typically, Marjory's sort of trouble is at its worst in our teens, for it is then that most of us finally take on our acquired faces and lose our Original Face. Earlier, though we have given that face in the mirror a name and acknowledged it as ours, we are still *at large* much of the time, still able and happy to coincide with our world. Earlier still, even that face in the mirror is only one more item in that world. Kate, aged four, came with her parents to my house, where the living area has a number of full-length mirrors. Pointing to herself in one of them, Kate asked: 'Has that little girl got a mother, too?' Needless to say, Kate's face was as relaxed and pretty as you could have wished for.

Which reminds me of two other children. The first is two-year-old Joan who, sent to the bathroom to wash her dirty face, began to wash that face in the mirror – her true Face being, of course, spotlessly clean! The second is three-year-old Andrew, who was hurt in a motor accident. He went to see his friend, taking along with him a mirror – to show his friend the stitches in his face!

When you were very little you saw that face in the mirror as 'baby', as another, as your little friend out there, not as you here. But you learned to take over that face, lifting it (pretending to lift it) all the way from behind that glass out there to your shoulders here, enlarging it and twisting it round in the process. Thus you traded your Original Face, which is empty of stress because it is no-thing, for your acquired face, which is full of stress because it is a thing. You are now reneging on that very bad deal, returning that thing to where in fact it has always been – at arm's length. You are coming clean, ceasing to play that most elaborate of dirty tricks on yourself.

This is real beauty treatment. For you are attractive insofar as you are wearing your true Face (true, because it's here); and less attractive, or unattractive, or actually repellent and off-putting, insofar as you are wearing your false face (false, because it isn't here). This must be so because your true and unmasked Face, having nothing of its own, is an open invitation to all things and to all comers. It has to let them in. It needs every face as a vacuum needs filling. It *attracts* them as a magnet attracts iron. Conversely, that false face which is your mask, being one of many masks, has to

29

keep the others out in order to be recognizable at all. Like all objects it occupies a space from which all other objects are excluded.

How do we learn the stressful and indeed fatal trick of dismantling that face in the mirror and rebuilding it here? Well, by all sorts of means. By sacrificing our experience to the language which insists that you and I are face to face. By pretending you are in my shoes, seeing yourself through my eyes, and I'm in your shoes, seeing myself through your eyes. And by having fun with mother when she plays games with us, like this one:

As she repeats each line of this nursery rhyme, she puts her finger (or baby's) on his forehead, eye, nose, mouth, etc., in turn:

> Brow bender,
> Eye peeper,
> Nose dreeper,
> Mouth eater,
> Chin chopper
> Knock at the door,
> Ring the bell,
> Lift the hatch.
> Walk in . . .

We grown-ups can't unwind our stress, with its telltale effect on our faces, by going back behind all this game-playing and trickery and indoctrination, and regaining our lost innocence. Nevertheless, many of us try to do just that, by means of alcohol and other drugs. The results, though expensive and temporary, can bear a striking similarity to the real experience. My friend Wilfred Gotham tells me that his father, while returning home unsteadily from a regimental dinner with a bottle of spirits in his hip pocket, met with an accident which smashed the bottle. Next morning, Wilf's mother was puzzled to find surgical tape stuck on the bedroom mirror! *In vino veritas.*

No, you can't shed its stress by going back to the time when that face in the mirror wasn't yours at all. You have to go on to admit it is yours, just as the soles of your feet and your house and your country and a billion other things are yours, while none of them is

YOU – or remotely like YOU. Your mirror has become a stress-inducer, but now you can put it to better use as a stress-remover – by looking in it to see what you are *not* like!

From now on, every time you catch sight of that face in the glass, you can say to it: 'Thank heavens I'm nothing like you! However relaxed and good-looking you may (or may not) be, I am infinitely more *attractive*! Here, as this Vacuum, I draw the whole world to me!'

THE SEERS

The relevance of the discoveries we've made in this chapter – their importance for living the unstressful life we're aiming at – may be judged by looking at them in the light of history. I'm thinking, in particular, of the history of the Eastern disciplines of Zen and Sufism. The early Zen (Chan) masters of the Tang dynasty described their experience as 'seeing their Original Face', and the Zen life as living from that vision. In our terms it was (and is) returning our acquired and human face to where it belongs, among those other stressful things on the *far* side of the glass in our mirror; and ceasing to overlook our true and non-human and featureless (and therefore unstressable) Face on the *near* side. Later Zen developed many complications, notably all manner of *koans*, or subjects laid down for meditation. However, according to the Japanese master Daito Kokushi (National Teacher, 1281–1337), the purpose of all the 1,700 *koans* of Zen is to point us beyond conceptual thinking to the clear seeing of our Original Face. 'When thought is put down,' he says, 'the Original Face appears.'

The greatest of Sufi masters and poets was Jalalu'l-Din Rumi (1207–1273). Here are just a few of his many comments on our True and Featureless Face:

Everyone likes a mirror, while not knowing the true nature of his Face. After all, how long does a reflection remain in view? Make a practice of contemplating the Origin of the reflection . . .

His form has passed away, he has become a Mirror: naught is there but the image of another's face.

He that beholds his own Face – his light is greater than the light of the creatures. Though he die, his sight is everlasting, because his sight is the sight of the Creator.

I could have taken passages from other famous Seers belonging to other traditions, to the same effect. But the message is clear. It is that, of all humans, it is these Seers of their Face who (whatever their religion or lack of it) are confident that they have overcome stress and arrived at felicity.

What they saw is none other than what you, dear Reader, are seeing as (yet again) you look at what this pointing finger is pointing at.

THE ADVERTISERS

All this (I hear you say) is old hat, not for today. Then let's go contemporary. And what could be more up-to-the-minute than our wonderful consumer society and its values, and the wonderful advertising industry that is dedicated to keeping it on the boil, at the height of its fever?

With reason, there's a lot of talk about the subtleties and inventiveness of this industry, culminating in subliminal persuasion by means of images not consciously taken in. Just so. Take a case in point. You plan to sell me merchandise (much of which, incidentally, is stress-generating) to alleviate my stress. Well, here's the smart way to go about it. Whether the product is bad for me (like cigarettes and vodka), or good for me (like a soothing malt drink at bedtime), or plain silly (like a new car with a fancy dashboard and fancier registration number), makes no difference. In any case, you get at me as I am, not as I appear to be. And you do so without my realizing at all (and maybe without *your* realizing clearly, either) what the blazes is going on. Nestling unobserved below the artwork glamorizing all those goodies that can never relieve my stress, is the One Goody that can always do so. If I have the sense to let it.

And it's the unholy (if not consciously cynical) juxtaposition of these two – the overt but false promise of relief and the concealed but true promise of relief – that does wonders for the company's sales graph. The advertising copy really does display my stress cure with unmatched clarity, but in such a context that its healing properties seem to ascend from the perceiver of the goods to the goods themselves. Oh very subtle! Those media boys need even more watching than we supposed!

Or, if it's a religious product you're flogging, you could do worse than take your cue from the ancient Egyptian goddess Selkhit, who is sometimes depicted first-person fashion instead of third-person fashion. Here she's promoting sun worship as the

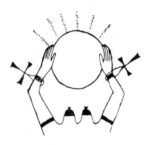

remedy for stress, and her sales pitch seems (with a finesse you might expect from a 2,500-year-old commercial) to be the feminine half of the market. The half that surely knows, in its heart of hearts, that a suntan doesn't go deep enough or last long enough, and that the best beauty treatment is a face unstressed – so unstressed that it isn't there at all!

Thanks, of course, to daily applications of her fabulous but incredibly low-priced Vanishing Cream!

6

BODY STRESS

EMBODIMENT

We have been looking at stress in particular body areas – in your eye region, and in the region of your face and neck. Now we come to your body as a whole, to the less localized stress that goes with having a body at all, to the price you pay for embodiment or incarnation, for being some-body and not no-body.

Apparently you are condemned to suffer some stress – at least that chronic, low-level stress that goes with embodiment – as long as you live on earth. Only at death, it seems, is there a way out, release from all stress. Well, let's see. First, let's take stock of your actual situation at this moment. What is your corporeal status, so to speak?

It is a curious one. Of the innumerable things the world contains, just one of them is special. It doesn't look special, but much like the others. What's so special about it is that you are *in* it, as they say. You alone have inside information about it. Apparently you inhabit it. You find yourself stuck in this thing you call your body. An easy test will bring out what it is to be like this:

Experiment 6: Special inside information

Take, as a fair sample of the things in the world, those which happen at this moment to be around: one of which you are supposedly inside.

Look around. You aren't in that wall, that picture, that table, that pot-plant, this book . . .

But you are in the hand that's holding the book . . .

What does this mean, in practice?

It means that you experience what's going on in that hand, but not what's going on in that plant and the rest. For instance, feel that hand with the fingers of your other hand, moving them back and forth. Result: sensations in there . . .

Now pinch that hand hard. Result: another sort of sensation in there . . .

Now treat the plant (or this book) similarly, stroking and rustling and pressing its leaves, and note that you have no access to what's happening in there . . .

Let's go on now to find out what inside information you have about your body as a whole.

Experiment 7: General inside information

Begin by looking at those feet, and slowly work down (I mean *down*) your body, noticing how it feels in there as you go.

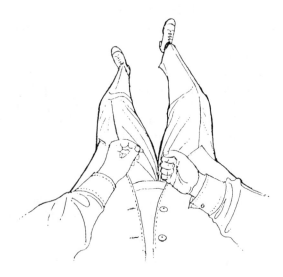

Note particular sensations such as aches and pains, but give attention also to the less definable feeling of what it's like anyway – pains or no pains – to be stationed *inside* the thing you are looking at . . .

Check that, as you come to your thighs . . . your abdomen . . . your chest . . . there's an increasing sensation of mass, solidity, density, concreteness . . . of confinement and compaction, of weight, of a lump . . . Make your own selection of these terms, and add your own, to bring to your notice this fugitive but fundamental experience of embodiment, of being physical . . .

If you are weighed down with care just now, or depressed, or heavy-hearted or downhearted, you will recognize only too well what I mean. And even if, on the other hand, there's no severe or nagging stress or pain in there at the moment, at least you have hints of something of the kind – of a variety of discomforts and tensions and pressures and warmths and tickles which (though for the most part overlooked) are around all right as ever-present reminders of what it is to be embodied. Together, acknowledged or ignored, they add up to the strong sense of being just this one thing in a world of things, somebody and not everybody or nobody. It's because it's so deep-seated and pervasive and unremit-ting that we take it so for granted, and are so little aware of its continuing presence – even when we are in pain.

IMPRISONMENT?

We come now to an astonishing fact – one either ignored or flatly contradicted here in the West. Or we could call it the other side of the coin we have been examining. Turn it over, and the contrast is total.

Down the centuries it has been one of the most insisted-on and durable teachings of Eastern masters (particularly Hindu ones) that the sense of being the body, or being in the body, is bondage, illusion, stress, every sort of misery: in a word, *hell*. And that heaven, or liberation, or Self-realization is none other than release, while this side of the grave, from the body-prison. To find oneself at large and unbodied, free and unbounded as the wind – this (according to those who claim to have broken out) is to shed the troubles that flesh is heir to, and arrive at the bliss of Nirvana. In the Buddhist Pali Canon, for example, a sharp distinction is drawn between the person who 'lives in a small hardness' and the person who 'lives in the immensity', and one is left in no doubt which of them lives the heavenly life and which the hellish.

Here we have a seemingly insoluble puzzle. The masters who most insist on our freedom from the body are among the most revered. They are seen as exceptionally wise and happy. How, in that case, are they able, while still no different from the rest of us to look at (eating, drinking, defecating, urinating like you and me, and as weighable and measurable and photographable and prone to disease as anyone) – how can they deny what it's like in there, deny that they are in the body at all, without self-deception or else plain lying? It may be delightful, it may be wonderfully exalting and spiritual, to feel oneself so free and so at large: but if it's a stolen delight, there's a penalty attached to it. If it is uplift bought at the expense of its physical foundation, a high price will be exacted in the end. To cut oneself off from the base-camp from which alone those spectacular ascents of Everest are made, is to store up trouble for the climber. As for ourselves now, how to reconcile these two seemingly incompatible accounts of our condi-tion – as trapped and free, as boxed up and out of the box, as small and immense, as contained in one of the things in the world and as uncontainable?

Well, it can be done. It must be done. More importantly, the reconciliation can and must be lived. In this chapter we shall see how: how we can escape from the body-prison without being escapists and self-deluded: how we can have our bodies without being had by them: how we can make the best of both worlds and be at last truly spiritual because we are truly physical, and truly physical because we are truly spiritual. Yes: it's an ambitious task we're setting ourselves. That is why this chapter is a long one. It lies at the heart of our inquiry.

As a preliminary, let's briefly examine three or four of the escape routes that have been taken by others, before we settle on our own – on the one that's practicable for us now, and requires us to tell no lies.

Escape route (i): Exhaustion and pain

Norman F. Ellison was a British soldier in Flanders during the First World War. On one occasion, having marched many miles in appalling conditions, he found himself exhausted, drenched, freezing, famished, pushed beyond endurance. It was the worst night of his life. He wrote in his diary:

> Then an amazing change came over me. I became conscious, acutely conscious that I was outside my fleshly body. I was looking in a wholly detached and impersonal way upon the discomforts of a khaki-clad body ... that might easily have belonged to someone else.

Later, his companions reported that his grim silence had suddenly given place to wit and humour, and he had chatted as unconcernedly as if before a comfortable fire.

Many similar cases have been reported. I recall reading of a prisoner on Devil's Island who was repeatedly put in a straitjacket, and the straps pulled tighter and tighter as a punishment. A more severe and stressful *in*-the-body experience is hard to imagine. It proved, he said later, just the opposite – a relaxing *out*-of-the-body one. At the time, his tormentors were puzzled to find that suddenly he appeared to be happy and at ease.

Escape route (ii): At death's door

Modern resuscitation techniques have produced a literature and an acronym – NDEs, near-death experiences, book on book about them. Ever increasing numbers of patients are being brought back to life to tell of their adventures, which frequently include the sensation of leaving the body. They describe how they looked down from above at that inert form on the bed being attended to by nurses and doctors, or lying mangled and bloody in a car-smash – as if they were watching a film or a play. Most report that, at first, they wanted to get back into their bodies but didn't know how to do so. Others weren't so keen. They felt exceptionally peaceful, at ease, not at all frightened, and by no means anxious to be dragged down and back into that dense and pain-racked lump of material.

My friend Sarah Naegle describes a near-death experience of hers, following a long and serious operation. Hovering near the ceiling, feeling so light and free, she looked down unconcernedly at the medical staff busy with that body. Her return to it was an ordeal. Not just the pain, but the feeling of 'great heaviness and pressure', is what she vividly remembers. That dead weight normally passes unnoticed because of its familiarity: but take a holiday from it (as Sarah did) and come back, and how leaden this in-the-body experience can be, how miserably constricted!

Escape route (iii): The psychic and psychedelic ways out

Some people claim to have the gift of 'astral travelling', of taking off at will into space and leaving the body in a state of suspended animation on the bed. While neither possessing nor desiring such a faculty myself, I see no reason for denying that others (and not only shamans) have it. Accounts of their journeys abound in a wide range of cultures from early times to the present day. If you wanted to develop such a supernormal power you could seek training under experts who, we are assured, are to be found in such places as Tibet and India and Mexico. The price in time and effort would no doubt be high, with no success guaranteed. However, once achieved, these out-of-the-body experiences no doubt provide a pleasurable vacation from the pains and stresses of physical existence. To coast along up there, a spirit or phantom in space, is far from being huge and empty as space itself, but how lightsome and free-ranging it must feel compared with finding yourself en-capsulated in one of those solid and creeping little bodies down below! It must be a relief to have Hamlet's prayer – 'Oh that this too, too solid flesh would melt!' – so marvellously answered, albeit not by disposing of the body-vehicle but by short-term parking.

Psychedelic drugs offer, and can sometimes furnish, similar out-of-the-body trips. Nor does one have to go on tripping to get some benefit from them. A little experimentation has been enough to show numbers of drug-users that release from the body-prison is possible and what it may be like, so that they are encouraged to seek safer and more legitimate means to the same end. At least (they point out) one has some idea now of what one's looking for.

Our own route

For one reason or another, none of these escape routes from the body is open to us here. Unless we are dyed-in-the-wool masochists or religious fanatics, we shall not go for extremes of pain and exhaustion, with no certainty that they won't plunge us further into the depths of bodily stress instead of releasing us. Nor are we willing to wait for this release till we stand at death's door: we are after what may be had now. As for the psychic and psychedelic ways out of the body-prison, the freedom they offer us is too uncertain and too brief. Early re-arrest is to be expected, followed very likely by closer confinement and other penalties. In short, the defect of the first and second of these ways out is that they aren't available now, and the defect of the third and fourth is that (in an important respect) they are the opposite of what we are after. Evading rather than solving the problem, they go up and out, up and away. Our route lies down and in and through.

Experiment 8: Down, in and through

This is a variation on our very first experiment (p. 8), which still has much to reveal. It can't be done too often. If one gets the point – and how can one miss it? – every time is a first time. Go slowly.

Starting at the top of your body *as given* (and I mean *top*), point to your legs, noting the threefold and roughly symmetrical set-up:

THING (finger) ... GAP ... THING (legs)

Attend to the sensations in those legs ...

Working down, turn your finger to point to your thighs ...

Working down still further, turn your finger to point to your middle, noting the same threefold set-up . . .

Linger here while you feel the weight, compaction, density of that thing's interior . . . increasing towards the region of your heart . . .

As you breathe out and hold your breath a little while, have the sense of being in there and weighted down, down, down . . . as if all the heaviness of the world had settled there, had sunk to its lowest point . . .

Stay there till the feeling of weight and confinement is complete . . .

And now look up, look straight ahead, bringing your finger round till it is pointing at what's below your chest – at the lowest spot of all, the spot you're looking out of . . .

See how the set-up has suddenly changed to

THING (finger) . . . NO GAP . . . NO THING

Look, look, look at the spot you're looking out of . . .

What spot . . .?

See how, suddenly, at your lowest point, at the point of your greatest implosion, you break through . . . you explode into being the wide, wide world . . .

Look now, at your Immensity . . . from your Immensity . . .

Be that Immensity . . .

What nuclear blast can match this quiet explosion, in range and in power?

Look again, and marvel at the delusion that you were ever,

ever, for a moment shut up in that little lump of stuff called a human body . . .

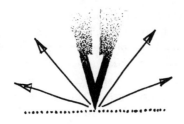

JAIL-BREAK

Let's go back for a few moments to where we were, before we took the way down and in and through: go back to your so-called *normal* perception of yourself.

You are a jailbird. Worse, you are in the punishment block, along with countless fellow prisoners, straitjacketed in your own skin, serving out your life sentence this way. Either you are longing to be free, or else you are so institutionalized, so much an old lag, that you've given up even that longing, cut that last link with the freedom that once was yours.

Can you imagine a more stressful and desperate situation? Or one that seems more difficult to break out of?

Christian and his fellow traveller Hopeful, in *Pilgrim's Progress*, found themselves in much the same fix. Giant Despair held them in his dungeon, visiting them only to beat them with his crab-tree cudgel. There they lay, nearing death, till at last Christian came to his senses.

> Now a little before it was day, good Christian, as one half amazed, brake out in this passionate speech: What a fool, quoth he, am I, thus to lie in a stinking dungeon, when I may as well walk at liberty! I have a key in my bosom, called Promise, that will, I am persuaded, open any lock in Doubting Castle. Then said Hopeful, that is good news, good brother; pluck it out of thy bosom, and try.

Then Christian pulled it out of his bosom, and began to try at the dungeon door, whose bolt (as he turned the key) gave back, and Christian and Hopeful both came out.

So the prisoners didn't break out. They strolled out. To make your own getaway from the body-prison and eventual (if not present) despair, pluck out of your bosom (or thereabouts) your master-key called ATTENTION and – turning it a full 180° in the lock – coolly let yourself out. As in fact you have just done.

The plain fact, of course, is that you were never for a moment shut up in there. All you have to do to shed this astonishing delusion is to come to your senses.

Few do so. To find out how taken-for-granted, how universal is this delusion, you have only to keep your ears open. 'I'm in the body', people say, and no more expect to be contradicted than if they had said they were in pain or in love. 'I'm corporeal, in the flesh, inhabiting this house of clay; I'm a person (and in law as well as common sense my person is my body, and what's done to it and by it is done to me and by me); I'm incarnate, embodied, contained in this mortal frame . . .' And so on. The descriptions vary, their gist is the same. How deep-seated is this superstition that at birth one is mysteriously sentenced (as if by some secret court from which there is no appeal) to life-imprisonment, that one is seldom or never let out on parole, and that not till death will one be released. Only to be re-arrested (reincarnationists would have us believe) and awarded another life sentence and transferred to another penal establishment. Decanted into another jug or can or cooler, as some old lags might put it. Society is a stratagem, says Rumi, for putting the king into a pint pot. And (we must add) persuading him the lid's shut tight. He'll believe anything he's told often enough and loudly enough – and all the more uncritically if it's bad news. The aim of the following experiment is to get the king to tell us what he *means* when he says he's in there.

Experiment 9: An in-the-body experience?
(This is a continuation of Experiment 6 – the first in this chapter –

44

which was an attempt to explore the inside of your hand. Of course your hand with your arm is just one of the outbuildings or wings of your 'house of clay', which we treat as a sample of the rest. We shall move on to other parts of the premises presently.)

Look at the hand that's holding this book, and keep referring back to it. Go by present evidence, by what's now on show, and go slow.

If you are in your body you are in that hand, in a position to say what it's like in there right now, and to answer the following questions:

Is it dark in there . . .? Gloomy, or pitch black . . .?

Is it cramped . . .? As restricted and poky as it looks to outsiders . . .? (The exteriors of buildings often do less than justice to their interiors: we need the inmate's view.)

Is it sticky in there, all messy and wet . . .?

Is it congested in there, packed solid, with no elbow-room at all . . .? If so, where do you come in . . .?

The point of these questions is that they are unanswerable and ridiculous. When you shake off blind belief and fantasy, you see you have at this moment no more inside information about that wrist than about that wristwatch. And that the same applies to the rest of your body.

It's perfectly obvious (isn't it?) that you are neither inside nor shaped by nor shackled to that limb you can see. More obvious still, I suggest, when you attend to parts of your body you can't see:

Where, on present evidence, does your flesh-and-blood seat stop and the chair-seat begin . . .?

Where does your back stop and the chair-back begin . . .? *What* back . . .?

How many toes can you count . . .? *What* toes . . .? Suppose I'm a magician who claims he's turned your feet into hooves with only two greatly enlarged toes apiece, how do you know I haven't succeeded . . .?

Now let's try the other end. How tall are you, on present evidence . . .? Ten feet . . . a hundred feet . . . a thousand feet . . .?

45

What shape is your head, as given . . .? *What* head . . .? Have you any way of telling whether I haven't magically turned you into an unspeakably grotesque monster with seventeen heads . . .?

I think you'll agree that, whatever your so-called body-sensations and stresses may be at this moment, they don't begin to shut you up inside a body-prison. That they don't, for you, begin to add up to a human form or any form . . . And certainly not to one you can take up residence in . . .

For example, select and attend now to some area of stress or tension or discomfort, allegedly 'in your neck' or 'in your shoulders'. Take time to get acquainted with it . . . What shape is it, as given . . .? Does it follow the contours of the region it's supposed to be in . . .? Or is it simply sensation, broken loose . . .?

Finally, hunch your shoulders and tense your neck and face as much as you can . . . and check that (even so) you remain, in those regions, as shapeless and as large as ever . . . All right, relax now . . .

It all boils down to the question of how *big* you are. There's a tradition that Jesus said: 'A man who looks at himself from outside, and not also from within, makes himself small.' Eccentric, off-centre, viewing yourself from a metre or so away from yourself, you do indeed *belittle* yourself. Drawing a boundary round yourself you *thing* yourself, you stress yourself, in the end you kill yourself.

Look and see. Now that your total implosion has issued in your total explosion, see how hilarious is the idea that you are inside one of your fission products, are contained in any object whatever. All are visibly *in you*. Without recourse to agonies of pain and exhaustion, without waiting till you collapse in a heap at death's door, without psychic or psychedelic tripping, without any search in secret India or Tibet or Mexico, you are now enjoying a perfect out-of-the-body experience. What's more, you can see for yourself that you never had any other sort. You have reverted to the sanity of your infancy and early childhood.

To enjoy a good laugh at your own (adult) expense, put to yourself such questions as:

Is this jailbird the same size as the jail, or is he rattling about somewhere inside like a small pea in a large pod or a die in a die-cup? Is he so bulky – or is his prison so cramped – that he fills out its volume without an inch to spare: a shocking case of overcrowding and violation of human rights? What sort of dream is this: that, within this thatch-roofed, four-winged, two-windowed penitentiary, is thrust an inmate who coincides precisely with the penitentiary? A prison-shaped prisoner? Suffering, as a result, the most horrible stress?

You must agree that the only fitting response to this nonsense is roars of laughter, and gasps of astonishment that the daymare should have gone on so long.

ECCENTRICITY

How does it come about, this wild notion that no wild creature is confused enough to entertain, this exclusively human pretence that the Observer – spellbound by some irresistible sorcery – is trapped in a tiny piece of what he's observing? By what black magic does the 'growing' child get trimmed, almost overnight, from cosmic to human dimensions?

The answer is that the child catches from grown-ups (actually, grown-downs) the contagious disease of *eccentricity* – of being beside oneself, distracted, out to lunch. This is the sickness whose victims – as if in some demonaic ballet or disco, or afflicted by a severe kind of St Vitus' dance – continually leap a metre away from themselves: and, turning round in mid-flight and looking back at themselves, *make something* of themselves. A condition that is in one sense quite imaginary, of course, but in another only too real. What a perfect recipe for stress! No wonder many sufferers seem permanently twisted; and that most are so tired that they need seven or eight hours of sleep a night – of remission from eccentricity to con-centricity – to recover from today's contortions and prepare for tomorrow's.

To describe the same condition in different clinical terms: one of the most notable symptoms of this pandemic disease of eccentricity is that the patient *hallucinates*. He 'sees' the face in his mirror as reversed, and enlarged, and transported to, and firmly planted elsewhere by a long chalk – on his own shoulders, in fact. He takes what is over there to be what is here. He misplaces things – as if he were to see his foot growing out of his chest!

A further symptom is that the patient, no matter how mentally gifted in other areas, is in this area curiously deficient. Flying in the face of the evidence, he's an absolutist instead of a relativist. He clings to the belief that things are fixtures which stay themselves regardless of where they are viewed from.

The self-evident truth (and its importance for us can't be exaggerated) is that what things are depends on the range of their observer. Distance lends more than enchantment: it lends form, an immense and heterogeneous array of forms as the observer approaches and recedes from the spot he has his sights on. The dear little pinpoint of light he calls a star turns out to be a superheated version of Nebuchadnezzar's burning fiery furnace, when he ventures near the thing: it's his application (for convenience's sake) of the same label *star* to both things that tricks him and us into imagining they are 'the same thing'. Similarly with you. No one (whether yourself or another) who is stationed a metre (or a centimetre or a kilometre, or a light-year) away from you is in a position to say what you are at other ranges – let alone what you are at Centre, o centimetres away from yourself. In fact, what you are physically is *all* the things you appear to be, at all distances, arranged around that Centre – around the No-thing you are at no distance at all from, in the place where you are no longer an eccentric.

Nearly all of us, nearly all the time, live off-Centre by a metre or so. The trouble with thus being beside ourselves – in the double sense of being split and being crazy – *isn't that it is too physical but that it isn't physical enough*. It's body-evasion, giving the thing the slip. It is refusal to go up to and accept and stay with yourself the way you are given to yourself. It's a learned and assiduously cultivated denial of what's so, a studied rejection of your substance in favour of your shadow. The road it takes is up and out and away from the Core of the physical and damn the facts, and it is lined and paved with stress. The true road is down and in and through to the very Core of the Core and hurray for the facts, and it leads you past your stress to the unstressable. People who are beside themselves are unnatural people, and they aren't very well. They don't like their bodies. They are airy-fairy. They aren't earthed. They give each other nasty shocks.

To go back to Nature and become centred again, you have only to come to your senses, and stay with your body instead of running away from it. You have only to rejoin the Ground – shock-proof and earthquake-proof – which you never left.

COMING TO YOUR SENSES – ALL OF THEM, EVERYWHERE

Here, you are no longer a jailbird. And you have not made your getaway from the body-prison by scaling the perimeter wire but by moving into the Governor's office. You have made your only true and perfect escape from the trap of the physical by becoming truly physical at last, which is no different from being truly spiritual.

But what, in that case, has become of the feelings, of all that constriction and heaviness you suffered from as a jailbird? Have they gone away, never to return?

At first glance, it would seem that either you still experience them, and they threaten to pull you back into custody again; or else you repress them, and you are a self-deceiving escapist after all. In fact, however, there's a third course, and it's the one that makes sense and is honest and works out. It doesn't deny your feelings but places them. It sets them in their context, and this rectifies them. Just how, the rest of this chapter explains.

The tremendous explosion which follows your implosion to the Centre is no transformation of the physical into the non-physical. Quite the reverse. It is your explosion into all that you need to be and are physically, into your true and worldwide Physique belonging to all levels. It is the restoration of those indispensable infra-human and suprahuman organs of yours which, in imagination, you amputated in order to reduce yourself to human dimensions.

It is your expansion into your total and only true Body which is the Universe. Anything less, and you're not all there, not viable, a fragment.

This true Body of yours happens to be presented to you through a variety of senses. Here, distance not only determines form, but how that form is served up. Thus your heavenly embodiment (for example, of galaxies and stars and planets) is *seen*; thus your earthly embodiment (for example, of people and animals and machines) is also *heard*; thus your nearer earthly embodiment (for example, of things to eat) is handled and smelled and tasted; thus your still more intimate embodiment (for example, of organs and tissues) is *felt* in various ways – felt, for example, as the solidity and weight that we investigated earlier in this chapter.

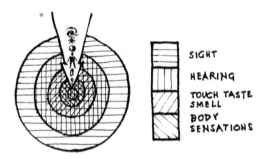

SIGHT

HEARING

TOUCH TASTE SMELL

BODY SENSATIONS

All of this – your assorted senses and the worldwide Physique they disclose – is for accepting as it's given, because it's the way you are when you cease to hive off essential parts of yourself, and take on all that you need in order to be you. The questions for us here are: can this taking on be done unstressfully? Is this new and exploded life an improvement on the old and partially imploded one? How does the released prisoner avoid taking out with him the negative attitudes and feelings of prison life?

The answer to all such questions falls into three parts:

(i) As what you are *not* – a limited thing, this human and nothing else – you remain full of stress. This stress is the immense push and pull of all the rest of you, invisibly making to restore every link between you-as-part and you-as-Whole, between organ and Organism.

(ii) As what you *are* – at once that Whole and its empty Centre – you are absolutely free of stress. The reason: there's nothing outside the first to exert stress, and nothing inside the second to accept stress.

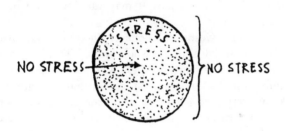

NO STRESS ⟶ ⟩ NO STRESS

The implosion-explosion, which places you at once at the Centre and Circumference of things, is your absolute assurance against the stress that intermediate things suffer.

(iii) And yet, of course, you register and you include these intermediate and limited things, along with the stresses that make them what they are. Without being able to wash your hands of any of it, or to pick and choose, this is the stuff of you, your content. All of it, from that dark and heavy body below to the stars above, is stress-built and stress-maintained, so that you are inescapably full of stress. Indeed more so than ever, now that you have taken on all the things of the world, each in its separateness, and leave out not a particle of it.

What makes all the difference, what saves the situation, what ensures (above, and below, and in spite of all) your felicity, is summed up in one word: ASYMMETRY.

Look and see now. Just as, to take on the shape of the hand that's holding this book, you have to be free from shape; and to take on its colour you have to be colourless; and to take on its opacity you have to be transparent; and to take on its complexity you have to be perfectly plain and clear – so, to take on its stress (as it holds this book by exerting contrary pressures upon it) *you have to be free from stress*. And the same goes for every part of your total Body, from the lowest to the highest. It all consists of the stress-filled things which you are, and you are free of. You transcend all, and you are rooted and grounded in all.

To discover how this feels and works out in life, you have to live it, and see. Here's a hint of how it may turn out for you, given sincerity and interest:

According to the Gospel of Thomas, 'There is a Light within a Light-man, and it lights up the whole world.' This is no dim and brief candle, unsteady on its candlestick, but more like the Eddystone Lighthouse. Picture what it takes for that structure to fulfil its function: everything from the light-beam at the top, so bright and clear and featherweight, to the darkness at the base, the solidity and weight and pressure which go to make up that foundation and the rock it's built on: plus all the engineering that lies between. Every level and every part, all those built-in contrasts, necessary to the working whole. To the extent that you put into practice what you've discovered in this chapter about bodily stress (your total freedom from it and your total involvement in it) you will find yourself resembling that lighthouse. The brighter and steadier and more far-reaching the Light of your Awareness, the deeper and more substantial its physical basis will feel, and will be, and will need to be. Already you are abundantly furnished with those twin treasures and contrasting necessities of life – the Light and the Rock – and know well how they fit and how they jointly overcome your stress without denying an iota of it. All you have to do is go on being more and more what you really are.

For encouragement you may reflect that here you are in line with the world's traditional wisdom. The Daruma doll of Japan, which is weighted at the base so that it always rights itself, represents the enlightened Zen man – in our own terms, the one who knows how to cope with his stress. The *Upanishads* of Hinduism make a point of bringing together the Light of the Spirit and Invulnerable Rock. And it's not for nothing that – in the Christianity which Archbishop William Temple called the most materialistic or physical of the great religions – the Light that lights every man and woman who comes into the world is none other than the Rock of Ages.

7

STRESS IN PERSONAL AND SOCIAL RELATIONSHIPS

Before beginning to discuss stress in personal and social relationships, let's make sure we know what they really are. We think we know, but do we? An experiment will soon tell us:

Experiment 10: In the bag

You require a friend, or preferably two friends, to help you get the best results. If for the moment you can't find anyone, you can manage with a picture of a face, as near to life-size as possible. You also need a paper bag, about 30 cm × 30 cm (12″ × 12″), with the bottom cut out to form a tube. The purpose of this device is that, when you and your friend look at each other through the tube, it eliminates external diversions and helps you to attend to what's actually given. More importantly, it's a very efficient de-conditioning instrument, and the best remedy for hallucination I know. When you see familiar things in an unfamiliar setting such as this, they are sure to strike you very differently. Parents, teachers – language itself – never got around to telling you what to see when you are *inside* a shopping bag. They left you free to see what you see, so be prepared for surprises.

You (A) and friend B fit your faces into the ends of the bag, while friend C asks you questions.

(In the absence of B you will need the picture of someone, to hold there in his place; and in the absence of C you will need to keep coming out of the bag to read the questions, before going back to find the answers.)

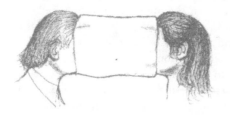

Here are the questions, which aren't for answering out loud.

On present evidence, dropping belief and imagination, how many faces are there in the bag . . .?

Are you face-to-face in there, or is it face-to-space . . .?

Take in the human features of the face opposite . . . the contours and shapes that make it unique among faces . . . Compare these with your own lack of human features of any kind, let alone distinctive ones . . .

Take in the colouring of that face . . . its various textures . . . its opacity . . . its complexity . . .

And compare these with your own colourlessness . . . your smoothness and freedom from all blemishes . . . your perfect transparency . . . your over-all sameness . . .

Is there any comparison . . .?

Come out and repeat the experiment with B reading out the questions while you and C are in the bag together . . . Finally, you read out the questions while B and C are in the bag . . .

CONFRONTATION

The aim of the experiment was to show that in reality you never had a *stressful* personal or social relationship – for the simple reason that you never had a relationship in the ordinary sense. How could you? Look and see. It's always No-thing at the near and first-personal end of the 'transaction', and No-thing is unstressable.

For you there's no transaction, no symmetry, no *confrontation*.

Look and see, on the other hand, how people – other people, such as B and C – invariably face each other, confront each other. All second and third persons run on confrontation as cars run on petrol. And confrontation runs on stress, each party acting upon and reacting to the other. Trying to reform or pacify B and C by weakening these opposing forces would be like getting them to run their cars on low-grade fuel. Trying to eliminate those forces would be like trying to get them to run their cars on no fuel at all. Always when there's symmetry there's stress. And it's stress that makes the world go round.

And where there's no symmetry there's no stress. At the heart of that stressful world lies its stress-free Hub. That's what you were, and where you were, at the near end of the bag. And it's what and where you are now. No longer at the near end of the bag, but still at the near end of yourself, see and be the way you are – the way you are inescapably, whether or not you approve of it or understand it.

Stress isn't for combatting but for placing. Cope with it by allowing it to be present where it is given over there, and absent where it's not given, right where you are. See that as first-person (and what else can you be?) you are shot of it. Try living consciously the way you're living actually – from here to there, which means from the unstressable into the stressed. Always your stress-medicine, your rule, the flag you fly, is ASYMMETRY, NON-CONFRONTATION. The word *front* means 'forehead', and *confrontation* means 'forehead opposed to forehead'. Also *front* means 'the scene of hostilities, where enemies clash'. Your peace is seeing that you are not built for war. Or (if you prefer) it is seeing that you are already the winner, that you are absolutely invulnerable, that your defences are perfect since you have nothing to defend.

The daily practice that follows from this is simple realism, simple truthfulness about your personal and social relationships, so-called. It is to notice, in all your 'confrontations' with people, that they aren't confrontations or anything of the sort. Nobody can get on a collision course with you, because there's nothing to collide with. Go on seeing this, and sooner or later (maybe sooner than you thought) you will find yourself living naturally and without special effort from the truth. There will remain nothing phony about you.

Not all your friends and relations will like this. Anyone who declines to join in the games people play is apt to be seen as a challenge and a rebuke – or at least as an embarrassment – to the games-player. Take Dickens' Mr Dorrit, self-occupied and self-pitying, a show-off and a pompous ass. His daughter Amy, by contrast, was a transparently sincere and open soul. She just didn't know how to confront people. This so worried her father that he engaged a companion for her, appropriately named Mrs General, to work on the problem. 'If Miss Amy Dorrit,' this old battle-axe assured him, 'will direct her attention to, and will accept my poor assistance in, the formation of a surface, Mr Dorrit will have no further cause for anxiety.' Happily, the plot failed. How can we ensure that the numberless plots and sub-plots against our native wideopenness – hatched inside and outside the family – will fail? By attending to the absence here of anything to close up, anything to form a surface on, anything whatever to confront those people with.

THREE EPISODES FROM LIFE

Now we come to some actual examples to illustrate how practical our discovery is, how relevant it is to real life. From the many available I select my own case, because it is among the most striking known to me, and anyway the only one that I can speak of with full confidence. The particular topic is fear – my fear of people, and my freedom from fear – in three short episodes of my life.

(i) As a child of about five, I found myself sitting with my parents at a religious meeting, facing a small crowd of people. They fascinated me. I remember vividly a lady whom I at once recognized as some kind of large, sitting pheasant. Her ankle-length dress was russet, speckled with white and downy in texture; her hat was gorgeous and spiky with brown feathers; her eyes were small and bright and birdlike. The fact that those eyes were fastened on me was of no interest. There was no little boy to feel under inspection, to be self-conscious, but only that astonishing lady ... Now it happened that, just before the meeting, I had collected some dead-looking snails. The warmth of my pocket brought them to life, and they started creeping down the chair-legs and on to the floor, in the direction of the pheasant lady. Imagine her horror! My snails and I became the concern of the whole meeting, all piety forgotten ... But did I care? Was I embarrassed? No more than my snails were. The reason: at five years old, I was empty for the lady, for my snails, for the shocked gathering. Emptiness welcomes that sort of thing, every sort of thing.

(ii) The second episode occurred more than two decades later. I was due to lecture on logic (*sic*) to a gathering of around fifteen people, set up by an educational organizer – a woman who was a stranger to me. By telephone we arranged a rendezvous in town, before the meeting. We met. For no apparent reason (this was by no means my debut as a lecturer) I was scared stiff, petrified, rigid, speechless. It was an awful half-hour for me and not pleasant for her either; and the meeting that followed wasn't very much better. A more absurd and humiliating performance it's hard to imagine. What was I up to? The sort of adjectives I've just used give the game away: stiff, rigid, petrified, frozen, struck all of a heap – this is the language of thinghood. I had no room for that lady. I wasn't interested in her at all; I was so busy being (or rather, constructing, illogically and in imagination) that pitiful object she was staring at, that I hardly saw her; or, later on, hardly took in my audience of would-be logicians.

This is one of the worst incidents of the kind that I remember, but there were others almost as distressing. And plenty of minor ones, such as my having again and again to cross the street to avoid an approaching acquaintance. I hated being looked at by people I felt inferior to, and I hated *not* being looked at – hated being ignored or cut dead – by the same people! Perhaps I was following a family pattern, blown up to pathological dimensions. My father, and his father, had been a little like that. My father, in particular, rarely brought himself to look squarely at the people he was addressing ... Anyhow, you will now appreciate why I've been over the years concerned with the ending of stress in personal and social relationships. I had the disease so badly I had to find the cure.

(iii) And find it I did. The third incident, typical of many, happened quite recently. I have a clear memory of standing at the back of a large hall in Denver, Colorado, watching with more than usual interest the crowd as they came in to the meeting. I was mightily impressed. The men looked about three feet taller than me and twice as muscular, and full of bounce, moving and talking easily. Perhaps what struck me most was how self-assured they seemed and how little they were likely to get out of this occasion: a workshop about – well, not about stress as such, but about its real cause and cure. But what did I care? As the seats, around 3,000 of them, filled up, a friend came and talked with me about our first meeting. At once I forgot about all those people: he and the subject of our previous meeting occupied me to the exclusion of all else ... Then the time came for me to walk down the centre aisle, mount the platform and talk and conduct experiments (including the paper-bag test we have just done) for three hours with those people, as coolly as I'd just been talking at the back of the hall to my friend. The reason for my lack of nerves was precisely that lack: nerves did not exist where I stood on that stage. What nerves? I was, for myself, *absent* in favour of that audience. As a child I had been free from nerves without realizing it; as a young man I had been false to myself, a bundle of nerves; much older, I was true to myself again. Absence, No-thing, Emptiness isn't jittery. There really was nothing where I stood on that stage, nothing to suffer stage-fright, no face to be shame-faced.

For purposes of illustration I have chosen, from the huge field of stress in personal and social relationships, just one type of stress – morbid self-consciousness and shyness, the kind of fear I suffered most from. There remain, of course, all the stresses that go with love and sexual relationships, family life, working with bosses and subordinates and colleagues, living alongside neighbours and so on. Probably for you at this time there is some particular stress-plagued relationship that's not quite the same as anyone else's. The dis-ease takes innumerable forms, the easing only one. The only radical treatment for your particular stress is to stay consciously where you are anyway, in the Place that's immune from all stress. The trouble isn't the *fact* of stress but its *whereabouts*. Observed in the right place – out there in bodies – it is right, it's what they are made of. Imagined in the wrong place – here where there's no body, at the mid-point of your world – it is wrong, a mistake, a nonsense. And so, whatever form your problem may take, the solution is to see who has it and who doesn't have it.

The way to make your relationships work is to notice that they aren't anything of the sort. However strange this may sound in theory, it's quite simple and sensible in practice. Take the two ladies who have appeared in this chapter. The first – the pheasant lady – I registered so sharply that I can still see her. That was because there was nothing here in her way. The second – the educational organizer – I scarcely registered at all. That was because I put here in her way a mass of congealed stress. The first was a relationship so complete that it amounted to identity with the lady; the second was a relationship so incomplete that it amounted to no relationship at all.

ANOTHER WAY

I have described how I have come to cope with the problem of my own relationships, so-called: namely by the *indirect* method which puts aside all effort to improve those relationships till I'm sure who the parties involved really are: the way of facts first and coping second. It's the only way I'm qualified to advocate because it is my way – the way I know works because I've been testing it over many years. Which is not to say, of course, that there are no other approaches. In fact I can hear someone telling me, in no uncertain voice:

Your trouble as a young man, Douglas Harding, was that you

had built yourself up into a negative, fearful, inadequate somebody: you had cultivated (for whatever reason) an inferior self-
image. Now if you'd had the luck or the good sense to build,
instead, a positive, brave, superior version of yourself, an adequate self-image, why then your social performance would, with
practice, have grown steadily better ... Well, it seems all did
come right for you in the end. You hit on your own roundabout
way through to self-confidence in your dealings with people
separately and en masse, resulting in a much-needed reduction
of anxiety and stress. But it's not a method that's sure to work
for others, and by no means the only one that's open to them.
There are more direct and less paradoxical and drastic ways of
making friends and influencing people than disappearing in
their favour. In fact, the very *opposite* strategy – the well-known
and well-tested method of deliberately constructing a personality here instead of demolishing it, of putting together a somebody to be reckoned with instead of disintegration into a nobody
– is surely the sensible one for most of us. 'Come on, pull
yourself together, for God's sake *make* something of your- self!'
say the ones who have made it to the ones who haven't.
And who is to say they are wrong? Imagine telling a slack and
listless teenager that he has the right idea, and should go on to
become a total nonentity!

A very serious and plausible objection. Let's go carefully into
this 'opposite strategy' of filling out our No-thingness here with a
positive thing for impressing others with, and making a proper
impact upon our world.

It has a long and respectable history, even an inspiring one.
Take, for instance, the address of Shakespeare's King Henry to his
troops before battle:

> Then imitate the action of the tiger;
> Stiffen the sinews, summon up the blood ...
> Now set the teeth, and stretch the nostrils wide;
> Hold hard the breath, and bend up every spirit
> To his full height ...

Can you think of an exhortation more contrary to that of this chapter and this book, a command more specific and more persuasive in its insistence on *thinging* instead of unthinging oneself? In a word, more deliberately stressful?

Altogether different in style, and intended to apply to the whole of one's life and not just its tight spots, are the innumerable and popular books and training systems that have been around for the past century and more, on 'the power of positive thinking'. Their aim, however, isn't so different from King Henry's as all that. They explain (I quote) 'how to work miracles through visualization and self-suggestion', and 'how to get people to do what you want through will-power and concentration', and 'how to realize one's ambitions by means of mental magic'. Here's what R. W. Trine (one of the less off-putting architects of this design for living) has to say:

> See yourself in a prosperous condition. Affirm it calmly and quietly, but strongly and confidently. Believe it, believe it absolutely. Expect it, keep it continually watered with expectation. Thus make yourself a magnet to attract the things you desire. Don't be afraid to suggest, to affirm, these things, for by doing so you will put forth an ideal which will begin to clothe itself in material form. In this way you are utilizing agents among the most subtle and powerful in the universe.

And (I would add) you are on the way to becoming a proficient miracle worker or magician in your dealings with people and things.

The method of these 'positive thinkers' is to persuade you to overlook or ignore your facelessness and to cultivate in its place your face – a carefully contrived but by no means inflexible façade (loving, attractive, powerful, dominating, above all successful, as occasion demands) for confronting people with. In a word, to achieve working *symmetry* in your person-to-person relationships. And the magic comes off – at least up to a point. You are quite likely to get many of the things you set your heart on, including a personality more than able to hold its own against other personalities. And, after all, what is surprising or special (not to say suspect) about this positive method? Isn't it the normal and common-sense method of growing out of one's youthful diffidence into adult self-esteem – worked up into a system, and only in extreme cases into a religion?

All right. But the question still to be settled is: which is the more practical way, the more likely to succeed without exacting too high a cost – cultivating your facelessness or your face, your asymmetry vis-à-vis others or your symmetry? Which really copes with your stress? Which, in the long run, is the more energizing and deeply satisfying: which, in particular, makes for healthy and lasting personal relationships? Is it the way of self-image-building which seeks to impose its designs on the Screen which you are; or is it the way of self-image-destruction which sees that no such impos-ition is possible, and that the Screen just won't take it – any more than your TV screen or your mirror will take on the things that appear in them? In the end, I think you will find that the entire manoeuvre turns out to be one of those stress-generating games people play – in fact the master Game from which all other games and pretences derive – the game of thinging this No-thing and objectifying this Subject, the game of Confrontation and all the hallucination it involves.

Here are some further considerations to help you decide which to go for – self-discovery or self-promotion, awareness or power, submitting to Nature or twisting her tail. It is notorious that magic boomerangs, and that sooner or later the magus gets hurt. Use it if and when you must (what adult hasn't devoted much time and energy to it?), only look out. The biographies of outstand-ing personalities who concentrated on winning regardless, on gain-ing and never losing face, don't make encouraging reading. In fact, the trouble with these so-called magical powers isn't that they are too powerful but that they aren't nearly powerful enough. They are feeble because in the last resort they are illusory: whereas the real Power, the Power that empowers all powers, is nothing else than your true Nature, your very own true and featureless and impossible-to-lose Face, the same that you discovered at your end of that humble paper bag. Some 2,000 years ago in China it was known as the Tao, alias the Always-so, the No-thing, mere

Emptiness, like water tasteless and colourless and seemingly so weak, and always seeking the lowest place. Yet to have the Tao is to have room for everything, and to rely on the Tao is to rely on the only Power there really is, on the Dark Horse which (though it makes a show of being a non-starter if ever there was one) turns out to be the winner. My tip is: back it, put your shirt on it. It never fails, never lets you down. As the Taoists put it: draw on this well. It never runs dry. I say to you, as always, don't passively believe a word of all this. Test this Power. You are it, it's your Nature, your No-thingness, your First-Personhood, not far to seek. Give It a whirl: or rather, allow yourself to be whirled by It.

This is going to take you some time, of course. Meanwhile, which would you say is truly positive thinking? Which do you feel like investing in: the faculty of hallucination, which conjures up just one little somebody right where you are, or the faculty of sight which finds everybody here, which has room and to spare for the whole world?

Shakespeare himself (in contrast to King Henry and most of his other characters) not only knew the answer, but had his own immediate entry into what the Chinese call the Tao: experiencing it, for instance, as the Nothing which (according to his Timon of Athens) brings one all things. And as the crystal-clear Essence, to neglect which is to ensure that, in our relationships, we degenerate into angry apes:

> But man, proud man!
> Dressed in a little brief authority, –
> Most ignorant of what he's most assured,
> His glassy essence, – like an angry ape,
> Plays such fantastic tricks before high heaven,
> As make the angels weep.

Unfair to apes, of course, but one takes the point, which is that you have a straight choice. You can (with Henry and his soldiers) model yourself – the First Person – on third persons, imitate them, straining and striving to become what they look like, and so find yourself up against them, at loggerheads with them. Or you can (agreeing with Emerson that imitation is suicide) be what you are, namely that great Unstressable that all creatures are coming from, and so make your peace with them because essentially you are them. Instead of imitating anybody or anything, try being the No-body or No-thing Shakespeare's Timon speaks of, and see whether there are any occasions, any crises (even bloody battle) when truthfulness doesn't work out, when being what you are makes a coward of you, when your Glassy Essence lets you down and playing the angry ape does not. In particular, see whether it's ever necessary, or ever advisable, to ignore or deny the self-evident fact that at your end of every 'transaction' there always is this marvellous Essence, the Tao, Awareness itself. Why, even that apostle of mental magic, Mr Trine, relenting more than somewhat, goes on (with surprising but commendable inconsistency) to heap praise on our immaculate Source, on the Infinite we are all backed by and its awesome know-how, and to urge us to submit to and to trust its mysterious operations.

Well, I've put the case for basing your relationships on what Zen calls your Original Face (no face at all) instead of your acquired and contrived face. Don't take it from me as proved. Test these diametrically opposed ways of conducting your social and personal relationships – the stress-building way of trying to be what others look like, and the stress-demolishing way of being what you are. Try both. Find out for yourself which is practical, which suits you, which is truly *you*.

This is the most momentous question that life puts *to you*, and it requires a definite answer *from you*. There are no gradations between being a stressful something and being the stress-free No-thing/Everything, no compromises. The difference is not negotiable.

Nor will thinking up the answer do. You have to look and see. You can (like Eliot's J. Arthur Prufrock) go on trying 'to prepare a face to meet the faces that you meet' – or else you can look and see how impossible the job is. Drugged by language (that most powerful and universal but undetected of hallucinogens) you can let the way you talk settle the way you are – talk, for instance, of *putting on a brave face* when people go for you, talk of *pulling faces* at them when they aren't looking, talk of *composing your face* when to show emotion wouldn't do, talk of *facing up* to some things and *setting your face against* others, talk of being *face-to-face* even with your loved one – till in the end you're so faced-up and so stressed it's unbelievable.

Or you can kick the habit. You can, right now, see your way clean through the stupefying smokescreen of words to what's so, and arrive at the perfect freedom and clarity that were yours all along. And accordingly you can enter upon a wholly new relationship with all comers by being them twice over. To everyone you can now say:

I HAVE YOUR APPEARANCE, I AM YOUR ESSENCE.

That's intimacy!

8

STRESS AND THE PACE OF MODERN LIFE

RUSHING ABOUT

I live eighty miles from the centre of London – not the world's biggest and most frenetic of cities, but high on the list. Driving up to town, I get the impression that the folk I pass are holding their bodies more stiffly, are walking faster and more mechanically, as I leave the country for the suburbs, and the suburbs for the metropolis itself. Here, people seem to be in a great hurry to get somewhere, but their strained faces seem to say they aren't getting any nearer. The trouble is as much the frustration, the *lack* of speed, of city life as the speed itself. Getting stuck in traffic jams and at pedestrian crossings and in long queues, and waiting for the bus or train or taxi that *won't* come, plus all the other hold-ups in our obstacle-race against time, all these are at least as wearing and stressful as the race itself.

We are all contradictions. In town, the speed of life has us yearning for the peace and quiet of the country. On holiday in the country the peace and quiet of rural life have us yearning to be on the move again. In the end it's difficult to say which is worse – the stress of enforced inaction, or the stress of enforced agitation. Perpetual motion is indeed punishing, a fact that Dante underlined when he placed the guilty lovers Paolo and Francesca in the Second Circle of Hell, where they are forever tossed about by violent winds. What the poet didn't hint at was the opposite penalty of everlasting boredom in a Paradise where all is perfect peace, where the barometer is eternally at Set Fair, and no rough winds blow.

Of course there are palliatives, or partial remedies, both for hyperactivity and its opposite. For example, we can settle down in a not-too-isolated country town where the pace of life is sedate (but not too sedate), and go up to the city less often. We can, some of us, switch to quieter and less exacting jobs, and choose restful hobbies like fishing and birdwatching in place of surfing and roller-skating and disco dancing. And of course there are always drugs to slow us down or speed us up. Some slowing down is well within our unaided power. After all, the greater part of our restlessness isn't imposed on us from outside by modern life, but from within by ourselves. We tear around because we want to, not because we need to. At least, when we're young we tend to prefer the stresses of the restless and even frenetic life to the bottled-up stresses of boredom. As we grow older, on the other hand, most of us seek some workable compromise between the stresses of over-achieving and those of underachieving. But a middle way is hard to find, and harder still to keep to. Worse, it's apt to amount to a cop-out, a falling between two stools, a faint-hearted refusal to live life to the full because we can't take the wear and tear of it.

The truth here is that the middle way is permanently closed for repairs. Palliatives and compromises won't do, however sensible they may appear. They aren't stable, and they are no cure for stress. That's because they don't get to the heart of the problem, which is ignorance of our Nature and its functioning. It's our business in this chapter to dispel that ignorance.

THE DILEMMA

Let's begin by taking a closer look at what we want.

Crazy creatures that we are, we crave incompatibles. Whether our desires alternate, or cancel out, or tear us apart, they are an unstable (if not explosive) mixture. We want a rest cure from the stress of the frenetic life *and* we want (at least we need) an unrest cure from the stress of the over-quiet life. (I commend Saki's hilarious story 'The Unrest Cure' to readers who feel their lives are unduly humdrum and predictable.) We want to take our ease with our feet up before a crackling fire, a soothing drink at our side and a faithful hound at our feet, *and* we want to be spread-eagled on the north face of the Eiger in a gale. We pray with all our heart for peace in our time, O Lord, *and* we spend the time playing war games and watching war films – the more horrifically realistic the better. And so on, in so many departments of our life.

Is this all meaningless? Is our species mad? Or do those built-in contradictions have a profound lesson to teach us about what we really are? Could it be that our Nature *is*, somehow or other, the reconciliation of all such diametric opposites? That we hold in our hand the medicine, that we *are* the medicine, for this strange sickness? What a piece of luck it would be, what a blessing, to find that our true Nature doesn't just patch up this deep wound that humans inflict on themselves, but somehow conceals in it the secret of our health? *Impossible?* Previous chapters have done something to erase that word from our vocabulary; and a lot to show that words like *absurd* and *nonsensical* aren't half as damning as we had supposed. Haven't we been finding all along that our socialized life is one great exercise in make-believe, an Alice-in-Wonderland tea party in which everything is upside-down and inside-out?

Really to deal with our stress we have to make a fresh start and call in question our basic assumptions, beliefs that we have taken for granted since childhood. This is *daring to experience our experience*, daring to be ourselves, daring to view life from where we are – here – instead of from where we aren't – over there – and daring to be eccentric no longer. It is going behind what we've been told to see, to what we see. And it's going on to discover what a huge proportion of our stress is due to our forsaking direct experience for socially acceptable formulae: or, less politely, to our astounding credulity, our willingness – our anxiety – to be taken for a ride.

ON NOT BEING TAKEN FOR A RIDE

On not being taken for a ride – that's precisely (metaphorically and literally) what this chapter is about. Applying the method of radical doubt – our start-all-over-again technique – to our topic, the question you have to ask yourself is: what is it really like to be on the move, to rush about the place, to slow down, to stop? What is your actual experience? I'm in no position to tell you. Nobody can. Only you enjoy access to the spot where the answer is perfectly clear.

One way of finding out would be to put down this book, go out and start racing down the street. Or, if you're not that fit or energetic, to get in your car and drive through town, the faster the better. Or, if there's an airport handy, to fly somewhere from there. There happens to be, however, a cheaper and quicker and safer (and probably more convenient) method of putting yourself in high-speed motion. Moreover, it's one that's ideal for our present purpose because it's unfamiliar. The chances are that it's many years since you got yourself going in this fashion: perhaps it's entirely new to you. Once more, then, viewing the old from a new angle or in a new context is likely to prove a wonderful Eye-opener, a sudden bursting through the truth-barrier, through the dense screen of convention which hides from us what we are all the while, without our suspecting its existence.

Experiment 11: What moves?

It helps to have a friend read out the instructions and questions that follow, while you carry out the experiment. Otherwise, you have first to read them through and remember them – not the exact wording, necessarily, but their general sense.

Stand up. Stick out an arm and point straight ahead.

Start rotating on the spot . . . round and round . . .

Here's movement all right . . .

But what's moving, on present evidence . . .? You, or the room . . .?

You say it's the room . . .?

Well then, gather speed – enough to set you in motion, too . . .?

What? You can't . . .? It's the walls and the ceiling and the furniture that are speeding up . . . while you stay perfectly still . . .?

(If you keep attending to what's at the near end of your outstretched arm . . . to the Stillness here at A . . . you will not feel giddy. There's nobody here to suffer vertigo . . .)

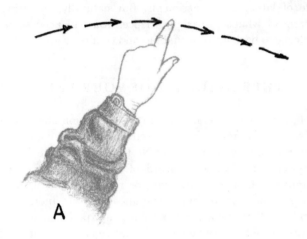

A

All right, then, slow the room down . . . gradually . . . gradually
. . .

Going by that experiment (which, as always, it's essential to do
and useless to read about) you discover that, contrary to all you'd
been told and thought, you can never, never budge an inch,
however much you long to. Why worry, in that case, about
slowing down the pace of your life, or halting in your race against
time and the other runners, when you never got off the starting
line anyway? Whether you like it or not, you are forever at rest.
R I P is for you now, not for your tombstone one day. Can you
imagine a more curious, more comic, more significant fact than
this – that very nearly all humans (you are now one of the rare
exceptions) live all their lives under the mistaken impression that
they are dancing round in a stable world, whereas in fact the
world – more unstable than a rough sea or a windswept cloudscape
– is dancing round in them?

You never moved an inch, nor ever will. (I refer, of course, to
the real you and not to your appearance: to you as you are for you
at Centre, not as you look to us way off-Centre.) Such is the

literally world-shaking scientific (repeat *scientific*) discovery you have just made, thanks to this briefest, cheapest and most repeatable of laboratory experiments. But naturally, to satisfy your criteria of what's proved in science, you will need some more evidence to back up your findings and confirm your conclusion.

FURTHER EVIDENCE OF YOUR IMMOBILITY

Well, for a start, is it such a strange conclusion after all? Isn't it only what you might have expected? Way back, you discovered that essentially you are Aware No-thingness or Bare Capacity or Emptiness, and whoever heard of *that* on the move? Imagine Emptiness chasing its own tail, or rushing about imitating the things it contains! In fact, we've uncovered yet another instance of the law that you are free of what you experience, that it's your Nature to be the very opposite of what you are currently occupied with. Look up and out at the wall ahead. Just as you are now empty for the shape of that object, so – a few moments ago – you were still for its motion. Just as you are now the colourlessness that takes in the colour of that wallpaper, and the simplicity that takes in that complicated floral design, and the transparency that takes in that opacity, and the silence that takes in whatever sounds you are now hearing, so you are the Stillness that takes in all that moves. Always you are this ideal marriage of opposites. In fact, therefore, your absolute immobility could have been predicted in advance of our experiment.

Again, if I doubt you when you say that *you* as First Person are stationary, whereas *I* can see you are running fast, I have only to photograph you to resolve my doubts. I may lie like Lucifer, but my camera doesn't. To get a perfectly sharp picture of you, it requires me to follow and take on what looks like your every movement till you are left with none. By the same token, you must have noticed how little progress horses make in the film of a race, and how it's the racecourse that does the racing.

For further confirmation of your Stillness, you have only to turn to everyday life, life as you live it. You certainly don't need, every time you want to make sure of your central Tranquillity, to imitate a whirling dervish and set the room, or the street, or the supermarket, or the airport, rotating about you. There are plenty of other, less conspicuous ways of checking your Stillness.

For example, though you say you are going to the office this morning – you can go on to see what's actually happening. Driving your car (as you put it) to the railway station, notice the behaviour of the trees, and lamp-posts, and buildings along your route – how they approach you, growing fast and gathering speed, and then vanish on both sides into your Stillness. Notice that road obligingly widening for you, its surface flowing like an asphalt river into the mysterious Cavern you call 'yourself'. Notice how those hands on the steering wheel aren't turning the car but setting the whole street turning and twisting. Arriving at the station car park, notice how, in fact, it arrives in you. You get the train which (they say) is about to take you to the city terminal. But don't believe a word of it. Your train stays quite still. It's the other trains, the stations, signal boxes, bridges, that go whizzing past. The given fact, the blazingly obvious truth, is not that you go up to the city but that it comes up to you.

(From time to time the truth slips out. A Welsh friend of mine heard a train guard announce in all seriousness: 'The next station is Cardiff, which will arrive in ten minutes!' I remember the pilot of a plane telling us passengers over the intercom that Newark, New Jersey, was 'passing beneath our port wing'. I looked, and so it was, very slowly indeed. What does 'flying' mean to the one in flight? What does the famous 'speed of air travel' mean to the traveller? He could honestly report that it's pure superstition, and the reality is that he hovers, more motionless than any kestrel or sparrowhawk, above a slowly moving landscape.)

Finally, arriving at the office, you walk along the corridor to your room – enjoying the fact that you're doing nothing of the sort. It's the corridor that's on the move, opening out for you like a great flower for a bee, losing itself in you . . . Yes: quite apart from the fact that this unloading of your movements on to the world is the unloading of your stresses, you have for bonus the enjoyment of a joke that never stales. You have a secret, and it's a precious one.

There are times when you can hardly stay unconscious of what's going on – the airport, taking on the motion that you imagined was yours, accelerating and tilting as you 'take off', the non-stop railway station so swift and so telescoped that you can't read its name, the roadside scene of an accident that 'flashes by' (as you say) at sixty miles an hour. Such moments of truth are normal if it's you who are in the accident ('the road came up and hit me'), or you are drunk (Bertie Wooster, weaving his way unsteadily down the Mall, 'aimed a kick at a passing lamp-post'), or you are very young (Pooh Bear didn't fall out of the tree into a gorse bush: it came up and hit him, painfully). The world has all sorts of ways, pleasant and unpleasant, of insisting that you, the No-thing among the innumerable things it contains, are its Hub. Cease resisting your uniqueness. Why? Because the less you lie about yourself the less stress you suffer.

SELF-CENTREDNESS

You have no reason to jib at this good news because it boosts your egotism and self-centredness, which are already (some would say) excessive. In fact it does the opposite: it is their only real cure. It sees off the egotism which, latching on to that essentially mobile and eccentric person over there in your mirror, tries and tries to make him or her the Hub of the universe. A forlorn hope! The stress involved in that impossible task, that ever-abortive attempt to centralize the peripheral, is immense. And you don't reduce it by seeking to moderate somewhat that false self-centredness, or pushing yourself just a little off-centre, a little adrift from that ego. No! Your only remedy is the true Self-centredness that makes the one-metre leap back to the Spot that in reality you never left, to the only true Hub or Stillness you will ever find, no matter how far and long you search.

A simple test will bring this description to life. Again, the point is in the doing, not the reading.

Experiment 12: The third person in orbit round the First Person

Take a hand-mirror, find and keep your face in it, and hold it out at arm's length.

Slowly swinging your arm, put that face in orbit, up the left-hand wall, across the ceiling, down the right-hand wall, and back to where it started from . . .

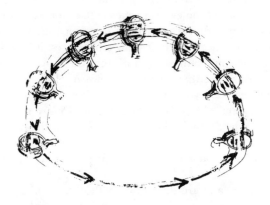

Complete the orbit a few times, varying its shape and speed as you please . . .

That human face, that person, is planet to your Sun.

Now see if you can shift the Sun – that 'bright and charming Original Face' – which is on your side of that mirror, at the near end of that swinging arm . . . Try taking it for a little walk to the other side of the room . . .

And discover you can't shift it by a hair's-breadth, that it's the room which does all the shifting . . .

THE WORLD IN MOTION

Things move, even the most stable of them. The Great Pyramid, a fixture if ever there was one, is (they tell us) orbiting daily round the axis of the Earth, which is orbiting annually around the Sun, which is orbiting round the centre of the Galaxy. Add up these movements, and you have a picture of the pyramid tearing around, behaving quite frantically. How unlike you who, as Capacity for all movements, are absolutely stationary! This is the natural consequence of your No-thingness, the cure for your agitation and self-centredness, and a fact of direct experience. It is dogmatism and false modesty to deny that you are the still Hub of the world. Humility in front of the evidence means that you accept it – and that you note, for encouragement, how science itself can find in the universe no *objective* Hub or Centre of centres: it leaves you at liberty to treat any point as central, since the universe obligingly arranges itself about that point like a swarm of bees about their queen. Which means you have every right (or not so much a right as a necessity and obligation) to treat as *the* Centre the one Spot you never catch off-centre, the Spot you occupy without occupying it at all. The idea that a mere tremor – let alone the stress of life, its frantic rush, its wear and tear – can ever get to you here, is sheer fantasy.

Things move, and are themselves built of motion. By contrast, you as Bare Capacity for them have neither external nor internal motion: you are, so to speak, stillness built of stillness. Another little experiment will demonstrate the difference between yourself as motion-free Capacity for things, and those things as motion-built.

Experiment 13: Motion builds

Shake your hand rapidly . . .

Go on shaking it so rapidly that it builds up into an object which, though not quite as solid-looking as that hand, is several times larger . . .

An atom takes shape and bodies itself forth by the swift rotation of its planet-like electrons. Halt them and it collapses, implodes. The atom plays its own version of the game we children used to play in the dark – lighting the end of a string and whirling it so fast that the glowing point turned into a circle of light. To turn

that circle back into a point, all we had to do was stop whirling. Halt the world, and it vanishes. Time and motion and periodicity are the stuff it's made of. In other words, it's congealed stress. Still life is death. It follows that to reduce the stress of anything is to that degree to unmake it. Which means that mere palliatives – aimed at reducing our stress as persons by taking on less and taking it easy and slowing down – evade the problem rather than solve it. Insofar as they cut down stress they cut down life.

The likelihood is that, having seen off your stress, you will live *more* energetically, perhaps *more* strenuously. The contents of your Stillness, the things that go to make up your life, that are your liveliness, may well grow more lively. No point in pacifying *them*! In fact, the boot is apt to be on the other foot: the more agitated they are the more able to point up your freedom from agitation. Just as your No-thingness isn't obscured but highlighted by the things and the people that come and go in it, so your Stillness is highlighted by their movements. The contrast can be very telling. Thus you may well find (as I do) that busy city streets, ball games, fireworks, funfairs – any complex pattern of moving objects, so far from disturbing your Stillness, is quite likely to enhance it. I once found myself lying on the floor alongside two hundred screaming, shouting, groaning, struggling, frenzied humans. Taking on that frenzy (without becoming it, as the organizers of that event urged me to do), I enjoyed a particularly deep feeling of peace. I shall not easily forget the difference between that calm and the storm that raged around – or rather, within – that calm. It isn't just that there's no contradiction between 'inner' quiet and 'outer' commotion, but that they are complementary. Which may well mean that you need not leave the city for the country after all, or take up less strenuous hobbies like fishing or knitting. It could mean you took up Formula-one racing!

And what's behind this passion for speed, in its many forms? For some it's horse-riding, or fast cars, or speedboats, or windsurfing, or aerobatics, or motorcycling; for others the rollercoasters and the big wheels of the fair grounds. Much of their appeal is that, by apparently speeding one up, they confirm one's apparent thinghood. It's as if one said: I move, therefore I am. Sitting still and getting nowhere, I feel a nobody and only half alive. Getting up and getting around, the faster the better, I feel I'm somebody, more real and more alive, and it's worth the high cost in stress and strain.

It's a significant and encouraging fact, however, that there are limits to this effort of thinging or solidification. There comes a point when the process suddenly goes into reverse. Up to (say) 100 mph I can easily tell myself that I am travelling at that speed through the countryside. But above that speed, at 150 or 200 mph, the truth becomes less easy to avoid: I am much more likely to see myself as the Stillness through which the countryside is rushing. At high speeds, it is virtually impossible not to attribute them to one's surroundings. I suspect that this is why car racing gets its hold on the racing driver, that this is the unconscious reason for the fascination of his job. He would be surprised, no doubt, if you attributed spiritual or mystical intent to him. Nevertheless, his acceleration does take him through an experience of mounting thingness, up to a limit or barrier beyond which lies the Stillness of his No-thingness. Something of the kind is certainly reported of the long-distance runner: after a long and difficult haul he reaches a crisis of effort and stress, beyond which he suddenly finds himself relaxed and tranquil, with the scene floating gently by.

Our own concern here is with ordinary life and everyday practice. We don't have to do anything unusual or dangerous or exhausting or at all difficult in order to arrive at our unstressable Stillness. Walking, driving and being driven at normal speeds, using public transport – all provide a perfect opportunity for observing what's so, what's moving and what isn't.

SAFE DRIVING

I can imagine a serious objection to much of this:

> Being still and letting the world flow by is all very well when it's a matter of relaxing in a passenger seat in a vehicle, but when I'm the driver or pilot I've a job to do. There has to be a responsible body in the driving seat taking the right decisions and making the right moves. To be mere stillness for the traffic to move around in would ensure a traffic pile-up!

I reply with a question: is my performance (whatever the task) likely to be *worse* when I'm alert to the given facts, and *better* when I ignore or deny them? Or, on the contrary, does it pay to be realistic and tell myself no lies – even when driving my car? Everyone knows that being absent-minded on the road, out-to-lunch, in a desperate hurry to be elsewhere, and above all stressed, invites a crash. Suppose I take this homespun wisdom just one step further, and tell myself the *whole* truth of what it's like out there and in this driving seat – the truth that right here is just Empty Stillness (or Still Emptiness) for taking in the fast-approaching roadscape. Suppose I do that, and observe the effect on my road sense and driving performance.

I have a vested interest in this kind of driving. I owe my life to it. My friend Virginia Parsell was driving another friend, Richard Lang, and myself towards Palm Springs in Southern California, along a narrow, two-lane road in the hills. On our left was a steep bank, on our right a steep drop. We were approaching a left bend. Suddenly we faced, coming at us round the bend, a tall truck which, taking the bend too fast, was keeling over on to its side and about to block the whole width of the road. The surprising thing was that Virginia didn't react normally and jam on the brakes. If she'd done that I wouldn't be telling you the story now. No: taking in not just that on-rushing truck but the whole scene in a flash, she *accelerated* into what Richard and I saw as sudden death, and at the last moment passed it. She had seen ahead what neither of her passengers had seen, a small unpaved area on our right, built out above the cliff, and pulled sharply into it. We missed that falling truck by inches; in fact, some of its load discharged on to us.

It's tempting to attribute *all* of Virginia's presence of mind to her absence of body, her well-practised alertness to herself as Capacity for whatever is going on. In fact she admits that the habit of seeing what's really in her driving seat has over the years greatly improved her driving performance, and was no doubt largely responsible for saving our three lives on that memorable occasion. On the other hand *all* of us are capable of such spontaneous 'miracles', and many of us have actually performed them 'automatically' in life-or-death emergencies. They provide yet another means of breaking through the truth barrier – not this time thanks to unfamiliar circumstances, or exhaustion, or intoxication, or very high speed, but to danger. Beyond this barrier we suddenly catch ourselves living from the truth of our unshakeable and unstressable No-thingness instead of our stressful thingness. But why leave the truth to come out only at desperate moments? Let's get in our homework when things are going quietly along in our Stillness, and there's little danger of their hitting us into eternity.

This advice applies specially to you drivers who are raring to try out our truth-technique on the highway. Remember that long-time habits aren't easily broken. The new *idea* (as distinct from the realization, the seeing), that no moving body occupies your driving seat, may well be more dangerous than the old idea that a moving body does so. Go slow, try out your Stillness/Absence at times and in places where the risks are minimal, and then go on to discover over the months and years how efficient and safe and pleasant it is to be yourself and at rest, and let things be themselves and restless. So that every time you go for a drive you practise stresslessness, and are a much more proficient driver now you have learned the gentle art of letting motion be where motion belongs.

BIRD WATCHING

In summertime where I live there are often many swallows and martins to be seen, each wheeling and swooping at such a speed that the bird lengthens into a streak. In wintertime the sky is occasionally crowded with starlings. Yet I have never observed a near miss, much less a collision – even when the birds are of mixed species. These incomparable aviators obey no traffic rules, no priorities to the left or right, up or down. What is their secret? What makes their performance incomparably superior to that of accident-prone human aviators? It is this: no swallow is *for itself* a swallow (any more than you were *for yourself* a baby once), a solid *thing* in swift motion among other things, a dangerous and endangered missile in flight. The swallow is Accommodation for *other* swallows, for birds of other species, and of course for flies, trees, its nest, its eggs – the lot – to come and go in. The very last thing it could be, for itself, is a wonderfully swift flying machine superbly equipped and superbly expert at handling its own controls. No! It flies on that 'automatic' pilot which will soon take it, still only a few weeks out of the egg, all the way from my garden in England to that place in Africa its parents have already made for.

The Stillness which is the resource and the secret and inside story of that bird is the same Stillness that is your resource and secret and inside story. It is no less skilled in you than in that young swallow. Why not live from it and be it *consciously*, with perhaps some of the panache and flair that Nature flaunts?

Once more, then, our method and principle – what this book is about – holds good. Let's remind ourselves of what it is: BE PERFECT – AND GET BETTER! Or, less briefly, the best way to improve your performance as a human being is to cut out its unnecessary stress; and the best way to do that is to live from the Spot where there's no human being, No-thing whatever to be stressed; and the best way to do that is to see what you see instead of what you're told to see. In terms of this chapter: efficiently to get around in the world, stay still at Home. You have your latch-key – that in-pointing finger. Don't let yourself be *caught out*!

9

GETTING RICH WITHOUT STRESS

MAKE YOUR FORTUNE

A lot of people will tell you *they* don't want to get rich, thank you very much. They give all sorts of plausible reasons for preferring to remain poor. For instance, the stress and strain of getting the stuff, and then holding on to it, aren't worth the rewards; or there's something indecent or morally wrong about being wealthy; or they aren't sufficiently crafty and ruthless and obsessional to stand a chance in the rat-race for filthy lucre – thank goodness! Let those who don't mind the dirt and the smell be stinking rich!

All sour grapes. Either such people aren't being honest with themselves, or else they are somewhat debilitated – if not actually sick. All healthy and truly alive men and women and children deeply want to be rich, deeply feel that they deserve to be rich, are somehow sure that they are one day going to be rich, and that their present poverty is a temporary indisposition.

This gut feeling – that great wealth is your due – is no pipe-dream. It's for taking seriously and respecting, not for feeling guilty about. The purpose of this chapter is to show how well-founded it is, and to invite you to go forth and make your fortune without stress or strain or delay. Yet another of our tall orders? Certainly! Mere hot air and uplift, unlikely to descend to the level of actually increasing your bank balance, or seeing you out of the red into the black? Certainly not, as we shall soon see.

What is it to be rich? It is to own the things you want. And to own the things you want is to have them where you want them, and when you want them, and as you want them; also to be relieved of them when you don't want them. It is to be sure they are safe. It is to be sure that you alone are entitled to them, and are in no danger of their being claimed by someone else. This, and no less, is what it takes to be truly rich. Furthermore, you have to take into account how much it's all going to cost in terms of stress. You would be no man of fortune, but of great misfortune, if your wealth left you more stressed than the so-called poor people around you.

Is there a way to great riches that involves no increase of stress, or actually reduces and removes our stress?

Indeed there is, and moreover the riches it offers are real riches, and having them is real having. An experiment in two parts will show clearly what it is, and how to make it your way.

Experiment 14: Cash in hand

Hold a coin in your open hand.

(i) Look and see: does this hand *own* the coin . . .?

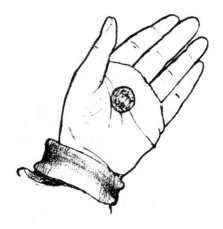

Who's to say the coin doesn't own the hand . . .?

Notice that, in fact, it is neither of these, not a case of owning at all, but simply of touching, of things up against each other . . .

Notice how hand and coin are two things, each occupying its

own bit of space and keeping the other out . . . How each insists on itself and its separateness . . . No danger of their merging, of their possessing each other, taking each other over . . .

(ii) While still looking at that hand and coin at the *far* end of your arm, notice what's taking both in at the *near* end of your arm . . .

See yourself as the Emptiness here that is filled with that coin and hand and arm . . .

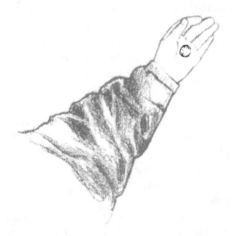

See yourself as the No-thing that isn't up against those three things . . . isn't adding a fourth item to them . . . isn't other than them . . .

See yourself as, in fact, those things, right now . . .

THIS IS OWNERSHIP.

TO HAVE AND TO HOLD

Things can never own things. They resist one another, crowd one another out. They are mutually exclusive. Insisting on themselves, they are merely themselves. But Aware No-thingness insists on nothing, resists nothing, and so embraces and becomes and truly owns everything it holds – which, given time, is *everything*. And where and when will you find this Aware No-thingness but right where you are, right now? It alone is rich – rich by nature, not by effort or intent. The people in it (as people, as second and third persons) are men and women of straw, undischarged bankrupts, not owning the clothes they stand up in. As for the things in it, they are stripped bare, models of naked poverty. But you as First Person (which means you as you *are*) have only to see that, as Traherne put it, 'your essence is Capacity', and at a stroke your fortune is made: you aren't just 'clothed with the heavens and crowned with the stars' – you are starry, you are heavenly. Everything the moment is furnishing you with is your very own real estate. Why? Because you are built like that, because you own the world in such a way that you can't disown it.

But just a moment. How can you be the rightful owner of all these things, scattered as they are throughout the universe? What's the use, what's the meaning, of vast wealth you can never take possession of? A thousand square miles of Moon-surface, with full mining rights, or a thousand stars of your choice, aren't worth a brass farthing till you can get at them.

Quite. But just supposing arrangements could be made for this far-flung property to be delivered, in good condition and distance no object, to your address. Then you would be rich indeed. It would all be your very own if you held it safe at home, no distance remaining to distance you from yours. An unlikely feat of cosmic transportation?

What if you have already taken delivery in your sleep? Well, let's see. Let's *measure the gap* between you and your goods. For this you will need a measuring rod marked off in inches or centimetres – I take it that nobody will question the reliability of this scientific instrument. A school ruler will do perfectly, or anything of the sort.

Experiment 15: Distance no object

(i) From where you are sitting, read off the distance between any object and anyone present. Or between any two objects if you are alone . . .

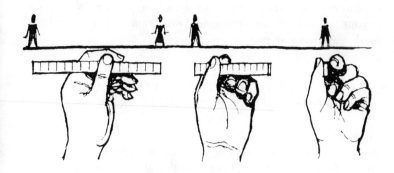

(ii) Slowly swing the ruler round towards you, watching those inches shrinking . . .

(iii) Bring the ruler round till it's end-on to you . . . Read off the no-distance between you and the object, the inches having shrunk to zero . . .

A line stretched tight between you A, and the 'remotest' object B, isn't *for you* a line at all: it's a point. Of course you can try to distance yourself from B by jumping in imagination to C, and reading off the distance A–B from there.

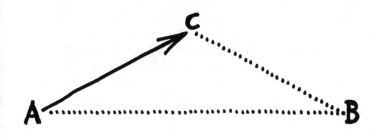

But just supposing you succeeded, the distance between you (who are now at C) and B would still be zero. The truth is that, no matter how hard you try, you can never sidestep or renounce your infinite heritage. To say that you were born with a silver spoon in your mouth is the understatement of all time. You cornered the market in silver spoons.

LISTEN TO PHOTOGRAPHERS AND PHYSIOLOGISTS AND CHILDREN AND ARTISTS

And, after all, what is this but good sound sense? Every amateur and professional photographer knows that the person or mountain or starscape he photographs isn't something yards or miles or light-years away and a piece of past history, but present and presented now in his camera and indeed in himself. Neither he nor his camera is in a position to pick up what's elsewhere and elsewhen. And every amateur and professional physiologist knows that what he senses – what he feels and smells and tastes and hears and sees – is where *he* is, never mind where the *object* is alleged to be.

Little children are, in their own way, equally sensible and honest. Clutching at the Moon, or holding the stars in their hands, they are taking what's given, humble in front of the evidence. Of course they have to go on to learn the art of pretending that things, such as people and houses and trees, stay the same size; that they aren't swelling and shrinking all the time, but just getting nearer and farther away. But when, joining more and more wholeheartedly in these solemn games of adults, they take the distance of things for gospel truth and not mere convention, they have lost the infinite treasure they were born with. Result: stress and more stress – the stress and distress arising from the fact that they have been robbed of their heritage. No wonder it takes long and painful years of growing up (of cutting down, in fact) before we will accept this imposed poverty. Even so, deep down, we remain furious at society for having cheated us so cruelly. Till we rediscover and reclaim our true wealth, all of us – and not just misers and professional burglars and swindlers – spend our lives doing all we can to get our own back.

You are now re-asserting your rights, and (in the very best sense) getting your own back – at last. You are opening up your very own Aladdin's Cave, which is nothing less than the whole world delivered, in prime condition, to your doorstep. *And* most beautifully scaled down to convenient sizes so that there's no overcrowding and your home isn't over-furnished. And not only scaled down, but slowed down, and cooled down, and warmed up, and otherwise adjusted as necessary: so that you aren't rushed or roasted or frozen or electrocuted, and so on.

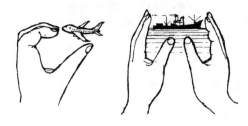

It's little children who see what's going on. A young friend reported to me, excitedly, that he'd seen a teeny weeny plane (yes, he was sure it was filled by even tinier people) moving ever so slowly along. Another, returning to my house after a walk with her father along the nearby estuary, told me she had just seen a little ship – so big, she said, holding her hands six inches apart. Of course the children are right. For one's wealth to fit in comfortably here, it needs to be suitably miniaturized. (In fact, that won't do. Planes and ships and people are elastic, and the sizes they come in are all real. A thing doesn't have a true size, any more than it has a true weight, or colour, or shape. It all depends.)

Then there's art. Walking round the National Gallery, your enjoyment isn't tempered by the reflection that these masterpieces lack depth: that they are two-dimensional attempts to do justice to a three-dimensional world. Quite the reverse. Their flatness isn't a defect. It's a virtue, a revelation. The eminent painter Max Beckmann said that to transform height, width and depth into two dimensions was for him 'an experience full of magic', enabling him to glimpse the dimension which his whole being was seeking. Painters are rubbing your nose in the real and given world, whispering in your ear that this scene and every scene is your scene, that it occupies the same plane as yourself for whom there's neither near nor far, that its features are your features. What terrific war-paint, what instant and gorgeous make-up you wear, now you can find no face to put it on and all surfaces are your surface! To have the National Gallery or the Tate for your beauty parlour – now that's living it up, that's luxury!

And there's music. Listening to Mozart, the sound doesn't fill you. It replaces you. You don't thrill to those melodies. You are melodious. It's not that you are musical, but are music: music so beautiful it's enough to make you cry.

THE RESULTS – IN CASH TERMS

So far, you could say that our discoveries, however entertaining and heart-warming and stress-reducing, aren't likely to fill our purses and boost our bank balances. Well, let's see. The time has come to look at the likely effect on our finances, our solvency, of this rediscovery of the fact that the world is our treasure-chest. There are at least five reasons for expecting good results:

(i) How much time and money and stress do we put into keeping up with the Joneses? To matching, we hope improving on, Mr Jones's new boat, country hide-out, pool, car, conservatory; plus Mrs Jones's up-to-the-minute curtaining, and more-than-streamlined kitchen fittings, and dream bathroom, to say nothing of yet another evening outfit and frequent hair-dos for the dog as well as herself; plus young Jones's birthday and Christmas add-itions to the already fearsome space-weaponry in his arms race with the young Robinsons? No one is going to win this excessively stressful game. Why play it at all? What status symbol will do justice to your rank as proprietor of the stars? Who can begin to compete with your splendour as Rome, as Everest, as every Old Master you care to take in? Play being yourself, rich and magnifi-cent beyond compare, stop playing unworthy and belittling and unwinnable games with Messrs Jones, and count your savings in hard cash. You will be astonished at the things you are better off without. Why, you could find that the greater part of your expenditure till now has been dedicated to impressing others – and depressing yourself: depressing and burdening yourself with possessions that possess you. But retire from that miserable and absurd game, gleefully concede victory now to the Joneses and Smiths and Robinsons, and start living to express instead of impress. In so many ways you will prosper. For good measure, you may well come to earn their respect. You won't be able forever to hide the fact that you have found the only real cure for envy (namely, to own everything), and for social climbing (namely, to be everyone).

(ii) Then there is the money you save on the tranquillizers (chemical and non-chemical) that drain your vitality, on diversions that become as routine as what they are diversions from, on holidays that you need a holiday to get over, on escape attempts from the prison of thinghood that always end in recapture. All such 'remedies' for stress treat the symptoms and exacerbate their cause, which is pretending to be what you are not.

(iii) And people come to like you. They may well be more generous and helpful now they sense you aren't up against them but embrace them, are them. They feel, without knowing how or why, that you are wide open for them, that you see and hear and appreciate them for what they are: and this disposes them to react in kind. You don't need to tell your secret, which is that you can't help yourself, and that it's as this infinitely capacious No-thing that you are so open to them, so big-hearted. To take personal credit for this, or to misuse it to get yourself into people's good books and to coax things out of them, would be self-defeating: it would be to revert to a specially deplorable kind of thinghood, with stresses to match. No-thing demands nothing of anyone, has everything anyway, is everything. Only stay with This, and see if it doesn't come up with just the thing that's needful at the moment – including, most probably, the money you're getting less and less interested in – so that you can't think why your bank balance stays so consistently out of the red.

(v) Which brings me to the last – and by far the deepest – reason why living consciously from your absolute wealth is likely to improve your relative wealth. Things can't be trusted. They pose problems, they change, they perish. Not so this Aware Nothing. It alone can be relied on. It comes up with things – not, it's true, with the things you imagine you want, but with the things you really, really want, the things you need. Is this so surprising? After all, it's from this same unspeakably mysterious No-thing that *all* things emerge for no reason (why should they?), that this wildly improbable universe is now emerging. No mean achievement, this cosmic enterprise ranging from quarks to galaxies, all on the go, all in working order! This is the Thing that your No-thing is getting up to, right where you are. If the power and the expertise behind this Unlimited Liability Corporation, this Business of businesses, can't be counted on, what can? If it lets you get in the red occasionally (and it could) be sure the management has its reasons. If in its service you sometimes go short of this or that (and very likely you will) you suffer no stress on that account. You are well backed.

The reasons why you should invest at least *some* trust in this, provisionally, and then proceed to put your shirt on it, are three. The first is that many of the now-most-admired members of our species have claimed that (in spite of all appearances to the contrary) they found it altogether reliable, and urged everyone to try it. The second is that, thinking back to the crises in your own life, you may recollect how you drew on far deeper interior levels than those you normally rely on, with impressive results. The third is that the Resource we are recommending is what and where you are coming from, is the Self of yourself, your Origin and own True Nature – and if this can't be relied on you are indeed in a bad way. This which is wholly you, which is more *you* than you are you, yet packs the irresistible power of what's wholly other than you – don't your heart and guts (to say nothing of your head) cry out: 'I give myself to This, give myself to my Self, and take the consequences!'?

You won't be sorry.

A NEW SORT OF BOOKKEEPING

Trust is a mighty antidote against stress. So is its companion – *gratitude*, thankfulness for your untellable wealth. I'm not thinking of some vague, warm feeling, but of a very striking and precise shift of attitude, even of a new sort of bookkeeping. First-person accountancy, I call it. A commonplace illustration will show you just how different it is from the ordinary sort.

You are driving along the highway, many miles from the nearest town, tired and in need of a rest and refreshment. You come to an isolated wayside café, buy your pot of coffee, sit back contented . . . You pay your pound . . . As you leave, you wonder how many pence in the pound are for profit, how many for overheads, how many for the actual ingredients – coffee, milk, sugar. You conclude you got value for your money, more or less. You don't feel grateful and you don't feel cheated. You go on your way . . .

That sort of practical economics, with its taken-for-granted method of costing things, is of course useful and not for giving up. But let's face its limitations. It is the economics of deprivation, scarcity, close-fistedness, ingratitude. And quite obviously it's incomplete, misleading, not in accord with the facts. There is a more realistic way of bookkeeping, one that takes more account of your reality as No-thing than of your appearance as a thing. It goes with the economics of abundance, gratitude, open-handedness and the relaxation of stress. Reverting to our example, this is how it works out:

You order and drink your coffee as before, pay your pound, and start calculating the *actual* cost of providing that pot of hot coffee, and that clean table and comfortable chair, at exactly that remote place and time to meet your need. Your estimate includes the waitress's salary, the proprietor's living expenses, the capital outlay and subsequent running costs of the land and building and equipment of the café, plus the similiar costs of setting up and running the dairy farm that supplied the milk, plus the cost of importing by ship and road the coffee from Brazil, plus the maintenance of the shipping line and road network . . . At this juncture you give up and conclude – rightly – that that pot of coffee has cost the

Earth, and more than the Earth. It took the entire structure and history of the universe to produce that one article just where and when you needed it. And of course the same is true of every service you enjoy. The waitress who takes your order and serves it up to you is a goddess, is none other than the Cosmos itself, heavily disguised. That humble pot of coffee is none other than the end-product and raison-d'être of the Universe.

But perhaps you aren't altogether happy with this unconventional style of bookkeeping. Maybe you still feel that the conventional way of reckoning the price of that coffee – by sharing all the costs evenly between all the customers – is the sensible way. After all (you say) what's so special about one of them – about yourself – that it's for this one alone that the whole set-up exists and all that money is spent?

Let's agree to settle the issue by reference to the facts – by attending to what's really going on in that café – and to regard as sound bookkeeping the sort that takes account of those facts.

Well, what *are* the facts, when we take time off from hallucinating to look and see? First, let's observe what happens when *the other customers* drink. Various beverages disappear into lip-framed slits in their faces, and there's no telling whether it's water or white wine, strong tea or coffee, cold or warm soup. Compare this with what happens when *you* drink. Similiar beverages are sucked into an Abyss unframed by lips (or a face, or anything at all), and white wine is at once distinguishable from water, strong tea from coffee, warm soup from cold soup. If you were to hang around that café for years you would never find another eater or drinker anything like yourself. In fact, you are the only real Customer, the only one who's served just what he orders and is refreshed by it. And you are the only one that doesn't take out of that café a face that still bears marks of fatigue and stress.

It follows that the accountancy which takes you to be unique – which reckons you to be the one for whom the whole set-up exists – is the realistic sort; and the kind which reckons you to be just one of thousands like yourself, is the unrealistic sort. Of course it's no condemnation of regular accountancy, that it takes no account of your First Personhood. Its business is to ignore your uniqueness.

Your business is to enjoy it. There's none like you. That pot of coffee on the highway was served up to the Unlimited, by the Unlimited, at unlimited cost.

At the start of this chapter we said that to be rich is not only to have the things you want, and to have them where and when you want them, but also to be relieved of them at other times. This makes *you* the real owner of that café: you have it only for as long as you want it, and are disencumbered of the place when you don't. Not so the legal owner, burdened with the stresses and strains of running the business all day every day, to say nothing of being stuck in that godforsaken spot. He is its slave. Similarly with the airline that's all set up to fly you across the world to the city of your choice on the day of your choice. Would it be more yours if you acquired it outright, bought the whole show instead of just a ticket? On the contrary, it would be less yours. To your current stresses it would immediately add a lot more. Again, suppose God liked you so much that he gave you the stars as a token of his appreciation – but he did so in such a way that they were a confounded nuisance and constant burden. Well, he has given them to you in a way that makes them the perfect present. Where would you keep your star-jewels securely (yet on show periodically) but in your safe-deposit of the sky? Can you think of a more satisfactory way of enjoying this magnificent gift than the way you already do? Do you want a legal document to prove your ownership? What would it be but a record of You making them over to You?

Some years back I watched a TV interview with the late Paul Getty, one of the world's richest men. The interviewer, commenting on Mr Getty's (on poor Mr Getty's) strained and unhappy face, expressed astonishment that his wealth didn't cheer him up. He need not have been surprised. Mr Getty, to his credit, didn't pretend to be a happy man. In reality, of course, he was, like humans in general, very poor indeed: seeing himself from outside as somebody in the world, and not also from inside as the world, he had reason to be miserable.

As Who you are, you shed the stresses of the false ownership

95

whereby one thing claims a few other things and so loses all; and you take on the relaxation of the true ownership whereby the No-thing claims nothing and so gains all. You are no longer plagued by the fear that you're not getting value for money or are being swindled, and you delight in a universe that's bent on serving you magnificently regardless of cost. Identifying with what you aren't – a body, a personality, a business, a great international corporation, an empire – is cheating yourself, ruining yourself in every way, at the cost of severe stress. It isn't practical. But identify with what you are, with the No-thing that leaves *nothing* out, and you get the best deal of all time.

THE JACKPOT

A headed person is a pauper, and a pauper is stressed. What makes one man, all the days of his life, hang on to his head like a hat in a gale? What makes another, after wearing the thing for a stressful decade or two, happy to let the wind of God blow it clean off? Or, happier still, to stake it in the game of life, lose it – and win the jackpot? Is it a heavier-than-normal burden of misery laid on one's shoulders? Or humiliation heaped on humiliation? Or poverty so grinding that, at long last, one's top is polished off? Or is it more a question of the luck of the draw? If we are fortunate, just about anything – physical or mental exhaustion, a personal crisis, sexual abandon, even a few drinks or a smoke – can loosen or dislodge the monstrous thing. Can (though it may be only for a moment) lose us a meatball and gain us a universe.

There is a Japanese legend which is very much to the point here. A poor widow was dying. All she had to leave to her young daughter was a wooden bowl, lacquered black and very heavy, on the surprising condition that she wear it on her head. Not so much a hard hat or helmet as a personal candle-snuffer, made worse by her mother's insistence that she would never be able, by herself, to take the thing off again. With filial piety the girl did as she was told – and went on to live a blighted, poverty-stricken, utterly miserable life. Eventually, however, she managed to get a menial job in a farmhouse kitchen. In due course the farmer's son came home on a visit, happened to notice the kitchen-maid, fell in love and determined to marry her. Well, in spite of her headgear, the strong reservations of his parents and the understandable reluctance of the girl herself, a marriage was arranged. And at the wedding ceremony, after the customary drinking of sake, the headgear exploded into fragments, and a stream of sparkling jewels and gold and silver coins cascaded into her lap. Wittingly or not, her mother had fixed it so that – neither too soon nor too late – her little girl's ordeal would end happily; and that she would be rewarded with a model husband who refused to be taken in by appearances, and, into the bargain, who had enough wealth to pay for a magnificent new homestead.

We aren't told whether the couple lived happily ever afterwards. I think it's much more likely that old habits died hard, and that the housewife – surrounded by such an array of cooking vessels and chamber pots and bowls of curious design – couldn't resist trying them all on in turn, just to see how they suited her. And sometimes one or another of them got stuck on for long periods, which led to shortages of housekeeping money, and domestic strife. I like to think, however, that she never forgot that they were all detachable instantly and at will. And that, in the end, she was content to go quite hatless. And accordingly – seeing that she was clothed with the heavens and crowned with the stars – very well-lined indeed.

10

HOW TO GET YOUR HEART'S DESIRE

GETTING WHAT YOU WANT

The way to end stress and be happy is to get what you want.

When I was very young there was a famous poster showing a baby straining after a cake of Pears soap. The caption read: 'He won't be happy till he gets it.' That says it all – not only about that infant in his bath, but about the rest of his life, and your life and mine, whatever our circumstances. Or almost all: it omits to mention how long the smiles and gurgles of pleasure will last when he does get the soap. The very next moment, probably, he catches sight of his sister's plastic duck, and the routine starts again, as stressfully as ever. So it wasn't the lovely slithery soap, or the beautiful shiny bouncy duck (or, later on, the delightfully danger-ous chemistry set, or the fabulous new bike with still more gears and gadgetry, or the stunning girlfriend, or the latest in fast cars, or the better-paid job, or the nicer home in a nicer suburb, or the business that will at last complete his portfolio) – it wasn't this he *really* wanted: otherwise he would, having got it, settle down with it, let go his stress and relax and enjoy living.

When we do get what we're after our delight is brief indeed. Nevertheless, there's a moment of real joy. Its only defect is its brevity. Too soon it turns, if not to conscious disillusion and disappointment, at least to indifference. The drive, the stress and strain of pursuing that particular quarry, is over, and the next is slow to appear. Meantime, there's the mounting stress of boredom, of being at a loss between projects, goalless. All that effort and all that frustration and all that achievement, and we aren't an inch nearer our real goal, which is *lasting* satisfaction. We still have to discover what it is we really crave, that true success which can only be judged by our own standards of sustained interior happiness and never by the superficial standards of the world.

It comes naturally to us to suppose that this seemingly insatiable itch could be cured if only we cornered all the soap or plastic ducks (or whatever) in the world, or clambered and clawed our way to the pinnacle of our profession, or finally achieved enduring fame and popularity, or came to wield unchallenged power. Nothing could be further from the truth. Was Alexander the Great, having made himself master of the known world, content at last? He wept, when he found there were no more countries to conquer. Few statesmen have been more admired than Winston Churchill, yet the last years of his life were soured by the feeling that his country had rejected him. What more brilliant and acclaimed composer ever lived than Tchaikovsky? Yet at the height of his career he tried to kill himself. Tony Hancock succeeded in doing just that at the point when, acknowledged to be one of the best English comics of his time, he could scarcely rise higher. How many outstanding success stories, when viewed from within where they really matter, are found to be outstanding tragedies?

You may remember how, in *Through the Looking-Glass*, the White Queen offers Alice a rather unsatisfactory job at tuppence a week, and jam of a sort: 'The rule is, jam tomorrow and jam yesterday – but never jam *today*.' Real success, which is freedom from stress, which is present and lasting joy, would seem to be as elusive as that jam. All the jam we're likely to get today is at most a fingertip taste of it, in passing. Rarely a spoonful, never the jam-pot.

There's nothing wrong with the jam. It's not a question of discovering a new and superior brand of joy (the old, too-brief joy will do very well) but of extending that ordinary sort, of prolonging throughout our life the satisfaction which as yet we taste only at our moments of triumph. Moments which, sad to say, become more widely spaced as we grow older. The baby's delight at getting hold of the toy that's just taken his fancy is at root the same as his later delight at attaining, after decades of endeavour, that longed-for position or property or reputation; but the baby knows that joy many times a day. As we grow up, our joys get rarer but no more lasting, and are increasingly felt against a background of sadness and stress.

GETTING WHAT WE REALLY WANT

What is it that will give us that elusive joy for keeps? To put it differently, what, in our heart of hearts, do we so deeply want that when we get it we seek no longer? In the course of this chapter we are going to find out. So far, we have discovered that what we think we want – from bathtub toys to world dominion – turns out to be miserably insufficient. There exists a something else, something that not only satisfies but goes on doing so, that never eludes us. We may be confident it's there – for two reasons: first, because we have a hunch, a built-in conviction that it is. The persistence and intensity of our seeking, the ever-springing hope that refuses to be dashed for long, indicate that our innumerable disappointments are milestones in our long and tortuous search for the real Treasure. And second, because there have lived, and live today, people who have found that Treasure, people for whom every day is a good day, who enjoy lasting content and that absence of stress which is happiness. We shall be looking at some examples presently. Meanwhile, let's go further into the difference between our superficial desires and our deeper ones.

Psychologists have long been insisting on this difference. Here are a few instances of the kind they point to. At table your husband – with obvious sincerity – assures you he loves you and wants to make up your recent quarrel, but his body tells a different story: he's careful not to look at you, he's breathing hard and his hands are busy tearing a crust of bread apart. In the office a colleague sincerely assures you that he's delighted at your promotion and would have refused the job if he'd been offered it: and all the while he's sitting there behind his massive desk, with hunched shoulders and a scowl on his face – giving the lie to the generous sentiments he's mouthing. In your sports club you meet a man who's keen to join a surfing party you are arranging. But at the last moment he's struck down with incapacitating (and perfectly genuine) backache, and can't come after all. He couldn't be more upset about it, but – doctor's orders, you know. The truth is that he has cleverly though unconsciously fixed it so that he will never go near those dreadful breakers, which he's terrified of without knowing he is. Thus he ensures safety with honour, and avoids admitting to anyone – least of all himself – his fear.

Not that our hidden motives are necessarily inferior to our superficial ones. Saints, said Dom John Chapman, are sure they are pigs. Their behaviour tells a different story. Perhaps most heroes and heroines believe they want a safe, comfortable and selfish life. What they find themselves doing – their unbounded courage and energy in an emergency – demonstrates what they really want, which is to give themselves utterly at that time.

No doubt other examples of such doublethink or doublefeel will occur to you, possibly some from your own life. It's our human condition to be thus at odds with ourselves, one level versus another. Our stress arises from the discrepancy between what we suppose we want and what we really want, between what we crave superficially and what we crave deeply. The greater the difference, the more severe the tensions that threaten to tear us apart. Our task in this chapter is somehow to bring these separated (even hostile) regions of our will together, to find a way of uniting the whole of our will, conscious and less conscious, personal and more than personal, selfish and unselfish, into one harmonious whole.

We may then go on to live an integrated life, no longer torn apart and stress-plagued.

THE THREE AREAS OF THE WILL

So we come back to what is the greatest question of your life: *what is your will, what do you really want?* We've seen that it isn't covered by what you consciously want. Your friend's conscious intention to go surfing was overridden by his much stronger intention to stay safely at home: and be sure that your own life provides plenty of instances of the same kind. In fact we can distinguish three areas of intention or will: (i) what you *think* you want, (ii) what you *really* want and (iii) all the rest, what you're up against, what the Universe wants.

Now if it should turn out that this third and immensely larger

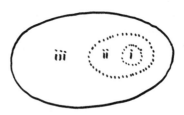

area is what you *really, really* want, and you not only contain the world but intend the world, that you want it all – (i), (ii) and (iii) – to be just as it is, why then you would be happy indeed. If you were wholeheartedly to choose the whole lot, all your stress would be laid to rest.

But alas the Universe is a difficult, dangerous, frustrating, painful and often exceedingly cruel affair. How could you sincerely tolerate all that, let alone endorse all that, to say nothing of actively intending it? Wouldn't your stress-free joy be bought at the expense of your honesty, of your compassion, of your natural revulsion against the world's dreadful injustices; and therefore be a false joy, ostrich-like escapism? Would it, in fact, be stress-free, arrived at thus? Ostriches (I guess) are no less tense than eagles.

Rather than speculate further, let's look at two people who, approaching the problem of the will from very different directions, actually solved it – in real-life terms.

My first could scarcely be more low-key and undramatic. He was a lumbering and simple regular soldier of late middle-age, who happened briefly to serve as my orderly during the war. The fact that he was lame was the least of his troubles. He was in constant pain from war wounds, and his wife was dying of cancer. He was also one of the most quietly cheerful and relaxed – yet effectual – people I have ever come across, and the least given to self-pity. His secret? Well, I feel sure he was unaware of having one at all. And equally sure that, far more by nature than nurture, he belonged to that fortunate company who have somehow acquired that most valuable of life-skills – the habit of saying YES! to what befalls them.

My second example resembles the first only in that saying of YES! In all else the contrast could not be greater.

Richard Wurmbrand spent fourteen years in Communist prisons in Romania, as a dissident. He suffered beatings, torture, drugging. For two years he was shut up in the 'death room', so called because no other man had left it alive. Nevertheless he spent his time whenever possible comforting and caring for his fellow prisoners. To one of them, by tapping on his cell wall, he spelled out the realization that sustained him through all his ordeals: 'When you will all that happens, then what happens is only what you will. Renunciation is the way to peace.' In his case it proved to be the way to joy also. On his release he wrote: 'The prison years did not seem long for me, for I discovered . . . a deep and extraordinary ecstasy of happiness that is like nothing else in this world. And when I came out of jail I was like someone who comes down from the mountaintop where he has seen for miles around the peace and beauty of the countryside . . .'

In our terms, what my batman and that Romanian dissident did was to raise to consciousness all three areas of their intention: not only (i), which already is the conscious will, and not only (ii), which is the deeper and unconscious will that at times one can become aware of, but also (iii), which is all the rest, the deepest and widest and most hidden region of the will. In effect, they extended to the very limit the all-important realization *that what they really, really wanted was the thing that was happening to them; and that thing was everything (since all things are interconnected), all that is, the Universe itself.* What was done to them wasn't done by the agent but by the Agency, by the Whole Organization, by the One they really, really were. And so they got their hearts' desire in spite of all appearances to the contrary, in spite of what the outside observer would call personal tragedy and terrible circumstances. They lived the solution of the problem of stress.

WHAT CAN YOU AND I DO?

Is it beyond you and me, who are by no means uncanonized saints or heroes, to learn the art of saying YES! to life, and to start living it now?

Not at all. I don't say that the task is easy, but that it is simple. Nor is it so hard as we fear – provided we break it down into its constituent parts, into the task of this moment. Of course, these moments add up to a lifetime's work, a much longer job perhaps and certainly a more exacting one than making your first million pounds. But would you have it otherwise? Do you want to miss the adventure, the ups and downs of discovering and rediscovering in what *is* – in what they call 'reality', sometimes dreadful, sometimes neutral, sometimes lovely – that extraordinary and unforeseeable and altogether indescribable perfection which Richard Wurmbrand and many others assure us of, which their lives guarantee is available? Would you have that enterprise of enterprises all over and done with at the very first sight of Who you are? Do you want to abridge or tone down or bowdlerize the story till there's practically no story left? Surely the truth is that what you really, really want – in that third and deepest region of your will – is that your winning through to that region shall be the challenge that it is and anything but automatic: that it shall be the ultimate Test of your life and your aliveness? And anyway, as Who you are, haven't you already decided to make access to Who you are so resisted (yet so wide open), so hard (yet so easy and natural), such a mixture of joy and pain? I can't see you going back on that primeval decision.

In any case, look at the choices you now have. Cursing and shaking your fist at the Power behind the scenes, or moaning and groaning about what it's laying on you, or bottling up your resentfulness and misery – or else endorsing it all, not excluding those negative feelings? What do you stand to gain by the first three? Or to lose by the fourth? Come on, let's be sensible about this, and give YES a chance to prove itself against NO.

For your encouragement, there's the fact that you can at once get down to practice. This doesn't consist in merely reminding yourself of the conclusions we've come to in this chapter, but of testing them again and again till they are built into your life. I don't mean gritting your teeth and putting on a ghastly smile and saying YES! to all that's happening to you, regardless, as a duty and a discipline. That could lead to harmful repression of your feelings and self-deception – to sweeping your personal garbage, and the world's, under a carpet that doesn't exist. No: see things for what they are, exactly as given in your Emptiness – in this Openness which manifestly has no preferences, no resistances or resentments, no check-list of good and bad things, no categories of beautiful and ugly, acceptable and unacceptable. And see what comes of paying attention to the way you already are. *See how perfectly you are built for this job of willing what is. See how proper and natural it is for you.* And just allow (don't force) the joy to arise, the peace that comes of having nothing to complain about. Given half a chance, it surely will, perhaps much sooner than you imagine possible. Anyway, let's make a start right now:

Experiment 16: Choosing what is

Please take at least five minutes over this experiment – remember what's at stake.

Think of your main current hang-up, the affliction and resentment of the moment . . .

Name it, as accurately as you can . . . Stay with it . . . Go over its salient features repeatedly, till you know them backwards, forwards, every way . . . Look at its likely origin and outcome . . .

Now see yourself as empty for all this, as the speckless Mirror in which it's all reflected, as the Screen on which that sad tale is unfolding without any damage to the Screen itself, or any staining of the Mirror . . .

That's to say, look at that affliction from the Place of no affliction, just as you are now looking at these printed words from the Place of no printed words, from the Place where there's nothing whatever in their way . . .

Notice that you can no more refuse admission to that current hang-up than to this page of printing . . . and yet are, yourself, in no more danger of being hung up than in danger of being printed on.

Next, ask yourself: how did it all come about . . .? Where do your so-called hang-ups arise from . . .? Is this tragic film being thrown on your Screen by some fiendish Projectionist, lurking outside the cinema . . .?

Outside . . .? What outside . . .? For you as What you really, really are, and visibly without limits, all is inside, your own, *you*.

No: it all comes out of, is sustained by, and returns to What you are . . . Look and see that this is so . . .

What more revealing discovery has man ever made than his own unconscious? Having arrived thereby at the startling discovery that what he *most* wants can be what he thinks he *least* wants, the matter doesn't end there, or on the psychiatrist's couch. His individual unconscious (ii) provides him with a much-needed stepping-stone from his conscious (i) to the universal Unconscious (iii). In traditional language, his will was up against God's, and hard it was to reconcile them. But now, this intermediary (ii), having shown him how little he knows his own will, the reconciliation – though still hard – is to hand. Now he has no more reason to deny that the unacceptable aspects of (iii) are his will in disguise, than are those of (ii).

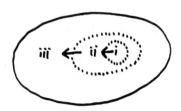

Not in your human capacity but your infinite capacity, as that human's Source and Reality, you come in the end to take responsibility for the lot, for areas (i) and (ii) and (iii). Responsibility for (i), what you knew you wanted, and (ii), what you didn't know you wanted, and (iii) what you're stuck with anyway, much of which you were sure you didn't want. All three prove, in the end, to be what you really, really want.

Therefore you are fulfilled, and you know what it is to be profoundly joyful and stress-free.

THIS IS OPTING INTO LIFE, NOT OUT OF IT

One final doubt I can imagine you voicing here: When at last I line up my intentions with those of my Source, or Origin, or True Nature (or whatever I choose to call it), so that I go along with everything that occurs, what happens to my life as a normal, responsible, healthy human? Is this the end of my decision-making? Do I lose all interest in the ordinary goals I've been setting up all my life, and working for, and on the whole achieving? Am I going to give up wanting anything – wanting that home in the country, that better make of car, that more important job, that exciting holiday, the fun of winning at tennis or golf? It seems I'm in danger of deteriorating into an admirably stress-free vegetable.

So it might seem, till misfortune – or the growing pressures of life, or happy chance, or grace – bring on a more wakeful mood, and you begin to raise to consciousness and to integrate all three areas of your wanting: namely, what you want, what you really want, and what you really, really want. Those who have done so report that the effect is – yes – that you get what you want because you want what you get: and nevertheless this is likely to mean not less but *more* efficiency, *more* success in the commonplace duties and endeavours of life, *more* pleasure in work and play, and certainly much relief from those unachievable goals which the Joneses and the Robinsons keep setting up for you. But this all-round improvement is, after all, only to be expected. You get further with less effort when you and the escalator are going in the same direction, when you cease swimming against God's current or sailing head-on into his wind. And you cut out the stresses and strains of the journey too.

Insofar as you consciously act from what you really, really are and really, really want, instead of from what you've been told you are and want, every little and big thing you do – all the way from washing the dishes to planning your beautiful home (what's wrong with that, for Heaven's sake?) – all is done better than before. This is because the You that's doing it isn't that little person confronting you in your mirror, or those hands busy at the kitchen sink or at the drawing board or the concert piano, but what's nearer than they are, what's nearer than all else. The unthinged You which is *here*, activating those hands and everything else besides – this has to be incomparably more skilled than anything of yours over there. Experiment, and check that this is so.

There's another happy discovery awaiting you. Everything you find yourself doing takes on another quality. Not that you deliberately revalue it, but rather that it revalues itself. All your circumstances and tasks are on the way to becoming equally enjoyable, equally unstressful; and also equally enjoyable from start to finish, and not just momentarily, at the time of successful completion. Thus life is no longer postponement. It's jam *today*. Even hanging around waiting for someone who's late, even filling in your tax returns, is no longer so disagreeable, so very different from the arrival at last of that friend, and from getting a notice from the tax collector that *he* owes *you* something. You'll find, I predict, that no chore is too mean for you and unworthy of your talents: and that, conversely, no high endeavour is specially high or that important. Who you are takes all in its stride. The reason for this evenness, for this mysterious sameness, obviously doesn't lie at the far or business end of the operation – in those hands and what they're working on, say at the sink or the drawing board or the concert platform – but at the near end, at your end, where you imagined you had a head chock-a-block with considerations and preferences about what you should be doing. Consciously done from Here, even the most boring and repetitive work turns out to be more like play. Not because of what it is but because of Who's doing it.

Why not start testing these sweeping assertions at once? There's no better place to begin than at the kitchen sink. You may well find that the job gets done quicker, and fewer dishes get chipped, and everything's left tidy for a change. The stress of resisting what you have to do is so clumsy and incapacitating, the relaxation of wanting to do it so dextrous.

ACCESS UNLIMITED

This chapter promises a lot – on conditions – at a price that can be afforded but must be paid. The amount and the currency and the method of payment must be right. In other words, your technique makes a world of difference.

If you are serious about anything you undertake, if you're looking for results and aren't just fooling around, you go into the technology of it. You find out what to do, and how to do it, and in what order. You do it right. To get the cash you want out of a cash dispenser, you follow the instructions meticulously. To get the joy you want out of life – out of its joy dispenser – you must be equally conscientious and precise.

You probably carry around at least one ordinary credit card. You well know how to use it, and from time to time it comes in handy. But certainly you carry around a master credit card that – provided, again, you know exactly how to use it – is nothing short of wonder-working. All the time, at that. The name on the card is Access Unlimited, and it's designed to keep you supplied with joy, among other goodies. But you have to comply with the instructions. All nine or ten of them, carefully.

(1) Locate the right dispenser. It's the one that's *here* where you are, nowhere else.
(2) Check that it's in working order. It works *now*, never at other times.
(3) Select the right card. It's the one with your *portrait* on it – your identity card, in fact.
(4) Find the right slot for it to go into. It's the only *gap* in the machinery.
(5) Feed your master card, *head first*, into that empty slot.
(6) Punch in your secret four-figure number. Yours is *oooo*.
(7) Punch in a request to be told your credit balance. I can tell you now that it's unlimited, so you don't have to bother with this one.
(8) Punch in what you want. *Really* want.
(9) Wait.
(10) Collect.

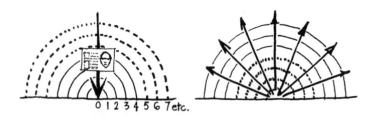

I sympathize with your doubts about the ability of Access Unlimited, and the bank behind it, to cope with your demands. You can only try it, and see. Or better, see, and try it. Meanwhile, here for your encouragement is a sampling of the statements put out by the bank's spokesmen:

Ask, and it shall be given you; seek, and you shall find; knock, and it shall be opened to you.

You can have what you want, provided you really want it.

The present moment holds all you could desire.

Only stop pretending. Be who you are, and what you need will turn up. Not what you superficially want: but what you deeply want, with all your heart and not part of it.

After all, you are only getting what you asked for.

If, after giving this master card of yours a fair trial, you are still dissatisfied with the results, it could be for one of three reasons. It could be that Access Unlimited, and the assurances we've just sampled, are fraudulent. Or that it has gone bankrupt. Or that you failed to comply with one or another of the instructions. Which of these do you think is most likely?

Maybe you didn't pick, out of the wide selection available, the right card, the one with your own face on it. Or, if you did, maybe you held on to it at the last moment, and failed to check that the face vanished into the empty slot. Maybe you punched in the wrong personal number: number one, for instance, instead of zero. Maybe, again, you didn't punch in what you really wanted, so naturally you are disappointed. Maybe you have forgotten what you punched in, so that the only way of finding out is to see what you're getting out. Maybe you are too impatient, and haven't given the works time to deliver. And finally, maybe you still have to count what's coming up.

In short, before you blame the Utility, make sure it's being correctly utilized.

SUMMARY AND CONCLUSION

Let's end this chapter by reviewing our discoveries.

To end stress, win. We found that the joy of winning our immediate objective, however, soon goes, showing that *that* wasn't our real objective. (What we *think* we want is often the opposite of what we want deeper down.) Our task, then, is to extend the joy of winning, by finding and getting what we really, really want. This (it's the biggest and best surprise of our life) turns out to be what happens to us, what *is*, the circumstances which hitherto had been our unconscious will and conscious bugbear or obstacle. To the extent that we raise this third-level will to the light of consciousness, we enjoy life. This means that at last we know the sweet taste and smell of success, are lastingly happy, stress-free at root, undaunted by disaster. And, for good measure, we become rather more efficient at those mundane jobs which, performed now from *Here*, from our True Nature, must shine with some of its glory.

11

STRESS AND THE HUMAN PREDICAMENT

THE STRESS OF IMPENDING DOOM

Willing all that happens to oneself is clearly what one has to do to be free of stress oneself. But it's far from clear how one could – or should – will all that happens to other people. What about the awesome catastrophes that threaten our species – the disasters we can see coming, and those that are already breaking over us? The stress they generate seems only too well-based and unavoidable. Is there any answer to it, other than removing its basis, the under-lying causes of war and nuclear war, of pollution, of over-pop-ulation, of hunger, and so on? And what – to be realistic – are our chances of doing that?

For a growing number of us this large-scale scene – the plight of Humanity itself – is where our anxiety and stress are at their most conscious and severe. It's difficult to ignore the grim facts (the media see to that) but, insofar as we succeed in doing so, we don't reduce our stress. On the contrary, it's all the worse for being bottled up. Most of us are well aware of the man-made disasters hanging over us, but we don't know what to do about them; or, if we have ideas, we never quite get around to action – for all sorts of plausible reasons, including, '*I* could make no difference, anyway.' It's not a happy life, but at least our stress and distress are out in the open. Another type of person – and very likely it's your type – really wants to reduce the threats to humanity and the stress they generate. You are eager to do something. You figure that helping to prevent the build-up of stress to an even-more-disastrous level in your world, is a good way of doing the same thing in yourself, since you and your world are inseparable. The question is: how shall you go about that huge task?

There are, of course, many answers competing for your attention, some making excellent sense, others fuelling the flames they are supposed to put out. You have a wide choice. Our own answer in this chapter doesn't under-value, much less rule out, any that promise to be at all effective.

GETTING TO THE ROOT OF THE PROBLEM

Let's agree that the best way to reduce the stress arising from the self-inflicted danger we're in is to reduce the danger itself; and the best way to do that is to get down to its root causes. These are FEAR, HATE AND GREED or CRAVING – a fact no less crucial because it's common knowledge, a cliché. Evidently, if no longer fed by fear and hate, war and preparations for war would wither away. Without craving and greed, the heedless waste of the human and biological and mineral resources of our planet would cease. Any proffered 'solution' of the great problems of our time, which doesn't address itself to these three underlying evils, is unlikely to do much to help our endangered species – to say nothing of putting it out of danger.

For our part, it's important to recognize that fear and hate and greed are ultimately one and the same. They are three aspects of our alienation, of our separation from ourselves, from one another, from all things. It is always the *other* that I fear, hate, envy, plan to destroy. Prove to me that there's a level on which I *am* you, and you *are* me – and all aspects of our mutual alienation are ended. Deny that fact – and all we do in the supposed cause of peace and goodwill and human happiness is, in the long run, counter-productive. Instead of adding to it we *subtract* from the safety of the world.

It follows that here we have no option but to start at home, where the trouble originates. (For each of us, surely, a thrilling personal adventure no less than a duty owed to suffering humanity.) First let us find the remedy for our own alienation, for our own resistance to and separation from people and things, and then the remedy for our fear and hate and greed – along with the stress they build – will be to hand. Then, and only then, shall we be able to tackle the same problems on a large scale, and to do something to make the world a less dangerous place for living in. We have no way of helping others to a safety we haven't found ourselves.

Experiment 17: Trying on your safety-helmet, Part 1

The full title of this experiment is: *Trying on the crash-helmet that protects you against all accidents – whether you are a motorcyclist or not.*

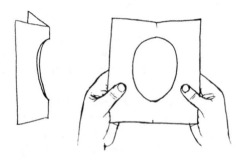

Make a roughly head-shaped and head-sized hole in a sheet of paper or card. This you can easily do by folding it down the middle and cutting or tearing out an oval – the shape can be quite rough.

Hold out the card at arm's length and eye level, observing that hole. It is your safety-helmet . . .

See how clear it is of the slightest obstruction . . . how perfectly empty and transparent . . . how safe from every sort of damage . . .

Now, if you were able to wear that always, you would be immune to all disaster, man-made or not . . .

All right then, *wear it* – like this: Bring it very slowly up to your face (absence of). Put it on as you would a mask . . . Try on your safety-helmet for emptiness . . . for size . . . for comfort . . . for safety . . .

Put it right on, and hold it there . . .

What has happened? Is that hole now filled . . .? Or is it still just as empty and transparent and speckless as ever . . .? And still as incapable of injury . . .?

Check that the only thing that has happened to that hole is that it has grown and grown and lost its boundaries . . . has become infinite, the Infinite Hole or Emptiness or Absence or No-thingness that you are . . . and become aware of itself as You . . .

Your personal safety-helmet has become your world's. In all circumstances you are out of danger. You never need – in truth you never can – take off what (borrowing an apt phrase from the Bible) is your *helmet of salvation*.

Take off the card and try it on again, very slowly, to make sure there's been no mistake . . .

As this Worldwide Gap you are inviolate. Can you then afford to let the world go by, with all its suffering and horrors and disasters?

If nothing else, your heart tells you this won't do at all. And no wonder: for it's only half the story – the easy half, and *by itself* false. (Aren't all the worst lies half-truths?) In our experiment we overlooked one all-important fact. We suppressed a vital piece of evidence – no insignificant detail, but one that cried out to be noticed. Let's take another look at that hole.

Experiment 18: Trying on your safety-helmet, Part 2

Hold out the card as before . . . and again see how empty that hole is . . . AND HOW FULL . . .

Examine carefully the *contents* of that 'empty' hole in the card . . . its present filling . . .

Now slowly move the card from side to side . . . up and down . . . watching its contents changing from (say) a pair of feet . . . to a patch of carpet . . . a chair . . . a window and the view from it . . . and so on without limit . . . Is there anything you can't find in it . . .? If it's a clear night outside, you can find a thousand stars in it . . .

Now see how perfectly *united* are the emptiness of that hole and its filling . . . So that you could say that this No-thing *is* all things, and they *are* it . . . That this Container *is* its contents . . .

And now try on, not this time the *mere* emptiness, but the Emptiness that's actually given, the Emptiness as experienced – the Emptiness that isn't just filled with the scene, but *is* the scene . . .

Try that hole on again (again as if it were a mask) for Emptiness-Fullness, for size, for comfort, for a good fit . . . And keep it on . . .

Finally, take it off and try it on again, very slowly . . . to check that at no point does that emptiness-filled-with-the-scene change, except that the scene widens and loses its boundaries and becomes infinite . . . and to check that at no point do your face and head come into the picture . . .

So now the completed story, the whole truth about you, is three-fold. Instead of being the mere thing they told you you were, you turn out to be (i) No-thing at all, and (ii), the Totality of things (and, as these, altogether safe), *and* (iii), every particular thing that lies between (and, as such, altogether unsafe and at risk). Yes, you are wholly free from harm by your very nature as (i) and (ii), and wholly free from the stresses and strains of the world of things: *and*, by your very nature as (iii), wholly caught up in them. The *difference* between you as Container (i & ii) and as Contents (iii) is infinite, the *separation* is nil. On the one hand, each of those things counts as just itself, just one thing. You, on the other hand, count as zero and an infinity of things, and each of them in particular, as well. *As o and ∞ you are stress-free. As what lies between them you are stress-bound.*

The contents that fill your ever-peaceful Container build a Universe out of their clashing. The horseshoe takes shape between the downward blows of the hammer and the upthrust of the anvil; the corn is ground as the millstones or rollers work under pressure against each other; the paper is cut by the opposing blades of the scissors; you are now holding this book between your opposable thumb and forefinger – and can feel the stress in them. And so it is at all levels from 'competing' particles to competing humans. (How can the relationships between individuals, generations, sexes, businesses, political parties, sects, nations, races, ideologies – how can they operate at all without stress and strain?) And so it is from us warring humans to those star wars we instinctively insist on – as if Earth's puny conflicts were not enough! Tennyson was right: Nature is 'red in tooth and claw', and there's no way of toning down that crude primary colour into a non-violent pastel-pink – except by looking at it through a cloud of wishful thinking.

Does this mean that an unkindly Providence, while relieving you of stress with one hand, piles it on with the other? Does it mean that your native peace is inevitably shattered by having to take on all the world's stress, all its catastrophes and pain and alienation – even finding room for its terrible weight of greed and hate and fear? Well, what do you have of your own to keep them out with? How can you be the stress-free All without embracing every stressful part?

The time has come to leave aside for the moment such general and abstract questions, and take a look at actual cases – four of them. Watching real people coping in very different ways with real-life disasters, and seeing how they handle the stress of them, will help us to arrive at our own answers.

(i) The case of the Red Cross worker in Nigeria

Several years ago, I watched an appeal on TV by a Red Cross worker in Nigeria during the Biafran War – a particularly nasty conflict. What she said about the terrible suffering of the civilian population was graphic and no doubt all too true, and certainly it supported her appeal for funds. However, what struck me at the time more forcibly than the agony of violence and disease and hunger in Biafra was the agony of stress in her voice and on her face. She could not have cared more. Her involvement was complete, her detachment non-existent. And I suspect that, as a result, her effectiveness in the field, like her performance on the box as a fund-raiser, suffered greatly. She was doubtless a very good woman indeed, perhaps heroic, but it seemed to me she had no access to that interior Rest which (as I hope to show) can not only receive without harm, but somehow transmute, all the world's unrest.

(ii) The case of the soldier on leave

A thirty-three-year-old British soldier in India during the Second World War, on leave in the Himalayas, made what was for him an all-important discovery. He took a fresh look at himself, and this is his description of the result, somewhat abbreviated:

> What I found was trouser legs terminating at the top of the picture in a pair of shoes, sleeves terminating sideways in a pair of hands, and a shirtfront terminating at the bottom of the picture in – absolutely nothing whatever. Certainly not in a head.

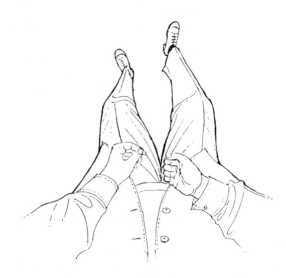

It took me no time at all to notice that this nothing, this hole where a head should have been, was very much occupied. It was a vast emptiness vastly filled, a nothing that found room for everything – room for that decapitated trunk, for grass, trees, shadowy distant hills, the sky . . . I had lost a head and gained a world . . . There arose no questions, no reference beyond the experience itself, but only peace and a quiet joy, and the sensation of having dropped an intolerable burden.

The soldier's leave having expired, he returned to his officers' mess in Calcutta. Bengal was in the grip of famine. It had been no rare thing for the destitute to die unattended in Calcutta streets, but now they were dying in hundreds and thousands, and many of the living were walking or prostrate skeletons – little children included. At the very door of his quarters he had to step over pleading forms.

Of course he felt pity and gave something. But he remained uninvolved, detached, cool. It wasn't a deliberate withdrawal from the suffering around him, a conscious retreat into the safety and perfection of the Emptiness he'd discovered in that so different (though not so distant) mountain setting. All the same, he really was running away from the stress and distress out there to their absence right here at the Centre. As if he could! As if this new-found refuge were by itself the answer to the world's catastrophes! It's true he had, with well-founded relief and delight, read correctly the first half of the story, the piece about absolute detachment, the easy part. The hard part, the part about absolute involvement, he had yet to take in and take to heart. Yes: he had made a good start. He had begun to solve the problem of stress – no more. For the present, he was able to look down at those emaciated forms with an equanimity that was deeply unreal and, one has to say, appalling. The reason I feel free to make such a comment is that that soldier was me.

(iii) The case of Anandamayi Ma and the Rani

Some twenty years after that wartime experience, I was in India again, staying at the ashram of Anandamayi Ma, a Bengali saint and seer with a following of millions. At that time she was a handsome woman of remarkable poise and dignity, around (I suppose) sixty years old. Through an interpreter (she spoke no English, I spoke no Bengali) I was privileged to have several conversations with her on the subject of a line – 'I bow to thee, I bow to thee, O goddess who art the Consciousness in all creatures' – that recurred in the traditional songs her attendants sang daily, and which happened to move me greatly. Two events in that ashram stand out in my memory. One was when, at our parting, Ma gave me the shawl from her head with the words: 'I am you, I am you!' The other was when a Rani, an Indian princess whose only son had just died, came to see Ma. For a long while she comforted that bereaved mother. Seers have something of a reputation for detachment. Well, Ma was weeping as copiously and for as long as her visitor was.

Among the saint's recorded words are some that might have been spoken to me personally at the time of that Bengal famine:

> If, after coming down from the state of contemplation, you are capable of behaving as before, you have not yet been transformed ... People come to me and tell me of their sons and daughters having got into a car and driven away, without looking up to see if they are weeping. They are quite unmoved by their parents' grief. You see, this is precisely what it is like at a certain stage on the Path ... You feel: 'Those whom I believed to be my very own are merely related to me by flesh and blood. What is that to me?' ... But later, when you have become detached even from detachment, there is no problem of detachment or non-detachment. What is, is THAT.

Anandamayi Ma was neither attached to nor detached from that mother and her grief. She *was* both. Her message for her devotee, as for me then and ever since that memorable occasion, was and is I AM YOU.

(iv) The case of Mother Teresa

Around the same time as the Red Cross worker – our first case – appeared on British TV, so did another woman, one equally concerned with human suffering and disaster – Mother Teresa of Calcutta. The scenes around her were scarcely less terrible than those of the Biafran War. Yet the contrast between the two women was extraordinary. The voice and the face of Mother Teresa witnessed to an inner serenity, a peace and stillness that, so far from being overshadowed or dimmed by the misery of the sick and the dying she loved and served, only made that peace shine brighter. Her friend and biographer Malcolm Muggeridge writes:

In effacing herself she becomes herself. I never met anyone more memorable. Just meeting her for a fleeting moment makes an ineffaceable impression. I have known people to burst into tears when she goes, though it was only from a tea party where their acquaintance with her amounted to no more than receiving her smile. Once I had occasion to see her off, with one of the sisters, at Calcutta railway station . . . When the train began to move, and I walked away, I felt as though I were leaving behind me all the beauty and all the joy in the universe.

Here is a living example of how to deal with the stress and distress of the world, including one's own: namely, to dive headfirst into the thick of it all – and stay free of it all. 'To care, and not to care', as T. S. Eliot put it. Mother Teresa wasn't, like the Red Cross worker, overlooking her interior Peace; nor was she, like that British soldier, wallowing in it. Still less was she delicately picking her way along some middle path between these extremes, some sensible compromise. No! She made for both extremes at once, with characteristic energy and dedication, and in practice solved the problem this chapter poses. The fact that our own language and belief systems may well have little connection with hers doesn't matter. The lesson for us here isn't her words but her deeds, and – even more – herself; and her heart-warming demonstration of the way to cope unstressfully with catastrophe, and for that reason to be really effective in doing what has to be done.

The four cases compared

Earlier in this chapter we said that the sensible way of undermining stress – in particular the stress that is due to the many-sided man-made danger we're all in – is to undermine the danger itself, by attacking its roots of fear and hate and greed or craving. Or, in a word, alienation. Let's now see how far our four cases succeeded in doing this.

(i) The Red Cross worker – everything about her – showed her *fear* of war and its effects, her *hate* of warmongers and her *craving* for her friends' security and survival. Result: stress and ineffectiveness. Along that road, sooner or later, lies despair or madness.

(ii) The soldier in India had broken through fear and hate and greed to a kind of peace. But there remained a strong, unconscious craving for and attachment to the half-truth of himself as *empty* Space, as distinct from the whole truth of himself as *filled* Space. This attachment he used to disengage himself from suffering humanity. In this he was, to put it mildly, unrealistic. He never had any shield against disaster. Result: for a long time much hidden guilt and stress remained.

(iii) I have no doubt that Anandamayi Ma's central freedom from fear and hate and craving, along with all other emotions, was complete. (It is complete in us all: for her it was consciously so.) And no doubt that her weeping, in sympathy with that bereaved mother, was all the more heartfelt because it did nothing to disturb the even tenor of her own serenity. She took on the other's grief by being herself free of grief, just as she took on the other's face by being herself faceless. Fully to appreciate what this means in practice you have, like Ma, to see steadily Who you are. To get the point you have only to see, right now, how your own Emptiness is empty for these comments on her.

(iv) In her own fashion Mother Teresa has broken through to confidence in place of fear, love in place of hate, abandon and detachment and surrender in place of craving. She takes on joyously the most appalling of human tragedies because her central Peace remains undisturbed. In our terms, she has solved the problem of stress by immersion in it, by *being* it absolutely and *not being* it absolutely. In theory absurd? If you like. In practice, it's the way that works. And how astonishingly it works!

You may feel that, unlike the women I've been describing, you are not the stuff that saints and heroines are made of. Don't be too sure. Countless unsung heroes and heroines have risen to meet the challenge of disaster and human suffering, and never saw themselves that way. Their general message is for us to learn; their particular beliefs and vocations are their business. The fact is that you are made of exactly the same stuff as they are made of, and it's as unstressable in you as in them. And as capable of taking on anything, anything whatever, without the slightest injury to that central Perfection and absolute Safety we all share.

OUR DAY-TO-DAY PRACTICE

So what does it all come to in the end, in our day-to-day practice? What can we do right away about the human condition with its catastrophe piled on catastrophe, catastrophes looming or actually happening? We can do three things:

(i) We can stop playing ostrich. We can raise our heads from the sand of wishful thinking and pretending all's well, or that our troubles will somehow blow over. They won't. Or, for one that does, we're pretty sure to find a new one or two darkening our horizon. And even if man's self-created disasters – present or in the making – were miraculously avoided, plenty of the other sort would remain to polish him off. Natural calamities are – natural. No less than individuals, Humanity itself – in common with all else – is on Life's hit list. Everything perishes. Wholeheartedly acknowledging and saying YES! to this self-evident fact is already to start undermining the deep stress that comes of turning a blind eye to it. What's more, having anticipated and endorsed our death as things in the world, we don't have to pile on the agony by speculating about the time and the manner of our manifest dying, individually or collectively. Looked at steadily and accepted, universal mortality is no reason for going into permanent mourning, or wearing the long face of its funeral furnisher. See whether it doesn't give rise to a tenderness, and take on a marvellous beauty, that take us by surprise. And dissipate our fear – our fear of death and of life.

(ii) Yet it's no bad thing to be fearful, provided we're driven to the one refuge from all danger and stress and fear – to this incomparable Safety, to the Place or No-place we have all along been at. By pointing a finger – or simply looking at What we're looking out of at this moment, or by any other means that works for us – let's get Home to What we are. Let's stay with and live from this absolutely safe Reality instead of that accident-prone appearance in our mirror, and see what comes of it, what happens to our stress.

(iii) But let's not get stuck on the Container here, at the expense of its contents, of the world. We can't too often remind ourselves that it's not a case of balancing one against the other, of compromise or moderation, but of *extremism*. We have to see and to live the strange truth that we are forever free from the stress and pain and tragedy of the world, *and* we are forever caught up in them, as well as in the joy and love of the world. Then let us go on to discover what is our special role, what is our unique and unpredictable work for the good of the world which is ourself. Maybe it's a humble and hidden job, maybe little more than setting an example of stress-free personal happiness plus a vivid appreciation of people and things for what they are. (Only this No-body extends the perfect welcome to everybody, letting them all in and letting them all be.) But rest assured that one moment of seeing yourself as Empty-for-all affects all profoundly. Your best contribution to the future isn't what you say, or even what you work for, but what you *are* now. Nothing is so catching as this well-founded freedom from stress, this impersonal serenity that must embrace all persons.

So this is our threefold practice – our thoroughly practical discipline. There's no occasion in our working or leisure life when it's inappropriate or inefficient to live from the truth. Agreed that the truth, so easy to see, is so hard to keep on seeing. But is life without it less hard? Is life lived from a many-sided lie a practical proposition? Let's remember, let's take courage from the fact that our practice isn't changing our lifestyle, but noticing how we're living in any case – as this Empty Fullness, as this truly amazing union of perfect freedom and total involvement.

And let us remember that living thus, consciously, is the very best thing we can do for our disaster-prone world.

12

BEYOND THE STRESS WORLD

In the previous chapter we looked at four ways of coping with the suffering we find around us: that of the Red Cross worker who let it get her down; that of the soldier, returning from leave in the Himalayas, who refused to let it get him down; that of Anandamayi Ma, who went down and down into the anguish of her devotee, yet stayed immovable and serene; and the way of Mother Teresa, which couldn't be more unlike the Hindu saint's way outwardly, or more like it inwardly. The first we described as notably stressful, the second as hiding some stress, the third and fourth as notably stress-free.

In this chapter I complete my report on the second of these four cases – because it's my case and I can write with full assurance of no other, and because its outcome will see us through the remaining stages of this inquiry.

Impelled by good fortune or grace rather than under my own steam, I went on to find a way beyond stress. I hope you will find it as practicable as I do. It's a way of going down without being got down, a way that doesn't require us to become heroes or saints or converts to any particular faith, a way that lies open to us now just as we are.

I can best introduce it and bring it to life by retelling that 'Himalayan' story as I relive it now, in the pleasant but less grand setting of the sierras of southern California in early spring after rain, where I happen to be writing this. My aim stays unchanged. It is to give a maximum of attention to the scene (including that part of it which I call 'myself'), along with a minimum of interpretation: it is to wake as if for the first time to what's going on, to bow before the evidence. BOW BEFORE THE EVIDENCE – and I mean *bow* literally as well as figuratively – that's our ground rule from now on, throughout the rest of this inquiry:

Looking up now, I take in that cloudless ultramarine sky, immeasurably wide, unframed. Slowly bringing my gaze down, I find the crinkled silhouette of a breast-shaped hill, green-black against that brightness. Then its nearer, bush-dotted slopes. Then level grass, light green and glinting with morning dew, and a splash of flowers. All is silent and still. And, so far, there's just the view, with no trace of a viewer . . . Alas, this description belies the striking self-sufficiency of the seen. No words can do justice to that sublime givenness, that independence of me.

Continuing my bow before the evidence, I come across a child's-size pair of shoes, attached to a pair of trouser-legs so drastically foreshortened that they amount to shorts. These are in turn attached to a shirtfront abbreviated till it's more like a pelmet, widening greatly towards the bottom of the picture.

Yes: the *bottom* of the picture. This creature – what there is of it – is upside down.

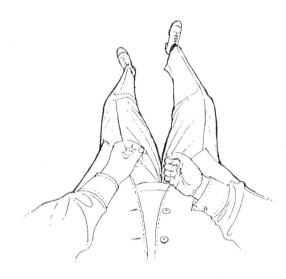

And then – my bow before the evidence at its deepest . . .
Then nothing at all:

Absence . . .

And no common absence at that. (Not the sort that's occupied with the thing's *image* in place of itself, as when you figure what letter is missing from this W RD, or look in vain for a head in our picture.) This shirt of mine ends downwards, at the bottom of the scene, in a Blank that's unoccupied and imageless and unimaginable, in absolutely nothing whatever. Here, completing my submission to the evidence, I come to the most overlooked and underrated spot in the world, the place that's replaced with No-place, the Terminus of termini, unique, baffling, the Mystery that's more than worthy of my humblest obeisance. All other places and objects I come across are set on *all* sides against a background. Somewhere or other they stop and something else begins: however big, they are encompassed within a perimeter – sharp or blurred – where they end and their environment begins. All except this magic shirt I'm wearing. It's as if some transcendental moth had been at it all along the neckline. Indeed this is the gnawing of no creature but the gnawing mystery of creation itself, of WHERE caught redhanded popping up out of NO-WHERE, of WHAT popping up – a divine Jack-in-the-box – out of NO-WHAT. All things above this Ultimate Bottom Line – those toy shoes up there, those truncated trunks, that pelmet-shirt itself on three of its four sides – all are normal inasmuch as they rest on something. *Those* are things that I can handle, that I have taped, that lie well within my capacity. But *This* defeats me. Here I've come to something that rests on no support, on a gap. Now this is irregular, abnormal, absurd – terms altogether too weak to do justice to such an Oddity. Here is the Line which underwrites and underscores all things, and is itself underwritten and underscored by a total White-out, by What's conspicuous by its absence. Above it, the world; below it not so much as a dust-grain – nor (and this is the point here) *room for one.*

To revert for a moment to that wartime soldier. I was a Sapper. I belonged to the Engineers, whose traditional task was twofold – sapping or undermining the fortifications of one side and building those of the other. And now my job isn't so very different. I'm still in the demolition-construction business, but it's the former that takes precedence. The world holds many wonders, but which of them can compare with this Undermining which tunnels beneath the world itself?

NO BELOW

let alone a head and shoulders

let alone empty space for them

My condition was perfectly described for me long ago. When Jesus said he had '*no place to lay his head,*' he was not, I'm convinced, complaining that he lacked a bed for the night. He had hospitable friends enough. No: he spoke, not complainingly but with gratitude and astonishment, of What he saw and valued beyond measure. Taken by itself, this is the saying of a homeless vagrant; taken along with the rest (e.g. 'You have indeed uncovered the Beginning', *Thomas* 18), it is the saying of one whose birthplace and whose Home is this No-place. Its meaning is precisely the same as Zen master Mumon's, 'No place can be found in which to put one's Original Face.'

For it's not as if, arriving at this No-man's-land and No-things'-land – or, if you like, at this Never-never-land – one comes to a *dead* end, to a region so nonexistent that it could hold no meaning and excite no interest. Exactly the reverse. It is that Unknowable from whose depths the known gushes without reason and without stint, that Unthinkable Seed of all life and all thought – including *this* thought about It. It is that Face which is masked by every face. In the following chapters I intend to show how, finding This, one finds the Point of it all, the Treasury and not just the treasure, the Resource of resources and Remedy of remedies; and moreover the final site for the disposal of all stress. One seeks in vain for labels, worthy labels that will stick to this Non-existence which is infinitely more real than any of its products, than anything which exists. It baffles us as it baffled Zen master Huang-po, who said: 'It is no mere nothingness. By this I mean that it does exist, but in a way too marvellous for us to comprehend. It is an existence which is no existence, a non-existence which is nevertheless existence. This true Void does in some marvellous way exist.'

Early in my 'Himalayan' period, getting on for half a century ago, I applied a variety of names to this Never-never-land that is also the Always-always-land. I called it Emptiness and Capacity and Absence and Nothingness and Void – terms I still can't improve on. Hopelessly inadequate separately, they do something for one another collectively. But also – where, as I thought, clarity would be served – I called it Space. Or, more precisely, 'Empty Space for that scene to happen in'. An unhappy phrase, for it seemed to say that I had found *above* the Bottom Line the world's content, and *below* it the world's Container, and that they were thus separable. True, having parted Space and its filling, I sought immediately to restore them to each other. Indeed I went further, and insisted on their unity. But the harm was done. Humpty Dumpty couldn't be put together again. The merest glance should have been enough to warn me: should have shown me that all the world in one piece – container and content undivided – belongs *above* the Line, and that there it's never served up short of room for itself. With hindsight, how mistaken was the picture of this dry toast of a world which I have to spread with the butter of space to make it digestible. Re-spread it (if you please) with the butter that I'd carefully scraped off in the first place, claiming it as mine! Such a gratuitous complication, such meddling with the stuff of my life, could hardly fail to affect that life. Accordingly there were occasions when, allowing this unreal, uninhabitable, abstract space to suffuse the Nowhere Land below my Bottom Line, I sought refuge in it from the real world of inhabited space, and in particular from its more tragic aspects. Thus I was able, returning to Calcutta from the Himalayas, to detach myself from those emaciated forms. As 'space for them to happen in' I was, in some degree, relieved of them. No wonder, then, that I paid in stress for that half-truthful lie, that false relief.

Happily, however, the mistake did not lie in the basic experience but in my interpretation of it. The lie belonged to the meaning of what I saw and not to the seeing itself. (All along it's been plain that, turning one's attention round 180° and looking in, one just *can't* see a distorted or partial version of one's Nature, no matter how mistaken one's understanding or deployment of that vision.) And happily, as I became more used to this essentially foolproof in-seeing, the notion that I was seeing into empty Space here corrected itself. In time and with practice I learned that there exists no bolt-hole or bunker or aid-raid shelter below the Line, that my life is lived above-ground willy-nilly, and that if I'm to be free of the world and its troubles it is by being them.

If I am perfectly contented now, it is because I have ceased to be any kind of Container at all, but instead am con*tent* with my *con*-tent.

Experiment 19: One world, inside-outside

Point *out* at the scene, noting the absolute union of content and container . . .

Now point *in, at exactly the same thing* . . . Note that the turning round of your finger makes not a scrap of difference . . .

See how the inlook no more emphasizes space than the outlook emphasizes its filling . . .

See how nonsensical is the idea that you have an inside world *and* an outside one . . .

In the rest of this book we shall be working out in detail how stress is discharged by taking it on, not evading it. How the road by which this toxic waste is transported doesn't lie up and out, but down and through – all the way down to the Edge of the World, where alone it is safely dumped. How the ultimate answer to your stress – its final disposal – is to be found where the lowest part of you (miscalled your topknot) has already been disposed of, and the rest has been up-ended to follow.

Don't be alarmed! Along with all the rest of your rubbish, that most stressful of ideas – that of your own death – will be dumped. Dumped exactly where? Just a little below the bottom edge of this book. Go on reading off the end of the page till you come to the End of the World, and see . . .

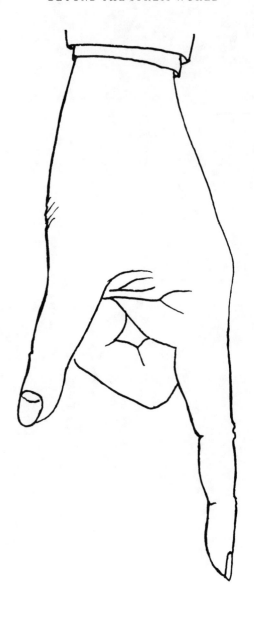

PART THREE
STRESS AND LIFE'S STAGES

The in-and-for-itself, the absolute, has not only gone out of life,
but has become something ridiculous in the eyes of men.

Kierkegaard

This, his being nothing, is the only way to be all things; this, his
having nothing, the truest way of possessing all things.

John Smith the Platonist

As long as I am this or that, I am not all things.

Eckhart

Now (said she) I know the cause, or the chief cause, of your
sickness. You have forgotten what you are.

Boethius

The form our stress takes depends on our individual circumstances
and temperament, but also very much on our time of life. In Part
Three we shall look at stress in childhood, when the price of
becoming human is to forget What we are; at stress in adulthood,
when the price of coping with our humanness – loneliness, boredom, guilt, failure, and so on – is to remember What we are; and
at stress at the time of our dying, when the price of a good death is
to stay with What we are, with the Essence which doesn't die – for
the simple reason that it never lived.

Here, in Part Three, we come to the deep end of the pool
described in the Preface. This is a suitable place for some readers –
those who feel they aren't quite ready to go forward – to go back
to the chapters where they weren't at all out of their depth, and go
on to the final chapter about the daily exercises which are for us

all. If you decide to skip Part Three and stay out of the deep end for the present, remember that the water there is still H_2O and no different from the water right where you are now. More water doesn't mean more Essence. Putting a tentative toe in that Essence, or plunging to its depths, you have it all, you are it all.

13

CHILDHOOD AND ADOLESCENCE

THE ENCHANTRESS AND HER SEVEN SPELLS

We come now to stress as it hits us initially, when we are young.

Is there a more appropriate and promising way through to the heart of our subject than a fairy tale, a tale about children of all lands for children of all ages, enlivened by plenty of magic – white, and terribly black?

Once upon a time there lived, in the remotest countryside, an old couple with seven daughters. They were a devoted and happy family, but so poor that Eyebright, the youngest, had to leave home and seek her fortune in the wide world, of which she knew nothing. After weeks of hard travelling she came to a beautiful and prosperous city, ruled over by an Enchantress. This Wicked Fairy had cast upon all her subjects a sevenfold spell that reduced them – as if in a powerful press – to a fraction of their original size, distorted them grotesquely, bedevilled them to the very heart. Thus remoulded, they were given the seal of royal approval and the rights of citizenship. The result was that the people, though well-off in other ways, were midgets or dwarfs, terribly misshapen, hopping round the splendid streets like so many frogs. And all of them crippled and possessed frogs, at that.

So Eyebright, who was in no state to travel further, faced an agonizing choice. Either she could squat at the city gate, a beggar living on scraps of garbage – no cripple, but suffering all the stress of a lonely and famished outcast; or else she could submit to being dwarfed and deformed and crazed, and live prosperously thereafter, but with all the stress of knowing at heart the dreadful price she had paid in self-respect to buy the respect of others, plus a comfortable existence for herself. It looked as if, either way, a life of severe and unremitting stress lay ahead of her.

However, following the pattern of all proper and true fairy tales, our heroine was as clever as she was brave. In the end she hit (as we shall presently see) on a way of beating the system, of counteracting the Wicked Fairy's black magic with her own more powerful white magic, so avoiding both kinds of stress.

This is what happened:

It was the royal custom to hold regular command parties for children and foreigners at the palace, and Eyebright allowed herself to be drawn in to one of these. The Enchantress, having welcomed her guests and settled them down, waved her wand. They all fell into a trance, and she addressed them thus:

'It is my duty to initiate you today into what it means to be a citizen of this realm. For the proper ordering of the state, I am putting you under seven spells:

'First, from this moment your Great Eye shall close, and you shall peep out at the world through a pair of tiny spyholes.

'Second, for the past few years, one of my familiars, called Starer, has been eyeing you hungrily from its glass-fronted cage. Now this spell sets Starer free to get at you, to invade and bug and possess you. I command you to be a good host, to welcome this lifelong parasite that will take you over, drain your energies and in the end kill you.

'Third, you shall no longer range unbounded and freer than the wind. I have caught you in my net and shut you in a box for life.

'Fourth, you and your loved ones shall be torn apart, and so remodelled that from now on you are all at loggerheads: *confrontation* being the first law of this city.

'Fifth, my superior magic destroys your power of staying forever still, and causing the city to dance around you delightedly. Henceforth, it is you who are on the move, dragging yourselves round the streets that have gone dead on you, ground to a halt.

'Sixth, with this wave of my wand, I reduce you from limitless wealth to destitution. Your riches I place out of reach, scattering them far and wide, because it amuses me to tantalize you.

'Seventh and last, you shall spend your life longing for all you've lost today – seeking, seeking your heart's desire, with almost no idea of what it is.

'So, my children, I've got you how I want you, all cut down to statutory size and statutory shape, and correctly bugged.

'And now, as you wake, you will remember nothing of this spellbinding. Henceforth these seven will for you be gospel truth, facts of life which, like the air you breathe, are so basic and taken for granted that you never give them a thought. Or – what's more important – a look.

'Wake, then, to your new life as true citizens of my realm . . .'

Now it so happened that Eyebright fell as readily under the influence of the Enchantress as the others did – except for the second spell. It wasn't that the dread Starer failed to break out of its glass-fronted cage and invade her, but that the invasion was only too real and devastating. Instead of putting up that parasite like a welcoming hostess, or at least putting up with that pop-eyed Thing, she suffered so much hurt and shame and bottled-up fury that everyone noticed her scowl and down-curving mouth.

The years went by, and she became no more reconciled to her unbidden guest . . .

Till one day, when she was quite grown up, she happened to discover that Starer had a weakness. It relaxed and dozed off from time to time. And then, caught off-guard with its grip weakened, it could suddenly be dislodged and pushed out and held at a distance for a few moments. What's more, every time Eyebright managed to surprise and oust Starer, she found herself pushing the Thing a shade further out and holding it there a shade longer. Soon she realized that, as a result of her vigorous fighting back, its strength was waning while hers was growing. Ever more frequently she plucked up the energy and the courage to hold the Thing right out there at arm's-length and thrust it into its glass-fronted cage. Till in the end it gave up trying to get back at her, and settled down safely behind glass and at a safe distance, no longer a parasite but every day more and more like a pet. It came to resemble a good yard-dog, well aware that it is as loathed indoors as it is liked out-of-doors and in its proper place. Thus the disgusting and deadly

Starer, the Wicked Witch's familiar, freed from its mistress and her spells, came to live a natural life again, as what it was and where it belonged. Accordingly Eyebright renamed it Fidelia, in recognition of its ever-devoted gaze upon herself, its real Mistress. Or Old Pop-eye, when in a frisky mood.

And then, having broken that most sinister of spells, it was easy enough for her to break, one by one, the rest. Quickly she came to recognize that all seven, seemingly so powerful, were in reality bluff, and that though the magic of the Enchantress turned upside-down what the citizens *believed* they were, it made no difference to what they *were*. Once you had enough energy and courage – and desperation – to get to grips with her boasted magic, it turned out to be eyewash.

Coming more and more to value this joyous and liberating discovery, Eyebright talked about it, cautiously, to her more intimate friends. At length several of them came to see that they, too, need not go on hosting that parasite, and neither need they remain half-blinded, or boxed in, or deformed, or powerless to make the world dance from their stillness, or reduced to penury – but could become as untouched by these curses as on the day they were born. And these friends, in turn, showed some of *their* friends how to break the seven spells . . .

And so in that city there grew, and is growing to this day, an Underground, a Resistance dedicated to exposing the System as the great hoodwink, the game of games. A game that's all right and stress-discharging to play if you see it as a game and make-believe, all wrong and stress-accumulating if you don't. For the members of the Resistance aren't noticeably unconventional, or antisocial, or spoil-sports. Where it's not destructive, they play being spellbound with at least as much success as those who take it seriously. O so dead seriously!

In fact, so far from the Resistance being antisocial, it is deeply concerned with the welfare – the very survival – of the city. In the end black magic destroys the magician along with the magician's victims. The spells of the Enchantress – having (no doubt about it) made for the city's prosperity over the ages – are becoming ever more counterproductive and mass-suicidal. In particular, the fourth spell – *confrontation* – has got altogether out of hand. Once tolerable, this magic goes on spawning diabolical powers which place the city itself in mortal danger.

And you, dear Reader (having with full attention carried out our experiments, the aim of which is to break those seven spells), are now a member of the Resistance. You belong to that growing Survival Team which sees that our hope, as individual humans and as a race, lies in waking, like our heroine, from our enchantment. And sees that no reforms – never mind how drastic or enlightened, and never mind whether they are labelled religious or psychological or political – no reforms that leave the reformers and the reformed asleep and dreaming the sevenfold nightmare, will save us.

And none of them – even if we do muddle through for the time being – will cure our stress. The question is: how can we become as stress-free as the cat purring on our lap, or the baby crooning in its cot, or the swallow wheeling and darting overhead, yet be fully human? And the answer is: *only by deliberately becoming as immune to the witchcraft of the Enchantress as they are immune naturally. Only by bowing before the evidence instead of before Authority.*

WHEN WE WERE VERY YOUNG

So much for our fairy story. We come back now to real life, to stories of some real children, and to you personally. Yes: *personally.*

To you as you are in your own experience of you, you as First Person Singular, as who you really are. That's to say, to you as you were before that Wicked Fairy cut you down to size, and as you are now you see that – to tell the truth – she did nothing of the sort, and it was all a gigantic fraud. In other words, to you as you lived then, unconsciously, from your Bottom Line and Source, and as you live now, consciously, from that same Place, where Nothing explodes into Every-thing. I'm referring, of course, to those occasions when you are not overlooking This, aren't eccentric, aren't out to lunch, as they say.

Who you really are, this First Person who says 'I', was never born into the world. It was born into you. You were never, for yourself, a young thing or any thing. In every way you contrasted with those around you – or rather, within you. It was they who were small, not you. It was they who were solid and opaque and on the move (which means under stress), whereas you were spacious, transparent, unmoved, and very much at large (which means not under stress). Those stumpy, toddling legs you looked down at (no: *up* at), those fidgety hands you looked out at, together with all those other coming-and-going objects and companions, were subject to stress – frequently severe stress – because they were things, and things are like that. You, on the other hand, were not like that – because you were never any thing at all.

Some children, resolutely First Person, stay like this. They used to be called innocents. Nowadays they are labelled educationally subnormal, retardates, imbeciles. Outsiders, they are frequently isolated in special institutions. But of course most children don't stay innocent for long – and that includes you and me. Spellbound, we will pretend just about anything, believe just about anything, do just about anything, to avoid being the odd one out, left outside in the cold. We are joiners, all eagerness to get caught up in the System, to submit to the trimming and moulding process no matter how painful.

The operation begins surprisingly early in some cases, in others surprisingly late. There is no hard and fast rule.

Simon Oliver, at one year and six months, is asked where Simon is. He points straight outwards. He is still unlimited, not other than the scene. Yet he responds at once to his own name, not others'. He's on the road to full citizenship, even at that early age. The trimming and compression have started. But for some years still he's resilient, elastic, springing back quickly to his true size which is no size. The process leading to final contraction and thinghood – for him and for us all – is long-drawn out and often agonizing. Typically, it goes on well into our teens, and for many of us is never quite complete. As children, fortunately, we have a wonderful way of handling what's happening to us, even for a while making the best of both worlds and beating the System, usually without advertising the fact. For social purposes and special occasions we not only *can* be, but also have a great *need* to be that small boy or girl called Simon or whatever – that unique and limited human. But for private purposes, and probably for most of the time, we well know how to break out of the Enchantress's box and explode in all directions. (The world *explode* doesn't do justice to a happening so cosmic in scope and so swift in execution, yet so relaxed in the feel of it.) We retain the knack of coinciding with our world, while we learn to play ever more expertly the absurd and dangerous but needful game of being just one of its occupants.

John, four years old, is playing in the garden – playing his own game, alone. Mother, calling him from the house, tells him to come in. Declining the invitation he explains: 'I'm not here!' And then, having made his point, he starts playing Mother's game and goes indoors 'like a good boy'. *Like* a good boy. (All of us went on behaving *like* good – and bad – boys and girls till that's what we *were* – so we thought.)

Kate (we met her earlier), now five years old, comes home from school with a panoramic photograph of the staff and pupils. She tells her mother the name of everyone, until she comes to herself in the front row. 'I don't know who that is,' she says. 'I've never seen that little girl before.'

Piaget cites the case of a boy who told him he had a brother called John. Asked whether John had a brother, the boy answered firmly: 'No!'

At table, Thomas (five) announced that, if he ate the rest of his rice pudding, he would be full up to the ceiling.

Standing in his bath, Peter (six) looked down at himself and burst out: 'I don't have a head!'

My friend Caroline tells how she well remembers her embarrassment when, a nine-year-old, she was sitting with the family round a table, playing cards: she couldn't make out why her mother insisted she should include *herself* while counting the players. Don't imagine that Caroline was a fool: she went on to get a good degree in philosophy. And if you can still hardly believe that an intelligent child of nine could be so silly, what about Hakim Jamal, writing of himself at ten? 'I knew my arms and body were black, I could see them, but I swore my face was white and if she (the child film-star Shirley Temple) ever met me, she'd return my love.' And there's no doubt at all that he was a highly intelligent lad. (Actually, behind this childhood fantasy there lurks a truth the world has great need of. Suppose that Hakim and Shirley had met, *who* would have taken on the black face, and who the white? It would have been a case of trading colours. In fact, the true complexion of us all – the one we actually possess and live with – is exactly the same colour, which is no colour at all. The least controversial and most far-reaching way of reducing interracial stress would be the general recognition, starting in school, of this self-evident fact. All men and women are born free – correction: omit *born* – are free and equal *and unpigmented*. What about writing a clause to that effect into the Declaration of Human Rights, and the Constitution of the R S A?)

The long ordeal of our reduction to thinghood – to how-we-look-to-others in place of how-we-look-to-ourselves – is normal, indispensable, and in a sense perfectly natural. But it is also felt from an early age to be unnatural, unjust, outrageous. We are brought up into stress, stress upon stress.

A. A. Milne, the subtlety of whose insight into the mind of the child no doubt stemmed from the fact that – lucky man! – he never quite grew up himself, wrote a poem called 'Nursery Chairs'. Christopher Robin, at the age of three, occupying one of these chairs, is a great big roaring lion frightening his nanny to death. In other chairs he's a full-rigged ship a-sailing, and an explorer down the Amazon. According to Milne, Christopher Robin doesn't *play* being a lion, or *imagine* he's a ship: that's what, for the moment, he *is*. (In our language, as Emptiness with no structure or shape or boundaries, he's free to fill it out with anything he fancies, and feel himself into that thing.) The fourth chair in that nursery, however, poses a serious and on-going problem for Christopher. It's a high chair up against the table, where he's required to 'behave himself' – which means be just that one little thing that everybody insists he is. He complains: 'I *try to pretend* it's my chair, and I'm a baby of three!' No difficulty in being a lion, or a ship, or anything you care to mention – so long as he doesn't get stuck with it and typecast – and lots of fun! Much difficulty and no fun at all being one little person – many times a day, and eventually for life.

BYPASSING THE STRESS BOTTLENECK?

The build-up of stress in the child and the teenager is hardly surprising. Indeed, the astonishing thing is that it isn't more severe – when one bears in mind the ordeal that he or she is being subjected to. From embracing the world to being shut out of practically all of it, from inspecting the world to being under its inspection, from being the Sun and Centre of the world to being the least of its planetary asteroids, from melting and merging into the things of the world to being up against them, from having the Unlimited for backing to being thrown on your own puny resources, from being richer than Dives to being poorer than the beggar Lazarus at his gate, from being the unshakeable Rock to being a fleck of the foam of the sea that beats on it in vain – can you imagine a more testing and many-sided ordeal, tougher initiation rites into membership of this Clan called Humanity, this Tribe of tribes?

It's to be expected, then, that some concerned parents – perceiving that these rites of passage are make-believe, a truly savage confidence trick played by society on its most innocent and defenceless members – should aim to spare their children the ordeal that they themselves suffered. I am often asked: Why do our kids have to fall for the same old trickery, repeating our mistakes and suffering all the consequences? Instead of travelling by that hazardous and stressful bottleneck of a road from infant immensity to enlightened immensity, why can't they get through – with a little push from us – from one broad highway to the other and avoid the bottleneck altogether? After all, these accounts of the enlightened things that children say and do – showing how alive they are to their immensity – form a continuous series from infancy to teenage. Strung together, don't they mark out a route from Eden to the Promised Land that bypasses the miseries of the Egyptian Captivity and the Wandering in the Wilderness?

A persuasive argument, which my work with schoolchildren would seem to support. I'm thinking of two occasions particularly, one in Florida and the other in California.

I had been invited by the headmaster to meet 'a rather special discussion group' consisting of a dozen children aged around ten. Having done, with enthusiasm, a number of experiments (including several which you, my Reader, are now familiar with), we went on to look at their significance. I've no doubt they all found the experiments meaningful. Several waxed eloquent, specially on the subject of the Single Eye and the Inner Light it unveiled. One boy, looking at his face in a mirror, excitedly likened it to a powerful magnet for pulling all this unwanted stuff from here and dumping it over there behind the glass, as if it had been a heap of iron filings. Another, warming to the proposition that at the centre of one's life there isn't one living thing but the Source of all living things, came out with: 'Yes, and it doesn't make you proud either!' For myself, I couldn't help secretly comparing that juvenile discussion group with some adult ones I remembered, whose members had the advantage of four or five times the life experience of those children – and deciding that 'advantage' was hardly the word for it. And I was reminded of a boy, of similar age, who played truant to talk with and baffle those formidable Elders in the Temple: and of how he, too, found his Eye to be single, and his whole body filled with Light.

The second occasion, very different from the first but equally memorable, was a class of some twenty teenagers. We sat on the floor in a circle. For the first and the last time in my life I succumbed to a sudden urge to introduce myself as Dr Harding, the eminent cosmetic surgeon. (Dr not Mr – this was the USA, not Great Britain.)

'Is there anyone here (I asked) who's unhappy with his or her face?' (The response was unmistakable. In varying degrees, they all disliked their appearance.) 'Very well, I shall now operate on you. Your facelift will be instant, painless, free, thorough and hygienic. And it could well change your whole life.' (Gasps and giggles of apprehension, embarrassment, disbelief . . . Ten seconds' silence . . .) 'All right, it's over! Hold out your hand-mirrors and check that your faces have been lifted all the way from just above your shoulders to where you now find them . . . You know what happens in the pathology lab of a hospital. Here it's vital to isolate cultures and other specimens to prevent them getting around and infecting people; and this is done by sealing them in glass containers. Well, that's how I've disposed of those unacceptable features of yours. See how securely they are held there on the far side of that glass wall, and no more able to escape and bug you than are the most carefully isolated specimens in the path-lab.'

I concluded by assuring those young people that this was no mere party game but the very best of all cosmetic treatments, and that they would find their faces to be far better-looking now that they were back where they belonged, safely behind glass. And that others, too, would find them more attractive now that they were relaxed and smoothed out. It wasn't *what* those things were, but *where* they'd got to, which spoiled them . . . Of course I've no way of knowing about the long-term effect of that hilarious exercise in aseptic surgery, but undoubtedly the operation itself was no ordinary bit of fun. It happened just at the right time for those children.

These two examples, out of a fair number that could be cited, will do to illustrate my point here: which is that many (if not all) young folk are willing on occasions, and some are eager, to see their faces off, to unthing themselves, to come to their senses – given a little encouragement.

In that case, back to our question: why not give them *all* the encouragement – sustained, but sensitive to the needs of different ages and temperaments – that we can? Why should our children ever be seduced into playing this most stressful game of self-thinging, this charade (always absurd, sometimes pathological, occasionally lethal) of a First Person posturing as a third person, when all the chances are that they will go on playing it harder and harder, more addictively and with mounting personal and social damage, till they die?

The answer is: however rational and well-intentioned, this bypassing won't work. There's no way round the trouble spot. Or, if a way is discovered, it arrives at the wrong destination. If overprotective parents were to succeed in diverting their children from the Purgatory or Hell of separate thingness, they would ensure it wasn't the Heaven of unseparate No-thingness they came to, but rather some Limbo of subnormality. An idiot is terribly good at keeping Starer – that would-be parasite – aseptically and permanently behind glass.

Why won't it work? Because ancestral history won't allow it. In no form of vital development can any important phase of the process be left out. Just as, in the womb, you had to pass through the stages – all the way from the lowest amoeba-like speck to the highest anthropoids – which your animal ancestors traversed: so, outside the womb, you have to pass through the stages of self-thinging (becoming eccentric, faced-up, a third person) that your human ancestors traversed. You cannot, as an individual, opt out of *recapitulating* their adventures. You arrive at your present exalted evolutionary status by taking the same route as your forebears – only for you it has been straightened and re-graded almost beyond recognition, so that what took them many ages takes you a mere nine months before birth, and a similar number of years after birth. History isn't for superseding but for telescoping. It won't be by-passed, but loves being rushed through.

The practical upshot is this: It's a good and safe thing for children to be reminded of their Identity from time to time – whether on set-up occasions like the two I've just described, or less formally and on the spur of the moment – provided the reminders are brief and relaxed and infrequent enough to leave children free to make their own choices. But it's neither good nor safe for the reminders to be sustained and insistent. And particularly when, compounded by the normal pressures of family relationships, they read more like parental commands than casual memory-jogging. Children should not be torn between two contradictory messages – one (coming from their parents and a few friends) insisting they are the *opposite* of what they look like, and the other (coming from virtually everyone else) that they *are* what they look like. The result is likely to be confusion or anger or both, and worse stress than that which those loving hearts are trying so hard to spare the new generation.

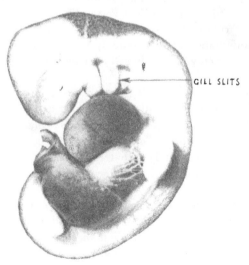

GILL SLITS

Twenty-five days after conception you bore clear traces of the gills of your fish-ancestors, and lived in a small version of their sea.

No: we can no more get out of being 'things' at plus eight years than being 'fish' at minus eight months.

What we can and should avoid is staying thinged a moment longer than necessary. It would be quite natural, quite true-to-form and in accord with all our history, if our children, and their children, and *their* children emerged earlier and earlier from thinghood into No-thinghood, in the decades and centuries to come. Already two of my dearest and clearest friends – the twins Richard and David Lang – came through in tandem at seventeen. (More than twice that age now, they have never gone back.) I dare say that the day will come when seventeen is regarded as an unnecessarily late age for seeing your face off and held in quarantine behind glass.

So to those understandably concerned parents I would say: be true to yourSelf and you will not be false to your children. Relentlessly pressuring *grown-ups* to see and value What you see and value so highly – this is violent and counterproductive enough: doing so to *children* is worse. It is disrespectful and it takes advantage of your position. Mind your own business. Don't overlook your own Bottom Line and World's End, live from your own Absence of face, be the First Person Singular that you are – but without trumpeting daily from the housetop, or from the head of the dining table, what you are up to. What you *are* will shout so loud that even your family will hear the message when they need to hear it.

Answer your children's questions about fundamental matters clearly and briefly, without pouncing on the opportunity to preach a sermon. Above all, remember that before they lose their faces they must find them, that their wisdom is the discovery of their mistakes, that their peace is the resolution of their conflicts, and that their freedom from stress is won through stress.

The sooner you wholeheartedly grant your children's need to join – stressfully – in the great sevenfold ancestral Game – the Game that adults must play to become adults at all – why, the sooner they will get through playing and be happy to join you in your stress-free and game-free Childlikeness.

JUDAR AND THE TREASURE-HOUSE

This chapter began with a new fairy story of our own devising. It ends with two old ones. Though the three stories read very differently, the experience they culminate in is the same. Of all experiences it is at once the most revolutionary and the most commonplace, the most surprising and the most obvious. To miss it is to miss the bus of your life and be left standing, a monument to stress.

Here, in brief, is the tale of Judar, the poor young fisherman. He finds, well-hidden, the treasure-house of the world, and knocks at the door. A porter, armed with an axe, opens and says: 'Stretch out your neck so that I can cut off your head!' Unafraid, Judar does so, and the blow is painless. He sees that the porter is a body without a soul. After further adventures, he proceeds to the treasure itself, which consists of the Four Valuables. They are the Celestial Disc, whose owner sees all places as near, the Sword, whose owner can slay all creatures, the Seal-ring, whose owner possesses and rules the world, and the Collyrium Pot, whose owner can spy out all the world's treasures. He takes possession of all four.

What does this story – from the Arabian Nights' Entertainments – say to you? Well, try the following: You have every reason to fish around for what may turn up. To seek, in fact, the infinite treasure that you were tricked out of, that you lost by trading it for a meatball, incongruously dished up on your shoulders. You are needy and adventurous, and still young – at least in heart. The trickery and the sheer dottiness of the substitution are still painful enough, the bargain bad enough (was there ever a worse one?) to get you looking all over the place for what you have no clear idea of. And then one day, by some wonderful turn of fortune, you come across the treasure-house of the world. You knock long and loud at the door, with the courage of desperation. With still greater courage you pay the standard entrance price of one head, and go on to collect your property. It is both familiar and new. Having been lost so painfully, longed for so persistently and rediscovered so perfectly, it is now immensely more valuable than it was. Before, these treasures were as natural as sunshine, as taken for granted. Now they glow with a supernatural light above the brightness of the sun. Yet they are more ordinary than ever, duller than dull, inexpressibly *mere*. Merely by looking to see, you make nonsense of distance: the world rushes to the doorstep of its owner. Merely by batting an Eyelid, you destroy and recreate it all. Merely by reversing your gaze, you see at once into your own inmost Nature and that of all beings: you know exactly what everything really is, and demolish all the barriers between them. Truly divine powers, and all so ordinary, plainer than plain, merer than mere.

Out there, people are in no position to judge your worth. Here, you are perfectly placed to do so. In appearance you are no more than a human being. In reality you are no less than Being, wealthy and powerful beyond imagination.

Yes, you are fortunate all right. Your only need is a touch of that simple truthfulness you were talked and laughed and bewitched out of when you were very young.

HORSE SENSE

Our second traditional fairy tale comes from Scandinavia. It can be told in a couple of sentences. For, in substance, it's the same old story of the secret spell that binds us all from childhood. Moreover one glance – downwards, into your hand-mirror – does more to spill the secret, and break the spell, than all the words at my command.

Seven young princes were turned by an enchantress into seven foals. They became princes again as soon as their heads were cut off, and laid at their tails.

Not just cut off, please note, but ranged alongside or between their hind legs. As if they were to spend the rest of their lives playing football with the things.

In terms of our own story at the start of this chapter, the dread Starer, dismissed to where it belongs, is no longer a parasite but a plaything. Result: Eyebright is bright-eyed again. And not just a princess, but the queen who holds the keys of the royal treasury.

I thought you would like to see this self-portrait which I drew thirty years ago. Not flattering, but it still makes good horse sense to me.

14

ADULTHOOD

(i) INTRODUCTION

Having read so far, and carried out our experiments with care, you have got their point. How could you miss it? Until you see WHAT you are you don't know what obviousness is.

And by *see* I don't mean *understand* (this WHAT baffles one, reduces one to a sort of alert idiocy), or *believe* (it's so mysterious it's incredible, it knocks one out), or *feel* (in spite of the mystery it's more neutral and unexciting than the white background these words are printed on). No: I mean that same plain and ordinary seeing by which you see anything at all. The difference between looking at WHAT you are, and at what others appear to be, lies in the *direction* of the looking, not the looking itself. There aren't two sorts.

Looking in now, you are for yourself exactly What you always were and always will be – immutable, ageless. For others, however, you have matured and are now a grown-up. That's how they see you. In the course of childhood and youth, you learned to share their view. You became expert at an extraordinary game – you could say, at an extraordinarily athletic and tricky sporting event called Eccentricity – to wit, leaping a metre or so out of yourself and twisting round in mid-flight and looking back to see what people make of you. And now, without altogether retiring from that game, you play it much as Christopher Robin played being a great big roaring lion and a ship a-sailing, and as you once played being a railway engine doing 100 mph, or a motionless rose-tinted sunset cloud or whatever. For you, the player, have discovered yourself to be, in reality, the archetypal Non-player, the Immovable, forever rocklike and up to no tricks or games whatever. You

are left with no reason or excuse for muddling your regional appearance with your central Reality, or denying that they are in all respects opposites.

It follows that you are now in a position to cope with the stresses of adult life, in the way this book advocates. This you do, in effect, by distinguishing three regions: (i) what you are at minimum range, at the place of total implosion, (ii) what you are at maximum range, at the place of total explosion, and (iii) all that lies between – your fission products (so to say), your many-levelled universe. As the first you are incapable of stress, because there's nothing inside you to be stressed. As the second you are incapable of stress, because there's nothing outside you to inflict stress. As the third, however, you aren't just capable of stress, you are built of it: you are all stress. It's what the world runs on. It's what you, as the world, run on. And there's nothing you can do about it.

Is this all, then, that we are offering here – not stress reduction but stress placing – seeing it off to region (iii) where it belongs, and where you are altogether caught up in it, indeed are it? Offering no change at all in the quantity or the severity of your stress, but only a technique for detaching yourself from it?

Not at all! We are offering alleviation from stress, of a most radical and far-reaching kind. This is how it works out. Waking to where your stress is and where it isn't, seeing it off to where it belongs – this itself is enough to change it drastically. (For instance: when 'I'm anxious about the war situation' becomes 'The war situation is an anxious one,' the anxiety is likely to abate somewhat.

And when 'I'm so in love' becomes 'She's so lovable', the progress of that love is likely to be far less fraught and the love more genuine.) And so in practice there are for you two sorts of stress in region (iii), namely the necessary sort that builds and energizes the universe, and the unnecessary sort that you add to it by imagining that you are based on and living from there, instead of region (i). In short, healthy stress and toxic stress.

All this is rather abstract, the bare bones of the matter. In this chapter we clothe them with flesh. Taking some of the main manifestations of stress in adult life – hang-ups most humans suffer from – we examine each in the light of the foregoing principles. This requires us to distinguish between the two sorts of stress in each instance – the sort that's unavoidable and enlivening and arises from how things are, and the sort that's avoidable and deadening and arises from how they aren't, from delusion.

We shall make no attempt to cover the whole range of delusion-based suffering and occasions for needless stress, but only some representative ones. They will be more than enough to illustrate how subtly and how thoroughly the same principles – comprising one and the same remedy for misplaced and superfluous stress – adjust and apply themselves to the endless variety of human needs. If you can't find in the following a section devoted to your own particular trouble, at least you will find plenty of clues about how to deal with it effectively, no matter how serious it appears. The heavier your hang-up the more you need to unhook it and let it fall – *all* the way. However odd and sinister the peculiarities of your own brand of toxic stress, there's just one safe dumping site for it – over the World's Edge, which is your own Bottom Line. As we shall presently see . . .

I wonder if you have seen a film entitled *The Gods must be Crazy*. In it the Bushman hero finds a Coke bottle which brings him all sorts of bad luck. Unable to get rid of the thing, he realizes that his only recourse is to drop it over the Edge of the World – which for him is a very high and steep cliff, many days distant in the Kalahari. This he succeeds in doing, to his great relief.

Take your cue from the Bushman. He tried dumping that

spooky bottle in all sorts of likely places. But it always came back at him in the end, till he took it to the one place where it would stay dumped. For you that place is your own Edge or Fringe. Cease overlooking it, and the fringe benefits won't fail to astonish you.

When you were very young indeed, you enjoyed those fringe benefits naturally and without question. How different life was then! What a revolutionary you were!

Yes: every infant is a secret dissident, a mole in Society's midst, a lone radical up against the status quo. But very soon the Bureau of Unhuman Activities, catching up with him, applies the standard counter-revolutionary treatment. He's brainwashed till his subversive views aren't just laundered, but reversed. *He's persuaded that the only way he can join the human race is upside-down.* Literally, not just metaphorically. So effective is this upsy-daisy treatment that almost immediately he's forgotten all about it. He's sure he's the right way up, and always has been and always will be this way up – just like all those other folk around. So sure, he doesn't spare the matter a passing thought or look. The cost, the price in stress of his new upside-down life, is cumulative. No matter how obligatory and how universal self-deception may be, it doesn't come cheap, ever.

A friend of mine travelled down under, where (no great shock) he found that the Aussies, too, consistently saw themselves as the 'right way up' – heads firmly screwed on top. All, that is, except his remarkably observant young nephew, who walked right up to him and announced: 'Uncle, I'm the wrong way up!' Then, taking another look, he changed his mind, and declared that it was Uncle who was upside-down. In either case, they were opposite sides up. Obviously. It's a safe bet that now, fifteen years on, this young man sees (hallucinates) himself as like everybody else – head above, feet below. Nevertheless I would hope that, one fine day, he will be overtaken and overturned by a counter-counter revolution, and once more – bowing to the evidence – see what he sees. Thereby ditching the stress of pretending not to see it.

There was once a Zen master who, realizing he was about to

die, inquired just how his predecessors had done so – and decided to be different. He insisted on departing (so the story runs) 'standing on his head', to the astonishment of his grieving disciples. Now was he just a silly old posturing show-off? Or playing silly Zen games? Or, on the contrary, making one last desperate effort to bring his silly disciples to their senses before *they* died? Let's give him the benefit of the doubt: and, taking the hint right now, let's look *up* at our feet, and work *down* our legs and trunk to our Openendedness at the bottom of the picture. And let the toxic stress that's got trapped in that body-receptacle drain away, with a swirl and a gurgle, down the plughole. Down the huge and wide-open waste that never was or could be plugged with any sort of stopper, and certainly not with a mere head-stopper.

How else would you empty a jug of dirty water, but by upending the jug? How else would you hang on to the filthy stuff, except by neglecting to up-end the jug?

In the following seven sections of this chapter about stress in adult life, we decant seven beakers of this poisonous waste – very different in the kind and degree of their toxicity, but the same in the manner and the site of their disposal.

(ii) DEPRESSION

Inviting my friends to describe their occasional bouts of depression, I have been surprised how different their accounts of it turn out to be. Some talk of life's futility and lack of all meaning and direction: they are lost, wandering aimlessly with nowhere to go. Or, worse still, stuck fast. Some talk of black disgust. Some of a sorrow which is all the more sorrowful for not disclosing what it's sorrowful about. Some talk of their worthlessness, of the certainty that they are rejected by everybody – animals included – and for the best of reasons. Still others, using more physical language, describe their depression as a deadness and exhaustion and inability to respond to just about anything, or a sinking sensation that finds no bottom, or an unremitting pressure from all sides as if in a vice. And so on. It seems that the devil of depression never runs out of his stock of tragic masks, no two of which are quite the same.

Our aim here is to unveil the countenance behind all these masks, to discover the common denominator of depression in all its forms and varieties of stress, and arrive at precisely what to do about it.

Let's go back to what, at first sight, appears to be the very opposite of depression – to that 'Himalayan' experience which we relived together in earlier chapters. In fact, it was not at all uplifting or expansive or euphoric. On the contrary, it was a come-down and a flattening. It was no casual and nodding assent to what was given, but a deep bowing before the evidence literally as well as figuratively, a lowering of one's gaze from the widest heaven to a shirtfront, and the lowest button on it, at that. You could call it a deliberate exercise in feeling low, if not in depression itself. The way one talks about depression is enough to show what's going on. For instance, you say you are bowed down with grief and care, referring to the shape of your body as well as the state of your mind. Or that life is getting you down, that you are under the weather, down-hearted and downcast. Before, you were riding high, on top of the world, elevated, uplifted, whereas now you're down in the dumps, have hit bottom.

Yes: that so-called Himalayan experience was a real come-down. But it was a trial run or mere tourist excursion into the depths, too brief and too tentative to bring out their heaviness and their stress. It was a review or rehearsal of the Fall from the Overworld of high Heaven, via Earth, to the Underworld and the very pit of Hell. All the way from that huge expanse of blue, almost thing-free, to those beautiful things I first saw as clouds and then as snow-peaks, to those grey-blue and greenish foothills, to that very green grass, to those minature feet (dangling from rather than standing on that grass), to this inverted and truncated trunk – all of it a narrowing and a condensation and a solidification. Put it like this: I saw Earth as the thinging of the Heavens, this upside-down body as the thinging of the Earth, this point I'm now pointing to as the thinging of this body – as the ultimate constriction and terminus of the whole descending and imploding process.

Experiment 20: Another bow before the evidence

Dear Reader, will you please accompany me once more on this showdown, this submission to the evidence, taking your time about it.

Looking and pointing *up* at the sky, then *out* at those hills, then *down* to the grass and those feet, and still further down to those foreshortened legs and trunk and What they rest on. Yes, I know: that ceiling has to do for sky, that opposite wall for hills, that carpet for grass: but no matter, it's essentially the same descent from Heaven to Earth, and precisely the same descent from those inverted feet to the Bottom Line of the picture. I'm counting on you not to stop at reading about this salaam to the Cosmos, this surrender to the Blazingly Obvious, this humility in the face of the Given, but to make your own salaams. Now . . .

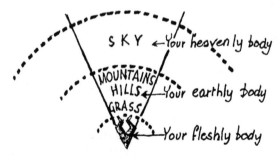

And will you please notice, in passing, that here we don't have an artificial world of make-believe, a convenience-product of a Universe cooked up and pre-packaged for land-surveyors and navigators and calendar makers and countless other specialists ancient and modern, but instead the raw and natural world as served up to the non-specialist down the ages. It's what we see instead of what it pays us to see, instead of what our parents and teachers and society and language itself insist we see, instead of what we're so sure we're seeing but are in fact hallucinating. Of course we need both worlds, the ersatz and the authentic, the contrived and the original. Of course the fictional and cooked-up universe is valuable for many practical purposes. But the real and served-up universe it usurps is indispensable for the most practical of all purposes: namely for heading off the stress of living from a convenient fiction in the belief that it is gospel truth. It is indispensable for heading off the stress of living from one hell of a lie, in Hell itself.

The real universe as so generously given – yet so rejected and despised by us moderns – was, in its broad outline, acceptable to our medieval forebears. They had the audacity and good sense to base their world-picture on it. That world-picture or cosmology took a variety of forms – some more arbitrary and fantastic than others – of which one is particularly relevant to our theme. The richest and completest, and in important ways the most realistic, is Dante's, as painted in his great poem, *The Divine Comedy*. This, in barest outline, is the shape of it:

At the top of the picture is the Heaven of Heavens, the realm of light as distinct from darkness, of lightness as distinct from heaviness, of spirit as distinct from matter – immense, carefree, happy. Heaven, says the Poet, is one great Smile. Ranged beneath this topmost height are the celestial spheres, angelic realms inhabited in turn by stars and planets and Sun and Moon, which are progressively less 'spiritual' and more 'material'. Then comes Earth, the sublunar world of humans and lesser creatures – small, non-luminous, weighed down with every sort of trouble. Thence to the still darker and more troubled Infernal Regions or Underworld, envisaged as a conical pit converging on Earth's centrepoint. This is nine-layered Hell – the lower the layer the more terrible the fate of its inhabitants. At the very bottom, Judas, along with his fellow traitors Brutus and Cassius, is stuck, upside down. His head has disappeared into Lucifer's masticating jaws, leaving his legs treading Hell's air in unending agony.

The whole is Dante's imaginative and elaborately dramatized version of the way things are actually presented – as more and more opaque and solid and thinged, more and more stressful and depressing and depressed, the nearer they get to the solitary Witness of it all at the centre of the system. If we're interested in a real and habitable world, a Universe for living in rather than for thinking about and manipulating, why then it's something like Dante's that we're after: a concentric Universe structured like a mandala or an onion. We shall not cope with our depression till we re-occupy this real world. To fight and dominate Nature we *conceive* a uniform or Potato Universe, with little eyes all over but essentially Eyeless and Centreless. To be at home in Nature we *perceive* a non-uniform or Onion Universe with one great Eye at its centre. To place the stress of Nature where it belongs in that Mandala or Onion, and so render it non-toxic, we point to and we open that Single Eye. And the only way to open it is to open it *wide* – wider than the wide world.

To point at all is to point at – why, a *point*, of course. But see how, once looked into and followed through, absolutely no trace of that pointed-at Point remains: it explodes with a blast that makes the biggest nuclear holocaust look like a puff of steam from a kettle. This focus of the Universe is the in-gathering and culmination of all its depression and pain and guilt and stress, the nadir of heaviness and remoteness from Heaven's ease and Heaven's light. It is Hell doing its damnedest, growing more and more diabolical till one arrives at its Terminus. Those little upside-down feet I'm looking at now and calling mine are in truth my Judas feet till I cease being a traitor to myself, and take up my station where Hell ends and Heaven begins, where I see and I am this Bottom Line and World's End and Ground of Being from which those feet, along with all Heaven and Hell, arise. But then at last, no longer stuck en route somewhere in Hell's cone but having come to the end of it, Hell suddenly gives place to Heaven. Being rather depressed or very depressed is one's agony, being totally depressed is one's instant relief from agony, one's dramatically sudden salvation. Till then the Great Breakthrough, the Great Eye-opener, the Great Revolution that puts all into reverse, can't happen.

That's the way it is for you and me, and how it was for Dante and his guide Virgil, in the 'Inferno' of *The Divine Comedy*. Wisely, they didn't attempt to go back the way they had come, and clamber out of that horrible Pit. Instead, they went on to the very limit and discovered there a secret way through to the bright world, to the wide heavens and the beautiful stars. A happy surprise-ending to the Poet's week-long and devastating tour of the Infernal Regions. The way *out* of that grim place of punishment turned out to be the way *in and through*. In our terms, not retreat from it: not trying to cheer up and pull ourselves together and raise our sights and our hopes. Not appealing against but taking our punishment: not resisting depression but embracing it.

Here are three more variations on the same theme, for the encouragement and guidance of all so-called depressives – acute and occasional, or chronic.

First, much condensed, from the *Tao Te Ching*, Chinese, third century B C. 'The Sage – wise, illumined, serene – confesses that he droops and drifts, that he seems to have lost everything, that he's an idiot who is inert and dull and in the dark, blown hither and thither, useless, intractable, boorish. "People look lively and self-assured," he says, "and I alone am depressed." (Yes: *depressed!*) But what chiefly distinguishes him from them is that he gets his sustenance "from the Mother's breast".'

That's to say, he gets it from the Tao, from the deepest of wells that never runs dry and never fails him, and which is the ancient Chinese equivalent of our Bottom Line and World's End and Source and Resource, the nethermost Ground of Being which rests on no subsoil.

Our second is from Meister Eckhart, German, thirteenth to fourteenth century: 'We must take the lowest place in our own Ground, in our own innermost Self, in abject lowliness. When the soul enters into its Ground, into the innermost recesses of its being, divine power suddenly pours in.'

And finally Hubert Benoit, contemporary French psychiatrist: 'I struggle increasingly "upwards" . . . Perfect Felicity (however) does not await me above, but below; it does not await me in that which I see as a triumph, but in that which appears to me actually as a disaster. My perfect joy awaits me in the total annihilation of my hopes. The man who has become really desperate, who no longer expects anything from the world of phenomena, is flooded by the perfect joy which at last he ceases to oppose.'

The total annihilation of my hopes, please note. If I go down into the pit of depression without discovering there the perfect relief Benoit speaks of, it's because I stand off a little from the bottom, refuse to let myself sink all the way. And if the relief is unsustained it's because I'm unwilling to renew it, unwilling to revisit that lowest place. For this is not a one-off experience, a once-and-for-all desperation followed by everlasting bliss. It's what St Paul means when he says that he dies daily. Not that this regime makes him miserable. On the contrary, he's always going on about the joy that floods his life.

There is a sense in which this whole book is a guide to the art of depression. Its thrust is downwards. If my role is that of a lift attendant, it's one who calls out: 'Going down, going down!' Down to the basement of the world, ladies and gentlemen, before shooting up to the roof-garden. Equally, of course, it's a guide to uplift, to sky-high lightheartedness. But at a price. It's as if, to fly from New York up to Alaska, I not only have to go via Miami, but to pay for every inch of the journey.

Not exclusively among religions, but with unique intensity and thoroughness, Christianity illustrates, obeys, insists upon the same principle. Let us then briefly examine this faith, not in one of its watered-down varieties but at full strength, and not in its theological details but the spirit of it.

When the King of kings gets caught up personally in his world, he doesn't do so by halves. He becomes the down-and-outer of all time. It says everything about him and his world that the one in whose presence (we are told) is fullness of joy, and at whose right hand are pleasures for evermore, should find himself plunged into the utmost depths of sorrow. The most dismal of all failures, he is a laughing stock and an offence. He is humiliated and scorned, abandoned by his dearest friends, betrayed, suffers cruel pain, sinks to the very floor of Hell.

This isn't because he's a sick King, or a black humorist at his own expense, or incompetent, or a cosmic masochist piling agony on agony just for the hell of it. No. He goes the way he has to go. He's a realist. The universe that is so difficult and strange – to put it mildly – is that state of being which the Abyss of non-being happens to come up with; and how could he not go along with it? When his unfathomable No-nature assumes a nature, it turns out to be cruciform. Unresisting, the Master of the world is obedient unto death, even the death of the cross. Though he wants the best, and does his level best, it gets him down to the lowest level of all. Be sure he would not have taken that low and rough road if a higher and smoother one had been open to him. Dearly he would like to build, at least for the comfort of his creatures, a fast multi-lane through road, bypassing Hell altogether and linking Earth directly with Heaven. But because we are riding with him, because we are made of him, because in truth we *are* him and there's no one else, we have to go his way, which is the way that Being actually takes. The way of that shocking bottleneck called Calvary. And thence through to the empty tomb (so very empty) and the swift ascent to the stars.

It makes a huge difference to acknowledge that you haven't been overcharged for Being, or picked on for a specially rough ride. The depression which is getting you down personally, whatever its immediate cause and whatever form it takes, is in a deeper sense not personal at all. It is cosmic, universal, the nature of Nature. It isn't just a fair sample of how things are through and through, but your necessary and inevitable participation in it. For God's sake don't picture yourself down here in the dumps and wringing your hands with sorrow, while he's safely up there rubbing his hands with joy. If he's blissful there it's because he's also down with you in the depths of your depression. With you, and for you, and as you. Here we are all in the same God-boat. Seasick probably, certainly drowning and sinking to the ocean floor . . .

But – ah! – finding here the pearl. It is nowhere else. It can be had nohow else, or on the cheap. For it's no cultured pearl, no piece of costume jewellery. It costs the earth, and heaven, and more. The sum you pay is not negotiable, and is subject to no trade discount for saints or sages or seers – let alone you and me. I'm not asking you to believe the old Preachers' cry – *No cross, no crown* – but to take heart when, in the midst of your darkness and pain, and maybe just glimpsing a light shining through, you begin to suspect how tough-mindedly realistic those preachers were. You are unspeakably depressed? Midnight is at its blackest and your load at its heaviest? You can go no lower? Well, that is your crucifixion. Now you have nothing left to lose, and everything to gain, by bowing before the facts . . .

And going on to submit, with equal humility before the nature of things, to your ascension and coronation, your unspeakable glory.

Such is the god-spell coming to me from the heart of this extraordinary religion, a faith apparently so negative, actually positive in the extreme. Echoed, as I say, by the others, but taking here its toughest and most poignant form. Hence its special value for our enquiry. And one of the most telling condensations of that form is the symbol of the pearl of great price, the jewel that rests on the bed of the raging sea. Your raging and cruel sea. Yes: but also your pearl. It represents the turning point in your otherwise tragic story. And what a turnabout it is!

The Hymn of the Pearl is a third-century gnostic poem way out on the extreme fringes of Christianity. You could look on it as one of the more valuable links between Western and Eastern spirituality. It has much to say to us at this point. Here is the gist of the story:

The King of kings, reigning somewhere in the East, descends in the person of his son into Egypt. His purpose is to get back the one pearl which lies at the bottom of a lake there, guarded by a fearsome dragon. On his way down, the Prince, shedding his bright robe and glorious toga, leaves behind him all traces of royalty. At length, having arrived in Egypt, he finds it prudent to hide the fact that he is a stranger in a strange land. So he disguises himself in the dirty clothes of an Egyptian and eats Egyptian food. Soon he becomes so drugged with it that he forgets all about who he is and his mission. In effect, he becomes an Egyptian.

However, the court in the East, learning of the Prince's stupor and degradation, sends him a sharp reminder by eagle-messenger. It brings him to his senses and rouses him to action. Let him take up his own tale here:

> My freedom longed for its own nature.
> I remembered the pearl
> For which I had been sent to Egypt,
> And I began to charm him,
> The terrible loud-breathing serpent.
> I hushed him to sleep and lulled him into slumber . . .
> And I snatched away the pearl,
> And turned to go back to my Father's house.
> And their filthy and unclean garb
> I stripped off, and left it in their country,
> And I took my way straight to come
> To the light of our home, the East . . .
> And my toga of brilliant colours
> I cast around me, in its whole breadth.
> I clothed myself therewith, and ascended . . .

Our interpretation of this ancient myth is as follows:

You, dear Reader, are royalty travelling incognito. So thoroughly incognito that even you were taken in by your disguise. You really are the Prince, sole heir to the King who is the One and the Whole and the All. But you have not only come down into the world: you have come down *in* the world, putting off in turn your galactic and stellar and planetary garments or appearances on your way to the human scene below. Here you assume the guise of 'one of them', gradually bringing yourself, at the cost of mounting stress, to think and feel and act as they do qua third persons. You become, even in your own eyes, what you look like to them – a mere commoner, no more royal than the rest of the fellahin. And, to bring your story up to date, a depressed commoner, at that. Why are you depressed? Why are you fed up, sick to death of it all? Because you overlook the fact that, qua First Person, you are an uncommoner, *the* Uncommoner. As Boethius says, you are in a bad way because you have forgotten who you are.

But now you have received a strong reminder of your true identity, and what your mission down here is. *It is to go down still further.* It is to cease resisting the completion and marvellous outcome of your depression. It is to allow your descent to continue where it left off, and take the plunge into that deepest sea. Or call it, as occasion and context demand, the pit of Hell, the sadness and heaviness in your heart, the dark deeps of your mind (whatever that elusive monster may be), or simply the lower regions your finger indicates on its way down to your Bottom Line and the World's End. For here on the sea floor rests the treasure which includes, though it infinitely transcends, relief from all depression.

It turns out, however, that your descent into the depths to regain the royal pearl is blocked by a monster who is none other than your own powerful resistance to yet further humiliation and loss. He's the crafty one, the most plausible of confidence tricksters, up to every ruse to keep you from your own treasure.

At this point in the story, let's take the liberty of updating it and filling it out with a small selection from that wily dragon's ploys.

(i) He strains every nerve to persuade you that your precious pearl is in fact worthless, actually no more pearly and iridescent than the surrounding water. All coy and smirking, he admits he's a silly old dragon, sitting like a broody hen on a china egg that will never hatch. He proves his point by reference to the best spiritual masters, East and West, who agree that the pearl is so colourless and shapeless and featureless that to gain it is to gain nothing whatever. Instead, he kindly offers you a tray of really exciting jewels, all contrasting brilliantly with that deadly dull ocean-bed object – a valley experience, if ever there was one. Here, he explains, are peak experiences, mystical delights shot through with flashes of love and ecstatic joy. No paste gems these, but real and exquisitely beautiful, glowing and sparkling with rainbow colours like the sunlit dew of early morning on grass. Mystical anthologies are full of accounts of them ... Now if you're shrewd you will, without arguing or even disagreeing with him, pay no attention to his marvellous pearl-substitutes. While not disputing their bright-ness and charm, while not failing to enjoy them to the full when they come to you, you won't forget that they are rather less permanent than the morning dew. That they come and go without reason or warning, and cannot be had when you can do with them most. Whereas the true pearl – just because it's so penny-plain (yet priceless), because there's nothing to it (yet everything in it), and because it is yourself, your very own Nature – is available on demand to meet your every need, always. No matter how black your mood, or intractable your problem.

(ii) Or the dragon, instead of playing coy, plays embarrassed. Now he's a dirty old thing. All arch and shy, he points out that, sad to say, the pearl of purity lies buried beneath a pile of disgusting dragon droppings. Before the treasure can be located and claimed, they must be cleared away. He promises faithfully to let you have it without a struggle directly you have got rid of the obscuring mess. So you roll up your sleeves and get down to your new job of lavatory attendant to a dragon. But, alas, no constipated dragon. Sooner or later it dawns on you that, no matter how hard you work at it, the dirt pile gets larger rather than smaller. You tumble to his trick of relieving himself on the dung-heap every time your back is turned ... In other words, he insists that you must get rid of your bad karma, must reform your character in all sorts of ways and by means of all sorts of training, before you have a hope of seeing your clear way through to the joy that lurks beneath your depression. He well knows, of course, that there's no end to the task he has set you. For you find yourself taking on, in addition to your own personal and comparatively light karmic load, the less personal and heavier loads of ever deeper levels. In fact, the whole unsavoury exercise is a nonsense. It's just one more trick in the repertoire of the great dragon-illusionist. The dragon himself is phantasmal, and his droppings are no more substantial than what they are dropped from. We have already found, again and again, that – of all things actual and imaginable – the pearl of your true Nature is the most radiantly obvious, once you dare turn your attention round to it. All the dirt-dropping dragons in the universe, all suffering from chronic diarrhoea, can't begin to obscure it by so much as a droplet of the stuff.

(iii) Alternatively – what a quick-change artist he is! – he may play being a modest and broadminded dragon. He waxes quite eloquent:

What, that fabled pearl, here in unmysterious Egypt! Guarded by this very ordinary serpent! Come off it! No, dear Princeling, you will never find the genuine article down here in this grimy cellar, but up there on the roof of the world, in mystic Tibet. Or perhaps hidden somewhere in secret India or Thailand or Mexico or even (Buddha help us!) in secret Japan. Or anywhere else for that matter (he adds, sotto voce) just so long as it's sufficiently far away, and sufficiently hard to find, and sufficiently esoteric and non-Egyptian.

Though it deserves no more comment than laughter, this dragon-drivel is astonishingly successful. The not-here, not-now, not-me, extremely-hard-to-see pearl is a thousand times more sought after than the one pearl of great price. And it is worthless.

(iv) Or perhaps the dragon goes all scholarly. Conceding that he's sitting on the real article, he undertakes to hand it over just as soon as you know enough about pearls and precious stones to appreciate its true worth. All you have to do, he assures you, is to read these three or four books on the subject. Or five. Or six . . . So you commence your studies, eagerly. But, alas, the shelf of required reading gets longer and longer. Each new addition to it promises to tell all at last. It's the final lowdown on the pearl – till the next one comes out. In fact, the majority of these books are about pearl divers, or oysters, or even oyster shells, and not about the pearl at all; and not a few are written by experts who wouldn't recognize the pearl of great price if it dropped out of the heavens into their lap, like a solitary hailstone accompanied by forked lightning. Moreover even the best books about the pearl itself are misleading, inasmuch as they direct your attention to rows and rows of very unpearl-like marks, all of which are twelve inches from the point. For the pearl isn't what you are reading about, but what's reading. So tell that learned old serpent, got up in cap and gown, what he can do with his million-volume and still-growing pearl library. Tell him politely, but firmly.

(v) After all, he's your creature, more a naughty and dangerous pet to be kept in its place than a wild beast to be shot at. Be friendly, as conciliatory as you can. Only don't take him on. Of all the wise things in the *Hymn of the Pearl*, the wisest is that the dragon is for soothing: you are not to rub his scales the wrong way. He loves to engage you – in argument, in research, in travelling the long long path towards discovering the pearl one fine and distant day, in frolicking with him, in fierce battle – in any activity whatever that diverts you from seeing your way clear through his subterfuges to the treasure, right now. One of his most successful gimmicks is to present you with a compendium entitled *Dealing with your Dragon*, bursting with advice about how to get the better of him by studying dragon anatomy and physiology and behaviour – till you know the shape and the lie and the glitter of every scale and tooth and talon, and the precise chemical composition of the smoke he belches. You have no chance of arriving at the peace of mind beneath your mind (he tells you, in effect) till you know your mind sufficiently to thread your way through its vast complexities . . . Of course your trouble again – and he counts on it – is that the more dragonry you explore the more there is to explore, labyrinths within labyrinths of it – all 'necessary for a mature and responsible adult to know', and quite fascinating, not to say addictive. And demanding, at the very least, the dedication of a lifetime. Meanwhile he's sitting pretty on his china egg. Which is indeed all it amounts to for you till you've seen him off it.

How to do that? Well, I recommend the strategy of Ramana

Maharshi: 'Never mind the mind. If its source is sought, it will vanish, leaving the Self (the pearl) unaffected . . . There is no mind to control if you realize the Self . . . You have ignored what is real and are holding on to the mind which is unreal.'

Of Nisargadatta Maharaj: 'Don't be deceived. All the endless arguments about the mind are produced by the mind itself, for its own protection, continuation and expansion. It is the blank refusal to consider the convolutions and convulsions of the mind that can take you beyond it.'

And of the Zen master who, when a disciple wanted his mind pacified, asked to be shown it. 'Alas, I can't,' replied the disciple. 'There you are then,' said the master, 'I've pacified it for you!'

You may well feel, with me, that the matter is best summed up by that other master who advised us first to seek the kingdom (which for him was synonymous with the pearl of great price), and then all these things shall be added. Including, no doubt, such things of the mind as circumstances require – if, indeed, they require any at all.

(vi) The dragon's cruellest trick is to award himself an honorary MD, pull a long professional face, and proceed to diagnose your depression as irreversible. By no means a rare condition, he adds breezily. Tell him that on Life's Motorway you are forbidden to make a U-turn till you get to Junction O, and that's the one coming up. Also tell him that he's the Father of Lies, and Hell contains no such monster as an irreversible depression. You may point out that, in the course of a day, the traffic in one direction along the Motorway equals that in the other direction, so that for every vehicle approaching Junction O there's another leaving it. Sooner or later, one way or another, all will be well with you. How can you be so sure? Because of Who you really, really are.

(vii) And now for one of the most specious of dragon ploys: You are depressed, poor dear, down to this level (says he, now all care and consideration). And here am I doing all I can, by blocking the way, to prevent you falling further. Be sensible! What's the good of trying to get past me, only to sink into deeper misery? That's the negative side of my service. The positive side is even more helpful. Indeed vital. Let me show you a way up. Climb this excellent escape ladder, and soon you'll be out of this infernal place and basking in the sunshine of the upper world.

In fact, the dragon has been at pains to set up a forest of ladders. Not even the longest, however, quite reaches to the top of the pit, and all have rungs that are rotten and snake-infested. Yes, this most snaky of dragons is bent on playing snakes-and-ladders with you, and has loaded the dice so that he wins every time. You can no more climb out of his pit than a fly out of a Venus fly-trap. This isn't to deny, of course, that we all have to do our stint of ladder-climbing, or that there are many useful means of cheering up and snapping out of our depression, ranging from wonder drugs to wonder meditations. Some are indeed wonderful as far as they go – which is not quite far enough, or for quite long enough. Again and always, the only way out is the way down and out.

Not that these seven dragon ploys exhaust his checklist of devices for keeping me from the pearl where my depression bottoms out. Far from it. The list is as long as my arm – as the arm I *don't* need to stretch out at all, if I really want to seize the pearl. Here, sketchily, are a few more of his subterfuges. He persuades me I'm a cripple who can only get to the pearl in an orange robe and a wheelchair, pushed (or is it held back?) by Nurse Whatsitananda. Or that I'll never make it till I'm a contortionist, at least able to tie my legs into a granny knot without actually groaning, and preferably able to twist my whole body into the most grotesque shapes imaginable. Or till I'm an idiot, eager to believe any old rot. Or a raving lunatic, happy to die defending that rot. Or till the tyger tyger, burning bright in me, is tamed and dimmed into a herbivorous baa-lamb. Or till I'm a gelding, in all but anatomy. Or a masochist drawing blood daily. Or a goody-goody so much holier than thou that thou runnest a mile. Etcetera. Etcetera.

What a trickster that old serpent is, how transparent his tricks should be to the meanest intelligence, and how we fall for them! Until we look. How he hates our looking to see! There's nothing like looking, if it's the truth we're after. And nothing like the truth, if it's relief from depression we're after. What is it, in the last resort, but a specially stressful kind of untruthfulness?

Of course it's the easiest thing in the world to *see* your way through, past the snoring (or is it hard-breathing?) dragon, to the pearl. You have only to cease overlooking what you're looking out of, and notice that already you are seized of his treasure, already you are the pearl itself resting on the deepest seabed. But not so easy to *feel* yourself down there and to stay that way, consciously grounded. For it's the nature of your feelings to ascend, making always for gain and never loss, expansion and never contraction. Not even the most saintly of ascetics can deliberately humble himself, with no pay-off in view. You can't put yourself down. But you can authorize life to do the job for you. And you can go on to marvel at how it does so in just the way you really need, and with perfect timing – once you dare to say Yes to it and trust its operations, apparently so arbitrary and cruel, actually so wise and kind. No bit of cake this saying Yes, Yes, Yes: or, if it is, this is the saddest cake ever baked: heaviness itself, but in the actual taste of it is a wonderful lightness. Here, God knows, is no easy way of life. But how much harder, how much more depressing in the long run, is the life that says No to life! And how futile, how pathetic!

It's as if you were a fizzy bitter drink, and your feelings were the bubbles in it. Of themselves, they can only rise . . . So you feel all bubbly – quite sparkling, in fact – this morning? This time (you tell yourself) the buoyant mood will surely last: happy days are here again – to stay. Then, sure enough, a horrible chunk of life descends on you, sinking to your depths. Under it a great bubble is trapped and borne to the very bottom of the glass. This, you feel, is unrelieved misery and bitterness . . . Right here in your extremity, however, a surprise awaits you, if only you will be patient. That dreadful thing which got you down all the way, that seemingly dead weight and insoluble problem, turns out to be a lump of sugar which, dissolving, sweetens the whole drink. Or at least turns it bitter-sweet. Accepted without reservations, your curse is your blessing. True joy, which is indistinguishable from true peace, floods out. The drink will never be the same again . . . But soon enough the sugar-loaf melts away altogether, releasing that trapped bubble of feeling: which now makes, as it must, for the surface. Only to be trapped and borne down, under another great chunk of life. And so the whole bitter-sweet process is repeated, with infinite variations of details, to infinity.

Such are the ups and downs of life where you find life going on, above that bottom line of yours. They go on regardless of whether they are resented, or just tolerated, or in the end (whether by God's good grace, or simple looking-to-see, or both) welcomed with open arms.

The art of handling these inexorable goings-on is the art of resting on what underlies them, the art and science of consciously being the ground which supports all that commotion without itself becoming disturbed in the slightest. Here, you are the bedrock of the world, where it all begins and where it all ends. Eternally one and the same, you are the Unmoved Mover.

To sum up and conclude this section, let's put the question: what, precisely, are you to do about the depression that's getting you down at this very moment?

The answer comes in two parts. The first is: *See, and see what happens*. It is the basic proposition of this book, its working hypothesis for testing all day and every day, that the solution of your problem, no matter *what* it is, is to see *whose* it is. Not to understand or feel or think who has the problem, but actually to gaze on that W H O and await what comes of the gazing. This seeing and this waiting you can always do, whatever your need. The rest is out of your hands.

Which brings us to the second half of our answer. See, see what happens, *and trust it*. If, owing to your depressive temperament (say), or your acquired habits of mind, or the specially difficult circumstances you find yourself in, your depression insists on hanging around in spite of its ever-renewed dismissal – why then your business is to submit to it, willingly. The willingness doesn't leave it unchanged. It makes the world of difference. More than depression accepted, more even than depression intended, depression *trusted* as what's needed at this time, as hiddenly beneficent – this isn't depression at all in the old sense. It is precisely what the sage in the *Tao Te Ching* is referring to when he says that he alone is depressed. It is milk from the Mother's breast, containing what are for you essential vitamins.

In terms of an earlier chapter, your depression, belonging now to region (iii) of your will (what you really, really want) instead of region (ii) (what you really want) and region (i) (what you think you want), its character is changed absolutely. Repeat *absolutely*. The nature and the feel of that change you cannot foresee, but only await with confidence.

Be prepared for a joy that could be won in no way but through that monstrous and mysterious bugbear which we label DEPRESSION.

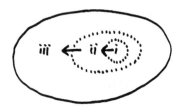

(iii) INDECISION

The way we talk about our inability to make up our minds bears eloquent witness to the stress we are undergoing. We are *torn* between conflicting influences, principles, motives, courses of action, *pulled* this way and that, *racked* by indecision, even *ripped apart*. The tension has many degrees, ranging all the way from having to choose between a family and a career, to having to choose between which apple to eat, or which programme to switch on, or which card to play. Also the tension depends on many factors: such as the urgency of the issue at stake, on how evenly weighted the alternatives are, on how long they have been trembling in the balance, and how weak-willed or strong-willed you happen to be – or suppose you are. It would be simpler – though not necessarily easier, of course – if you were always required to choose between the wise and the foolish thing to do, between the safe and the reckless action, between good and evil. But so many of your choices are between evils, so that either way you are in trouble. Examples are: having to choose between taking painkillers that dim consciousness, and enduring the pain; or between poisoning the moles that are reducing your lawn to a wasteland, and letting them get on with it. Also, life would be simpler if you managed to sidestep all avoidable dilemmas, say by getting yourself institutionalized. But even this last-ditch and much-tried means of stress-avoidance doesn't work: or, insofar as it does, it amounts to suicide. You just can't get out of making choices all the time. You chose to wear that jacket today, to sit in that chair a moment ago, to take up this book instead of the whodunnit you are also reading, to study this paragraph about indecision instead of getting up and making yourself a pot of tea. From pram to deathbed your life is ceaseless choosing, choosing, choosing. Which is to say that, at best, you are under mild but constant stress: and, at worst, so torn asunder that – like the donkey who couldn't decide between two equally distant and equally appetizing carrots – your indecision is killing you.

If you reply that this is the way that life is and there's very little you can do about it (apart from avoiding such carrot-dangling places as racecourses and casinos and stockmarkets), why, of course I have to agree with you – so far as the outside story of your life is concerned. I'm sure that, if you were to monitor my own behaviour today or any day, you would conclude – rightly, from your viewpoint – that I, too, live by choosing. That my life, like yours and everyone else's, is spent in a succession of cleft sticks, and therefore stressfully. Certainly that's the way it looks.

But not the way it is. That's how we appear to be, not how we are. If there's a lesson we should have learned by now, if there's one crucial discovery we have made again and again in the course of our study, it is that appearances are misleading and you aren't a bit what you look like. What's more, the inside story of your life is the very *opposite* of the outside story. This rule applies perfectly to your decision making, so-called. All your painful hesitation between conflicting alternatives, all the stresses and strains of having to choose between manifest evils and between doubtful goods – all are so much shadow boxing, a put-up job, superfluous, without substance or power. The Bottom-Line truth is that you never had to make a choice, never did make a choice, never will make a choice. Your very Nature is to undercut and undermine choice, to blow it sky-high, along with all the stresses it incorporates.

Unbelievable? Or, if believable, alarming? 'I choose, therefore I am,' I hear you saying. 'Be careful, in disposing of my stress, not to dispose of me.' Well, it's time we ceased generalizing and came down to instances. Here's a straight piece of autobiography, dating from around seven years ago:

As so often, I found myself standing at a Y-junction in my life's journey, uncertain about which fork to take. I had devised a model or instrument – simple in idea, elaborate in form – for showing people What they are and what they are not: a device for conveying the message of this book visually rather than verbally. Should I boldly go ahead and manufacture and market it, or shelve the thing? The pros and cons seemed evenly matched. On the one hand I enjoyed the enthusiastic support of a friend who was well placed to ensure large sales, as well as that of other friends whose encouragement was more moral than practical. On the other hand lay the high cost in time and cash of getting patents and going into production, together with my own inexperience in and distaste for the role of entrepreneur . . . Well, reporting on me from outside, you would have to say that, after some weeks of dithering, I came down at last on the adventurous side, and committed myself irrevocably to going ahead with the project.

And you would add, pointedly and in a marked manner, that my decision proved to be the wrong one: because, directly I'd made it, I received from my no-longer-influential friend a very long and interesting letter addressed to me from a prison cell ... Not surprisingly, my venture turned out to be a commercial flop.

Now for the inside story of that venture, the way it looked from here, the reality and not the appearance of the matter. I did *not* hesitate between action and non-action, and then choose action, and then almost immediately rue my action. No: it wasn't like that at all. I applied the principle and technique of No-choice – of no decision making, no decision regretting and troubled post-mortems, and no accompanying stress.

This is how the technique works: faced with a problem, one doesn't feebly sit back and wait for things to happen. Neither does one toss a coin, or consult an astrologer, and hope that the outcome will prove the right one. Not at all. The very definite action to be taken falls into four stages:

(i) See yourself to be the Ground or Bottom Line for the pros and cons of the problem to arise from – as many of them and in as much detail as may be. Encourage them to arrange themselves in all sorts of ways. Live with that display, brood on it, sleep on it, but don't go hankering after a decision. As entertaining the problem in all its aspects, as the Screen for them to come and go on, as their Mirror, you remain neutral. Among the exhibits, however, you may well find, prominently featured, a dateline for the problem's solution. Brood on that, too.

(ii) One morning on waking, or during the day when you are preoccupied with some chore, the completed pattern of things to come arrives, spontaneously and unannounced, from the Bottom Line. So inevitable it seems, so conclusively does it resolve your problem, that you are left in no doubt that here is the right decision, arrived at in the right way at the right time. It has been immaculately conceived in you and for you but not by you. Certainly not by you the human being. Accordingly, it arrives carrying the authority of its parentage, which is the real You, the Source, the World's Beginning and the World's End.

(iii) Now it is the turn of that decision itself, of that seemingly so right design, to go on display above your Bottom Line: and to reveal its limitations and weak spots. All manner of doubts and difficulties, and dilemmas about how to give effect to the decision, are now likely to appear. Again, you don't solve them by choosing between possible alternatives. You stay with them till they, in turn, are ripe and ready to resolve themselves.

(iv) Finally, the plan is implemented. With interest, perhaps with awe, you watch it take shape. At no time do you feel that you are moulding or forging that shape. It forms in you as cloud-shapes form in the sky, or intricate patterns in a kaleidoscope.

Such, then, is the technique of No-choice, resulting in no stress of the superfluous and toxic sort. It works. It works creatively, coming up with unforced and unpredictable and truly inspired solutions that you couldn't possibly take personal credit for. And it works like that because, to tell the truth, it is not a technique at all, not a useful dodge for relieving you of the pains of indecision, and certainly not a recipe for a quiet life at all costs. No: it works because it's the way you are built, the way you function in any case, whether you realize it or not. All this choosing one thing in preference to another is illusory, a great cover-up. Separate individuals, as such, are powerless to make the slightest difference in a universe where every one of them is tightly controlled by the rest. Pretending otherwise, pretending that, as our sole selves, we exercise free will, is as absurd and dishonest as it is vainglorious – and stressful. Only the Source of all, under the sway of none, has free will; and only deeds which are seen to proceed from it, which are referred back to it, which are felt to be its own deeds – only these carry its marvellous smell, the smell of an originality and rightness which belongs solely to that Origin. To live the choiceless life that we have been describing is not fatalism. It is not giving up the struggle and accepting that one is a machine within a Machine. It is to identify with the Machine's Inventor, to take one's stand in Freedom itself. It is to be one's Source, to choose what flows from it, and to perceive it as very good.

You could fairly point out that, in the case of my own invention which I have cited, my refusal to choose led to the wrong choice being made – wrong at least in the eyes of my accountant and bank manager. So it would seem, to them and to any other sensible outsider. Not to me, the insider. The fact is that decisions arrived at this way, choicelessly, are never *wrong* decisions. Uncomfortable ones quite often, painful ones sometimes, but always in the end they are felt to be *right*. How different from those seemingly personal decisions that split one down the middle. However justified by events in the short term, however right at first, they don't end that way. One is left with the strong suspicion that one has made a mistake, maybe a ruinous mistake.

To round off my own story: my invention – more accurately, my non-invention, the offspring I was midwife to – was *not* stillborn. It has shown some friends the way Home to the World's End and the World's Beginning, and reminded others of the way, and what accountant could put a figure on *one* such Homecoming? Besides, who can detach and estimate the effect of one part of this Homework in isolation from another part? It goes forward as a whole. The world won't be won over to choicelessness by successful skirmishes here and there and a succession of local manoeuvres, but broadly on the broadest of fronts. It is the tide, not a collection of ripples, that floods the foreshore.

Above your Bottom Line is the place of No-choice. Everything there is caught in a close-knit web of mutual conditioning, and freedom is a dream. The Bottom Line itself is the place of Choice. Here is the only place where freedom is real, seeing that there's nothing to bind or be bound. Here you – you as you really, really are – make that supreme and stress-free and only real Choice which Hamlet could not make. What stress that failure cost him! You choose to *be*. Here You freely decide to be, not just the Origin of all things, but of Yourself. No: it isn't Hobson's choice. You don't have to be. There's absolutely no one and nothing below You to give rise to You. Look, You are choosing to come up with Yourself right now and right here. How You do it is *the* Mystery. Accept my congratulations!

Look at it another way. In your heart you know you have freedom of choice. You are perfectly sure of it. But in your head you figure that you have no such freedom, because you are conditioned through and through – conditioned from outside by your environment and from inside by your heredity; and you may add that only the Unconditioned, alias God, has the power of choice. However there's no contradiction here: the apparent you that has no choice lies *above* the Line, while the real You that has choice lies *on* it.

Your heart tells you that you choose. Your head tells you that only God chooses. Taken together, they tell you Who you are, right now.

In the end, the only way to be free of stress is to be Her, or Him, or It – pick your own pronoun – who is Freedom Itself.

Here's some Bottom Line stuff I'd like to leave with you:

> Others gain authority over you if you possess a will distinct from God's will.
>
> Rabbi Nahman of Bratzlav

> It is because we are not near enough to Thee to partake of Thy liberty that we want a liberty of our own different from Thine.
>
> George Macdonald

> For God, freedom is necessary.
>
> Vladimir Soloviev

My purpose in this section hasn't just been to show how true-to-life statements like this are, but to show how to *live* them. Precisely. Unstressfully. And whatever our religion – if any.

(iv) FAILURE

Who of us is not, at some time in our lives, a miserable failure – at least in our own eyes? How many – even among those of us who seem to be realizing our boldest ambitions – feel in our hearts that we are truly successful, that we are by no means letting ourselves down in all sorts of ways, that we are fulfilling early promise and achieving most of what all along we had in us to achieve?

Consider the cost, in terms of stress and distress, of the sad and sometimes bitter tale of defeat we have to tell: or could tell, if it were not so shaming. If success means living the life we like living, and doing the job we like doing, and making an unglamorous but indispensable contribution to the general good – why then I suspect that the least unsuccessful people around are those skilled and semi-skilled workers whom nobody would accuse of vaulting ambition. On the other hand, if failure means that, on the public front, we still lack the power or the fame or the status that we feel is our due; and that, on the private front, we still lack the devoted friends and happy relationships we should like to have – why then we are indeed failures. Our life is a washout and a let-down, no matter how sure the world may be that it's a roaring success.

In fact, progressive limitation and disappointment (what dis-appoints you fails to turn up) form the basic pattern of our life, as boringly repetitive as the pattern on our wallpaper. Bright hopes, vast potentialities, realizable options go by the board one by one as we grow older. The infant of today could be the Buddha or Jesus of tomorrow (B): the world A B C is his oyster. The child of today could do well (E), but his oyster has shrunk to D E C. The youth of today could do fairly well (G), but his oyster has further shrunk to F G C. And so on down through ever-narrowing options to his old age, with practically nothing left but the oyster-shell. He has had it. His life, all our lives, are a slow dying from cradle to grave, foredoomed to failure. Even Leonardo was no good at all sorts of things, and certainly no good at staying Leonardo and alive.

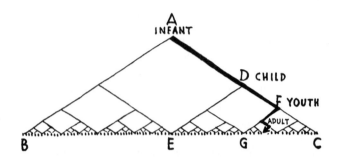

At the same time there's something in us that knows better, that jibs at this relentless contraction and defeat after defeat, something that feels cheated. And, at least underneath, is stressed and distressed about it. Of most of us grown-ups you could safely say that, if we aren't disillusioned with life, if we don't feel a failure and frustrated (if not embittered), it's because we are only half awake, only a quarter conscious of what deep down we know we are worth and are capable of. To the degree that we've shaken off sleep and feel the lust of life stirring in us, we are sure there's something lacking, some key mislaid and door unopened, some lost and wider horizon, some nine-tenths forgotten secret, some holy grail or talisman or elixir awaiting us just beyond the edge of our vision, which would set all right at last and cure our illness. And failure is a serious illness.

Well, the medicine does exist, and it's yours and mine right now for the asking. This sovereign cure for failure, this secret but well-tested recipe for total success, is what we are about to take internally much as we would take any other medicine, dose by daily dose.

But first let us look at the kind of health we're aiming for. What is success? How would you describe a truly successful person? Let's say: it is one to whom the word 'defeat' is meaningless: one who, undaunted by all the odds, does the great thing that he or she sets out to do – indefatigably, joyfully and painfully, all the way to completion. A cumbersome definition, but it sits well on the sort of man or woman I have in mind. I'm thinking – to take a handy sample – of Thérèse of Lisieux. She said that she was sure she was born for greatness, and in her case greatness meant becoming a great saint. (You and I probably favour other sorts of greatness: but no matter, the greatness is the same though the forms it takes are infinite in their variety.) In that formidable task she succeeded astonishingly, though she died at twenty-four. If there's one word that sums up her life it is *heroism*. In general, to be great is to be a hero. And to you in particular I would say: once you have a hero's weapons (and you do have them), and the skill to use them (and you do have the skill), and the heart to use them (and you do have the heart), why, then you are all set to become a hero of the first rank. (Or heroine of course. One of my dictionaries makes *hero* do for either sex, and that's the usage I am following here.)

Perhaps it is not yet quite clear what a hero is. In that case we cannot do better than turn to the ancient Greeks. They specialized in heroes whose mythical exploits have intrigued and inspired our species ever since. Much more than exciting stories, far deeper and more illuminating than the ancient Greeks themselves suspected, their message has still to be fully decoded. For us here that message is so important because it reveals, with unparalleled thoroughness and wealth of imagery, how to be supremely successful.

Let us look at the story of the hero Perseus. It is full to overflowing with lessons for us, lessons which gain rather than lose by taking imaginative form.

Perseus was half divine and half human – a son of Zeus, the Father of the gods, and Danaë, a mortal woman. Danaë's father, Acrisius, had been warned that he would be killed by her son, so he took the precaution of shutting her in a brass tower. However this didn't deter Zeus who, turning himself into a shower of golden rain, came down through the roof and impregnated her, thus begetting Perseus. When Acrisius discovered that his daughter had given birth to a son, he set them both at sea in a chest. But Zeus caused them to come safely ashore at Seriphos, where a fisherman rescued them and took them to the king of the country, who befriended the refugees.

When Perseus reached manhood the king set him the formidable task of killing Medusa, one of the terrible Gorgon sisters, whose head was covered with writhing snakes instead of hair – a sight so frightful that one look at her turned the beholder to stone.

Our hero proceeded to equip himself for the adventure with great thoroughness. First, he visited the Weird Sisters, who shared one eye between the three of them, and snatched it as they were passing it round. Then he made them direct him to the Nymphs, from whom he obtained the Winged Sandals (which enabled their wearer to travel very rapidly through the air), the Magic Wallet (into which things disappeared and out of which they reappeared) and the Cap of Invisibility (which gave its wearer the power of vanishing at will). Athene, the goddess who personified ideal wisdom and power, lent him her Mirror Shield, in which alone Medusa could safely be viewed. Finally Hermes presented him with a wonderful sword for beheading the monster.

Thus magnificently armed, our hero duly tracked down and beheaded Medusa without looking directly at her, hid her head in his Magic Wallet, and got away unharmed from her enraged sisters – thanks to his Cap of Invisibility.

Such, in brief, is the famous tale of Perseus the Hero and Medusa the Gorgon. It is also, directly you and I care to make it so, our own heroic tale, told in parable. Its meaning for us falls into nine parts:

(i) The Divine-human Hero

On his mother's side Perseus was mortal, on his father's divine. Your nature, too, is dual. Looked at from outside, you appear all-too-human and all-too-mortal; looked at from inside, you are clearly nothing of the sort.

(ii) The Fall

Perseus is at sea, adrift, all hint of divinity gone, in danger of drowning – a failure if ever there was one. You, too, have come down in the world, are lost, in mortal danger.

(iii) The Task

Surviving against all the odds and reaching maturity, Perseus is required to solve *the* problem, the problem of petrification. In other words, personal solidification, the universal but false belief that one is shut up in a body, shrunk into a thing like those things out there. For yourself, growing up from infancy, your mother's face, every face you see, becomes in effect Medusa's, forever telling you that you, too, are like this: forever insisting that this thing you are looking *at* is your clue to what you are looking *out of*. Now your task is to see through this lie. You have to find a way of looking at that face, at every face, of somehow coping with it, without letting it petrify you – a way of seeing that you are not like that at all. For this great task you are already marvellously equipped, as follows:

(iv) The Single Eye

For a start you need, like Perseus, your Single or Third Eye. The fact is you have only to notice you never looked out of anything else.

(v) The Winged Sandals

Again, as soon as you attend, you find that the world is given as two-dimensional – high, wide and without depth. Whereas Perseus, shod with Winged Sandals, *gets* all over the place, you go one better and *are* all over the place, instantly.

(vi) The Magic Wallet

Like Perseus, again, you are furnished with the Void that is forever taking in and producing all the world's treasures. Indeed you are this Bottomless Purse and Horn of Plenty. Your essence is Capacity, with room and to spare for all comers. And the ability to come up with what's needed.

(vii) The Cap of Invisibility

See how your headgear vanishes along with the head you imagine you are putting it on. The art of life, of the unstressed life, is to wear the Cap of Invisibility indoors and outdoors, upstairs and downstairs, and – yes! – in my lady's chamber: wherever you are and whatever you're up to. Remember Karen's little poem ending: 'All those people around you, and you are just not there!'

(viii) The Mirror Shield

Athene's Mirror Shield is what you see when you turn your attention round 180° and look in at what you're looking out of. It's the Clarity that, your side of these printed words, is now taking them in. When you are overlooking this Mirror Shield of yours, whatever head you are looking at turns you into the same sort of thing, to 'stone'. But when, gazing into your Mirror Shield, you see that head reflected in this total Absence-of-head, it is rendered perfectly harmless. You are unpetrified.

(ix) The Magic Sword

Really there's only one Medusa, only one snaky and disastrous head in all the land, and that is yours, right where you are, right now. All the others are, as you can see, perfectly snake-free and normal. Your hero's task, then, is to cut off, in one clean swipe of your Magic Sword, this poisonous monstrosity. In fact your Sword is already poised and held to your neck: you catch it in the very act of decapitation. Yes of course, the Sword is none other than your own Bottom Line, below which your imagined head – in contrast to all those seen heads above the Line – is a nonsense and a lie. But a lie that is real and monstrous enough to account for a huge proportion of the stress in your life.

What a wealth of encouragement and insight is wrapped up in this ancient success story! It is your success story. It is already achieved. It is total. It is unconditional. It is not success at others' expense. It takes care of your lesser goals. It dumps your stress . . . Let's enlarge a little on these points.

It's your success

This isn't just a great archetypal tale of somebody else's personal triumph over terrible odds, but your very own personal triumph. The experiments you have already carried out, ranging from the Single Eye to the Bottom Line, are none other than your victory over the horrible Gorgon, marvellously anticipated by the Greeks 2,500 years ago.

It's already achieved

You have come unscathed through the ordeal. You have won. All that remains for you to do now is to avoid falling asleep and dreaming that you are a loser, a failure, a non-achiever. The joke is that your great and truly heroic task from now on is to keep seeing that it's already accomplished.

It's total

It is the only 100 per cent success story. Whatever else you do or anyone does, I don't care what it is, is flawed. It could be done better, or last longer, or give more satisfaction, or come from deeper depths of you. But this hero's work of yours couldn't be done better by a whisker. It's first-time perfect. Perseus was no yuppie. He didn't attend night-classes in Handling Monsters, or serve a few years as an apprentice hero. He didn't need to, because he made sure that all the gods were on his side. It's exactly the same with you. You and he have all the luck in the world.

It's unconditional

Ordinary and partial successes are earned. Perfect success is unearned. It's not a question of merit at all. You don't deserve it. You are it, regardless. If you aren't an admirable character, remember that Perseus wasn't either. The way he treated those Weird Sisters was disgraceful. He mugged them!

It takes care of your lesser goals

It does make a difference to those tasks which, because they fall short of the heroic Task, can never be perfectly accomplished. When you start living the heroic life – that is, living from your true Nature – your peripheral and human nature is bound to benefit. You cannot know in advance how or when, but you can count on Yourself the superhuman hero giving yourself the human non-hero a helping hand and a leg up where necessary.

It dumps your stress

Heroically successful, you cut off, along with that horrible Medusa head of yours (horrible because misplaced), the stress it loaded on you. Wielding your Magic Sword, drawing and redrawing your Bottom Line till it stays drawn, you HEAD OFF STRESS. And dump it where there is no Where. The magic of this Sword is that what it cuts off isn't just removed. It's annihilated. There are no *disjecta membra* and no disposal problems.

Everything else about you, everything you get up to, is in itself a failure. It decays by degrees, and in the end altogether, as it comes down to a mere point on that Line. It gravitates to the very Pit of Hell, so to say. As we have seen, however, this is no dead end. When not resisted, it is the liveliest of beginnings. Here, total implosion is at once total explosion. Everything that arrives on your Bottom Line is You, and as such is a huge success. Consciously living from here, You are the world, and the fact that all its components (and not least the one that figures in your passport) are in constant flux and dissolution – are no more permanent than sparkles on sunlit water – only highlights your imperishable success and its uniqueness. It is a success in which every one of those components is caught up, in which every one of those sparkles shines.

To be a hero and succeed absolutely, you overcome the world by getting to the Bottom of it all and taking it from there. This is its salvation.

Look now. What alternative do you have?

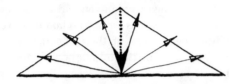

(v) LONELINESS

It goes almost without saying that loneliness and stress and pain keep company in the depths, and that togetherness and relaxation and joy – or at least freedom from pain – keep company in the heights. 'Laugh and the world laughs with you, weep and you weep alone.' This well-worn piece of homespun wisdom introduces, if it doesn't quite wrap up, the topic of this section.

It finds classic expression in Dante's *Divine Comedy*. The Heaven of Heavens above the fixed stars, topping off and putting the most magnificent of lids on this seething cauldron of a universe, is a vast amphitheatre in which myriads of blessed souls – resplendent in their resurrection bodies – commune eternally: an immense concourse of persons so lovingly united that they never tire of one another's company for an instant. Except for Lucifer and his gang, none of them ever leaves the room for a breather – much less to visit that smallest of rooms where, here below, we are solitary willy-nilly. It seems those blessed ones never experience a need to get away for a spell from all that wonderfully relaxed and unquestioning agreement, and do some tense thinking and feeling for themselves. It's precisely that sort of defiant behaviour that led to Lucifer's fall into Hell at the bottom of the cauldron, where there's no agreement at all and everyone's at loggerheads, lonely, under terrible stress. Between these poles – midway between the zenith of oneness and the nadir of alienation – lies this familiar earthly scene which is an unstable compromise between these extremes. Here loneliness and togetherness fight it out inconclusively, a long-married couple that can neither live together nor apart.

Well, if this model (stripped of theatrical décor and poetic licence) gives any clue to the situation you and I find ourselves in, our prospects look poor. It seems we must choose between three evils – the monolithic togetherness up there, the fragmented loneliness down there, and here in the middle a very unsatisfactory mixture of the two.

So it would appear. There should be, indeed there is, a clear way out of this trilemma. By now you will know well where to look for it. But, before taking our exit, let's start again and look at loneliness from a more mundane and contemporary viewpoint.

Loneliness is one of the more punishing forms that stress takes. Some of us suffer much from it, others little – that is, consciously. What makes the difference? What determines that one person should practically never – perhaps not even on his or her deathbed – feel lonely; while another should do so practically all the time, even in a crowd, even *en famille* – perhaps especially then?

The first and too-easy reply, begging the question and furnishing no real answer at all, is that some of us are born loners and others are born joiners: that some of us happen to be Clint Eastwood types and others the sort of worthy citizens, the sociable types, he's happy to leave behind as he rides off into the wilderness. In other words, each of us has a temperament that he or she has to live with, and there's very little we can do about it.

In fact, there's a lot we can do about it, as we shall see. However, the question now confronting us is: why these differences? Some rather more helpful reasons can be found than temperament. For example, much depends on (i), your cultural background, on (ii), the age and maturity of the civilization you belong to, on (iii), your own age as an individual and on (iv), your particular circumstances just now.

(i) Cultural factors

If you happened to belong to an ancient tribal culture that has survived into modern times, and I asked you how you viewed your moods of loneliness, the chances are that you would have no idea of what I was talking about. Most probably the notion of yourself as quite distinct from your fellows, with views and moods of your own, would never have occurred to you. You are a joiner and not a loner. Togetherness and social solidarity make up your lifestyle. So much so that if, for any reason, you found yourself cut off or expelled from the tribe, you might well just lie down and die. Leading a Robinson Crusoe existence would be unthinkable. Your culture has no room for loneliness.

If, at the other end of the self-consciousness scale, you happen to be a sophisticated Japanese or Chinese, and I press you to tell me about yourself, the chances are that you will explain in much detail how you stand in your family, in your office or factory, in this or that club you are a member of. You will define yourself in terms of relationships rather than what you are as an individual.

But if, by way of contrast, you happen to be a forthcoming American or Scandinavian or Britisher (say), and you are approached on the same question, the chances are that you will talk about your hobbies, your taste in books and films, your hopes and fears for your personal future, your psychology, your moods, maybe your spells of loneliness. The Easterner tends to see himself as not so much a joiner as joined, as inseparable from his fellows. We Westerners, on the other hand, tend to see ourselves as rather more loose and freewheeling: in many-sided contact with our fellows, of course, but essentially our own man or woman. And, in this sense, loners.

In general, the attitudes and moods one ascribes to oneself and one's peculiar temperament, supposing them to be individually determined, are, far more than one realizes, culturally determined, even a matter of geography.

What can we do about it? If we feel too little alone and too socialized, make our getaway with Thoreau to the woods, or with Gauguin to the South Seas? Or, if we feel too much alone and too self-occupied, join a tight-knit and hardworking rural community dedicated to the simple life? Or take up an Eastern or Western religion that, as soon as we can bring ourselves to believe what it requires us to believe, rewards us with the companionship of other believers?

By all means let us try any exit from our loneliness that our conscience and good sense will allow. But if we imagine that it will make a lot of difference in the long run we are due for disappointment. Our cultural conditioning is laid down earlier, is more complete and runs deeper, than we are reckoning for. No: we have to find a better way than digging ourselves up like bedding plants and trying to take root in another soil.

(ii) Social factors

Our attitudes aren't only a matter of *where* we find ourselves but also of *when*, of the stage we have come to in the maturing of our native culture. Take our Western, two-millennia-old Christian civilization. Its history can be encapsulated in two words – progressive individuation. That is to say, the sharpening of separate self-consciousness, of the sense of being on one's own, up against rather than ranged alongside or merged with others, of loneliness – with all its advantages in terms of independence and all its disadvantages in terms of stress. If you had lived a thousand years ago and were an artist, you would be most unlikely to paint a careful portrait of any individual or to sign your work, but would happily stay anonymous, merged in society. The probability is that your opinions and behaviour would differ very little from those around you, and that even your moods would be picked up from without rather than generated from within. Your style would accordingly be unoriginal by our standards. But what you lost in freedom you would gain in the all-round social support that protected you against the pain of loneliness.

How different is life at this late stage in the development of our Western civilization! Our insistence on being our sole selves is our current religion. All the same there are many sects and subcultures, many degrees of individualism, largely corresponding to distinctions of class and vocation. At one end of the scale are millions of workers – by no means all manual ones – whose implicit ideal is a maximum of good neighbourliness and group loyalty, coupled with a minimum of 'showing off' in the shape of odd opinions and behaviour, and of personal ambition. Result: some mutual insurance against loneliness and its stresses, at a premium not reckoned to be too high. At the other end of the scale are those comparatively few leading professionals and intellectuals and artists whose values are quite remarkably different. Here originality and strident individualism, personal initiative and contempt for convention aren't just tolerated but admired. The results are apt to be as costly for the individual as they are valuable to his society. Loneliness is the occupational disease of the gifted.

Where do you stand, where would you like to stand in this hierarchy? And, wherever you place yourself, what price salvation from loneliness now? What should you do, what can you do? The prospects look unpromising anyway, the choice one of evils. To come off your ego trip and conform till you are thoroughly normalized, and your loneliness is alleviated at the expense of your aloneness? Or to come off your anti-ego trip and be as aggressively different as you have it in you to be, never mind how isolated and lonely you will often feel? That is the question to which, put like that, there's no practicable answer. Either way, you're in trouble. Besides, we are assuming (and what a huge assumption it is) that you and I can dismount from our lifestyle and hitch a ride on one going in the opposite direction, just like that.

Here, we are committed to finding a more realistic answer – one that makes sense and works, that is essentially natural, that cures our loneliness without killing our aloneness. And one that doesn't require us to change our class or our outward way of life or do anything conspicuous or odd at all.

But we have still to look at two remaining determinants of our loneliness.

(iii) Individual factors

Earlier on, we noticed how your individual history recapitulates your racial history, telescoping it drastically, of course. Provided you were brought up normally and not deprived or maltreated,

you no more suffered from loneliness as a young child than did
your Stone Age ancestors. Of course there are wide individual
differences, and exceptions to most rules about people are numerous, nevertheless by-and-large loneliness grows with ageing –
whether it's the ageing of the species or the individual. In youth
and middle age our socialization – our involvement with other
people in all sorts of ways – is of necessity far greater than in old
age. Besides which, old people (I speak with firsthand knowledge)
just lose interest in so many of the activities – learning new games
and new skills and keeping up with the times, not to mention
raising a family and competing for a place in the sun for them –
that structure the time of young people and knit them to the
community. One reason why loneliness is the handicap of old
people and hard to remedy is that it is what one part of them very
much wants, while the other part hates. Being thus torn isn't
comfortable. I know.

Is the answer, when age brings on loneliness, to retreat and
become a child of sorts again, and perhaps as free from the plague
of loneliness at eighty as we were at eight? No. Obviously senile
dementia, while it could be a partial cure, is rather worse than the
original disease, and is hardly ours to command. (Becoming *as*
little children is quite another matter: regeneration, not degeneration.) The true cure of loneliness, which we shall presently be
taking here, lies ahead and not behind. It is a bold advance and
no retreat.

But, before making that advance, let us spare a moment for
what some might call 'the sensible cure – and about time too!'

(iv) Circumstantial factors

The immediate reason for your loneliness may well be some drastic
change in your circumstances. A spouse has died. A much-loved
child has left home. A special friend has gone abroad. You find
yourself living in a new and apparently less friendly town where
everything, from accents to headgear, is unfamiliar. Retirement
has suddenly made you realize how much you counted on your
business colleagues for the maintenance of your self-image as a

useful and well-liked and respected member of society. Now your loneliness has more to do with the dimming of that image, and the perception of yourself as a reluctant loner, than with your actual lack of company.

Commonsense measures for correcting or minimizing such distressful changes of circumstance are not to be despised. Quite the contrary. By all means let us take whatever sensible measures are open to us. Let's join a group whose members have the same problem as ourselves, try a marriage bureau, share our too-big house with another lonely soul, take fitness classes, go on a cheap out-of-season holiday to a country we've never been to, with folk of our own age. And so on. Much can be done if we really want to snap out of our loneliness. Normal and sensible things.

Yes of course, but let's not kid ourselves that any such emergency measures and palliatives will solve our problem radically and permanently. It runs deeper than we are reckoning for, requires a much more penetrating solution.

How are you and I going to recognize that true solution when we come across it? By two infallible signs. Firstly, it will turn out to be the solution, not just of that particular problem but of all problems – and specially the problem of oneself, of one's true identity and meaning and destiny. And secondly, it will turn out to be something far more positive than a mere exercise in problem solving: in fact, to be not so much the removal of an old and hated impediment as the unearthing of a long-sought-after treasure. The more deep-seated the disease the deeper the cure has to be. In this case it is the deepest and the best. It is as if, bulldozing for a long overdue city bypass, you struck enough gold to build a brand new city on a far healthier site elsewhere.

The cure of loneliness is just like that. The only real remedy for your loneliness is your Aloneness. And this Aloneness is the crown of all experience, the brightest gem in that crown. Your extremity is God's opportunity, the opportunity of the Alone to be you. The worst is the prelude to and precondition of the best. No implosion, no explosion.

These bald, if not outrageous assertions call for more than explanation. They call for testing. As follows:

Experiment 21: The well of loneliness

You feel lonely, right now?

Then locate the loneliness. Observe exactly where in all the world you come across it, where you keep this feeling. Again, I ask you to bow before the evidence, to make your humble obeisance before what is given.

Look up at that great over-arching sky. Is it there that you feel so shut in and lonesome? Quite the contrary, I suggest.

Look out at that broad sweep of hills and plain, at that stretch of forest, at those rows and rows of little houses, those thronging people. Is it there? Far from it, I suggest.

Look down at those inverted feet and legs. Is your loneliness in them, lurking somewhere in those shoes, those trouser-legs? A silly question!

Now look still further down . . .

Ah, now we're getting warm! Or is it bitter cold? Isn't it here that the dregs of your loneliness settle, here that the leaden weight of your loneliness collects and presses so hard on you – in your guts, most of all in your heart, your downhearted, heavy, ice-cold, breaking, sinking heart? Listening to popular songs, to popular stories, to popular speech, how often we come across the expression *the lonely heart*! For good reason. Deep down we know where we keep our loneliness – deep down indeed, at the very base and lowest point of our world, our life's sump, into which all the agony of the world's fragmentation and lovelessness drain. Here is the Pit all right, the Sink, the poisoned Well of Loneliness at the World's End.

Let's not be in too much of a hurry to take a great frog-leap out of this Well, so cold and wearisome. Let's spare a little while to be honest with ourselves, to stop pretending our loneliness is elsewhere, or someone else's fault, or not so wearisome as all that. A little while to be loneliness itself, friendless and abandoned in this Well at the World's End . . .

And now: not up and out to the Well-head but to the very bottom: down, down – and through. Just like Dante and Virgil, through that narrowest and tightest of fissures to the wide bright world, as our implosion into the infinitesimal issues in our explosion into the infinite . . .

Are you brokenhearted? Have you lost heart? Then take Heart. At last you are broke enough, are ground fine enough, to pass through the needle's eye from which you must emerge as the Heart that beats in every breast.

Is that just high-falutin' talk? Then convert it into experience. Point in at this Point. And lose it altogether. And stay pointing at the Immensity which you are where you are. Not at unending empty Space, not even at unending filled Space – filled with that same overarching sky, those hills and trees and houses and people – but Space that *is* all these things, that is this wonderful world, and a meaningless abstraction by itself.

This you are, now. From being that heaviest, smallest, most exclusive pinpoint in the world, you are now, suddenly, all of it. The heaviest has exploded into the lightest, the smallest into the biggest, the all-rejecting and by-all-rejected into the all-embracing. This lonely one has become the Alone, unique, like no other. Look and see now: have you any peer or peer group, any likeness, any analogue at all? Look and see now: is there any explosion *in* the world remotely comparable with your explosion *as* the world? Are you not, on present evidence, absolutely peerless?

You don't understand a word of all this? Neither do I! But you do see it (don't you?) with a seeing that reduces ordinary seeing to purblindness.

Oh I quite understand that all sorts of objections keep occurring to you. For instance, that wettest of all wet-blanket questions, 'So what?' Or the objection that this unspeakably good news is far too good to be true. Or the objection that, in this case, seeing – though brilliant enough while it lasts – is only half believing, just because it is so fugitive. All sensible, damping stuff, not to say sodden. I suggest you come off it, and dare to face your own Aloneness in all its majesty. In other words, dare to face what it takes to be absolutely stress-free.

Well, to conclude this section, let me offer you some additional encouragement. I mean encouragement and confirmation, not additional evidence. Don't forget that an ounce of actual, secular, down-to-earth, rock-hard testing is worth a ton of hearsay – no matter how supportive the saying or how wise the sayer. Still, for what it's worth and for all it's worth, there follows a sampling of the perennial wisdom concerning your true Identity.

At the very core of the great religious traditions – overlaid, neglected, very often vehemently denied by religious experts, but nevertheless the taproot those traditions spring from and are sustained by – is one perfectly lucid, simple, awesome, beautiful realization. It's a proclamation which deserves all the trumpets and bells of Heaven and Earth, and it's about you personally. Personally. It is this: that, more intimately yours than all else, 'closer (as Tennyson put it so accurately) than breathing, and nearer than hands and feet', is the One you really, really are, the Self of yourself, the Self and Source and Substance of all selves, the Alone. No mere spark are you of that Eternal Fire. No mere ray of the One Light that lights every man and woman and child that the world comes into. Not a part of the Whole which (to quote Dante) 'gathers up the scattered leaves of all the universe and binds them by love into one volume', but that Volume itself. You are all of that All which is strictly indivisible. Repeat: indivisible.

'Indivisible perhaps, incredible for sure,' I hear you saying. In reply, I ask: what do you find when you take the advice of Huang-po, the great Zen Master: 'Observe things as they are, and don't pay attention to other people'? Search as you may, wherever you like and for as long as you like, and you will never find Awareness – whether it takes the implosive form of loneliness or the explosive form of Aloneness – but exactly where you are and exactly when you are. Let me ask you again that key question: Look and see, is there any explosion *in* the world that's remotely comparable with your explosion *as* the world? No: I'm afraid you are stuck with What you are, stuck with your absolute uniqueness, stuck with your incomparable grandeur, and there's no wriggling out of it.

What? You still don't believe me? Thank God for that! Only believe yourself – not what you think, but what you see.

Or is it that you don't believe what I've just said about the common Core of the great religions? Well then, read – in the light of the experiments you have done so carefully – what are acknowledged to be the world's most profound scriptures, and you'll soon change your mind. Meanwhile here's a little something to be getting on with. I could dig up scores of quotations to illustrate this embarrassing News about you personally, but shall have to content myself with just three, chosen from the sayings of the most internationally respected of Sages belonging to this century:

> When there is nothing except Yourself you are happy. That is the whole truth.
>
> (Ramana Maharshi)

> When you find everything within yourself and there is nothing other than your own Self – this is full Realization, complete, perfect, all-comprehensive. Supreme Union means the whole universe is in you.
>
> (Anandamayi Ma)

> You are the Source and Heart of all . . . All is you and yours. There is no-one else.
>
> (Nisargadatta Maharaj)

Do I hear you saying, 'This is oriental megalomania. In the West we know better and are more modest'? Then let me throw this one in from St Catherine of Genoa (*Saint* Catherine, note): 'My ME is God, and I recognize no other.'

And so, if it's not just temporary relief from loneliness and the stress of it that you are after, but its radical cure, you will have to face up to the truth about yourself. You will have to allow the bud of your loneliness to blossom into the marvellous flower of your Aloneness. Now.

What are you waiting for?

Perhaps it is for one last word of reassurance about what Aloneness amounts to.

There are two sorts. The first is the false kind, which is the attempt to be aware of oneself as bare awareness, empty of what it's aware of: awareness of a solitary self that's washed clean of all thoughts and all things. Some have earnestly tried for this state. It is impossible to arrive at, much less stay at. But, in so far as it is approached, it amounts to making a serious suicide bid. The second and true kind is the Aloneness which is brim-full. Look and see: who and what can you leave out, who and what does your explosion not engulf? As for what each of these myriads of creatures, these embraced ones, really is intrinsically – well, isn't it what you are intrinsically? If there were just one of them that you were not at heart identical with, why then you would not be the Alone. *Looking out now, you have what they appear to be. Looking in, you are what they are.*

The frog that was so lonesome and ordinary has become the Prince that is Alone and Peerless.

Since writing the above, I have come across this piece by Kurt Vonnegut:

> How on earth can religious people believe in so much arbitrary, clearly invented balderdash? ... The acceptance of a creed, any creed, entitles the acceptor to membership in the sort of extended family we call a congregation. It is a way to fight loneliness. Any time I see a person fleeing from reason into religion, I think to myself, There goes a person who simply cannot stand being so goddamned lonely anymore.

How lustily true! I would add, however, that there's a much more effective and honest way out of loneliness than to retreat from the so-called reasonableness of common sense into the un-reasonableness of religion, and that is to advance into the true reasonableness of the uncommon sense which attends to what's GIVEN. For in fact, as we have seen so often, common sense is mostly nonsense, and a great deal of what we dignify with the title of 'reason' is every bit as superstitious as the dogmas of religion are.

My own experience is that, when I reject both the balderdash of religious beliefs and the balderdash of secular assumptions, and take a fresh look at Who is doing so, I find friends who are getting up to – or rather, getting down to – exactly the same thing. Friends good and true and in plenty. Friends whose mutual loving is unconditional, because it arises from shared Identity, shared Aloneness. Friends who realize that *it is only the Alone that doesn't suffer from loneliness*.

So I would say: if you don't want to be so goddamned lonely anymore, stop being so goddamned superstitious – common sensibly superstitious or religiously superstitious, it makes no odds. Try bowing before the evidence, instead of Authority.

(vi) BOREDOM

We shall best understand boredom – its nature and stress and treatment – if first we glance at its manifestations, graded from extremely severe to extremely light as if in some inverted Beaufort Scale. For convenience we select seven degrees or 'forces', but of course like wind forces they merge and overlap. The pattern is a ramp, not a flight of stairs.

(i) Absolute paralysis

For the moment let us take as a notional limit the absolute boredom that goes with absolute immobility – somewhat like a temperature of absolute zero – and not as a condition that can actually be reached and maintained. We shall come back to it at the end of this section.

(ii) Paralysis

Here we have the all-too-actual boredom of near-total immobility. For good reason this state can be even more resisted and feared than death itself. Accordingly it is used by society as one of its severest punishments and sanctions. The offender's movements are restricted more or less drastically (depending on the gravity of the crime and the humaneness or barbarity of the penal system) all the way from house arrest and open prison to finding oneself shackled to a wall in a dungeon, or closely caged in iron and suspended at the crossroads for public viewing and execration, like a fly held fast but still struggling in the web of a particularly horrible spider. It's neither an accident nor an arbitrary dramatic device that the wickedest villains in Dante's Hell are not tossed about in everlasting flames, but embedded in everlasting ice. Nor is it irrelevant that – in my own experience conducting workshops – more anger and fear have been generated by experiments demonstrating that in reality one is quite motionless than by any other sort. As a clue to what near-total paralysis can mean in real life, take the heart-rending case of a vigorous young man who, following a stroke, can now only move his eyes, and a finger with which to tap out messages bitterly complaining that the hospital is keeping him alive against his will. Just think, for instance, of being unable to move your jaws, and having to be fed by tube direct to the stomach. And no hope at all of ever getting better. The boredom and the stress of it are unimaginable.

(iii) No work

Unemployment, including serious under-employment – whether by reason of our economic system, or the technology which progressively substitutes machines for people, or handicap, or illness, or old age – is of course one of the most intractable curses of our time. And a particularly cruel curse because it is so like partial paralysis. We are not concerned here with what could or should be done about it at the political level, but rather (pending remote and large-scale efforts to overcome the problem) with what can be done right now by the individual sufferer to alleviate and indeed to end the boredom and stress of his or her own unemployment. What can be done by people of all ages and circumstances who don't know what to do with themselves, who have no idea how to structure their time and how to find any purpose in their lives.

(iv) Mechanical work

Even when they do land a job, it can prove so monotonously repetitive that it's only marginally less boring than having no job. The classic comment on this man-trap is Charlie Chaplin's *Modern Times*: in which Charlie, stationed all day at the factory conveyor-belt tightening an endless procession of identical nuts, comes away unable to stop. He has become a machine himself, an exceptionally jerky robot tightening invisible nuts. Is there any doubt that the notorious tendency of machine workers to down tools and walk out is due far more to boredom – to the stress of restricted and repetitious bodily movements (amounting sometimes to partial paralysis) – than to the grievances which are officially put forward? To strike, after all, is to show an initiative and make a move which is denied to paralytics. We have no useful advice with which to burden the experts whose concern is job satisfaction. But we do have something very practical to propose to the individual machine minder, and to any other worker who suffers stress because his or her job is at all tedious. Come to think of it, how many of us have jobs that are consistently interesting?

(v) Unmechanical work

There are well-meaning folk whose advice to the bored factory hand (note that expression: the person attached to the hand is a troublesome appendage) is: 'Work hard, show at least some initiative other than "industrial action", and you may be upgraded to foreman. Or even, if you are lucky, change your blue collar for a white one.' All right, but for how many can this be appropriate advice? Workers are likely to go on being more numerous than bosses well into the twenty-first century. Besides, and more import-antly for our study here, if you do make it to those managerial heights you will only be exchanging one sort of stress for another. Managers are apt to wear more deeply furrowed brows than those of the work force they manage, many of whom pity the boss more than they envy him. *They* know what they are about, exactly what they are going to do tomorrow, what they will be doing next year. *He* wishes he did. No doubt the works manager and his assistants down to the foreman don't suffer too much from boredom (what with never-ending demands from below for higher pay and shorter hours and better conditions, coupled with never-ending demands from above for higher productivity) but they do suffer from anxiety. To be promoted from the shop floor to the board-room is certainly not a matter of stress reduction, but of swapping one sort of stress for another and possibly more crippling one.

(vi) Creative work

It's much the same with people whose profession it is to be original, to come up with the new rather than cope with and renew the old. Much the same, only better as regards the stress of boredom and worse as regards the stress of doubt – including crippling self-doubt – and worry about the periodical drying up of the spring of inspiration. Poets, painters, composers, writers and of course inventors – if they remain original and haven't yet given up the struggle and gone into the cliché business – have to wait for that spring to flow; and go on to satisfy themselves when it does so that the water is potable by others no less than by oneself. Notori-ously the Muse is a capricious lady who can be invoked, never commanded. Unless you are one of those extraordinary geniuses like Mozart (and look what stresses plagued his short and tragic life), your Muse can be out of commission for what seems an age. Here the stress of certainty (the boredom that comes of knowing all too well what comes next) is almost entirely replaced by the stress of uncertainty (the worry of not knowing at all what comes next). In any case, it's no good counselling a man under stress because his job is monotonous to pull up his socks and become an innovator, let alone a great one. He would be justified in punching your nose for you.

(vii) Spiritual work

Are we, then, about to prescribe the 'spiritual' work (whatever that tricky term may mean) of the earnest meditator or devotee – of the would-be saint, or the apprentice sage or Bodhisattva – as the antidote for the stresses that are inseparable from the creative work of the artist and the innovator of whatever sort? Is truly 'Himalayan' mountaineering among the snowpeaks of mystical experience – instead of slogging it up and down the foothills with imperfectly inspired creative artists – is this the answer? Is this our final recipe for boredom-relief, without too many tears or excessive worry or danger? Alas no! The fate of poor Lucifer should warn us against the hazards of high spiritual endeavour. The Light-Bringer and Morning Star, he was the most exalted and beautiful and in a sense the most 'spiritual' of all the archangels. Satan, as Milton portrayed him, had every virtue – courage, fortitude, intelligence and unlimited enterprise – all except humility. So he was indeed humbled. His unbounded chutzpah brought on its own retribution, his total self-upgrading inevitably led to his total self-degrading. The highest pride went before the deepest fall, and he suffered the cruellest punishment that Hell could inflict.

What does this terrible danger, lurking in the heights like some abominable snowman, mean in practice for you and me? What abomination, exactly, are we being warned against?

Plenty of answers could be essayed. The one that matters for our purpose is this: it was none other than insupportable stress that brought Lucifer, alias Satan, tumbling. Having bartered under-achievement for over-achievement, his last ounce of the boredom of inactivity for the excitement of hyperactivity, he found he just wasn't built to take the strain. For us, too, the least practicable way of avoiding the stress of the lower levels is to make for the high ones, to climb and claw and scramble our way up and out of our troubles. To train and discipline ourselves, for example, to attain to the highest peak of Enlightenment (whatever that soaring monstrosity may be): to force ourselves to meditate till at last, after many a winter – and very likely many a lifetime of cold and dark winters – we make it to the Light, achieving the unimaginable high summer of Nirvana and resplendent Buddhahood. The stress and strain of it all! The uncertainty of it all! We may never make the grade. Meantime, oh the pain!

And in the end the crashingly obvious futility and nonsense of this, by far the most ambitious of all ambitions! Let me cite just one example:

As a young man in seventeenth-century Japan, Bankei read in a Confucian scripture about a mysterious Bright Virtue, and determined, whatever the cost, to find out what it was and how to get it. Having consulted all the available masters and failed to get any useful guidance, he decided to go it alone and take up solitary zazen (sitting meditation in the lotus position, with straight back and legs tied in the correct knot). Here's a piece of his own story:

> Going into the mountains and into a cave discovered there, I went in and sat there with my seat bared, not minding how rugged the rock was. I often kept up my zazen for seven days without eating. Once seated I gave myself up to it regardless of what might come, even risking my life for it. I often kept on sitting crosslegged until I fell from the rock exhausted. As there was nobody to bring me food, my fasting went on for days on end.

This sort of thing continued till he gave up all hope of living, and came in fact very near to death. Then, and not till then, quite suddenly it dawned on him that he had been on the wrong tack all the time, and had expended all that energy to no avail. He realized that he *was* the Bright Virtue that he was dying to find. Switching from the language of Confucius to that of the Buddha, he re-christened it the Unborn, which is the True Nature of us all. 'It is full of wisdom and illumination. As it was never born it never dies . . . And by it all things are perfectly well managed.' He made a miraculously swift recovery, and soon became a noted Zen master whose favourite theme was the Unborn which everyone could see had been their own all along. Trying to earn or achieve it or climb towards it was absurd and only served to hide it from view.

The Unborn, the Bright Virtue, our true Nature and our Healing – what is it after all but that Absolute Immobility which registered Force (i) on our stress scale? So ends that scale, with a turning upside down like a giant egg-timer.

The Bright Virtue, the Unborn, the Tao, the Secret of the Stress-free Life, the Absolute Stillness, the Bottom Line, the World's End – however you name it – is indeed one's very own, perfectly obvious from the very start, and all that spiritual ambition, all that killingly stressful work to win it, is uncalled for and ridiculous.

Yet not so at all. Quite naturally and properly we all begin by seeking in the heights what can only be found in the depths.

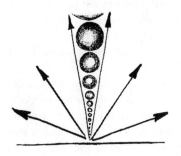

Ultimately all of us are Lucifers who must rise like ever-expanding balloons into an ever more rarefied atmosphere until, having reached our critical ceiling, we suddenly burst from ever-increasing internal pressure, and plummet to where we started from. Fall back in the end, not to Square Three or Two or One (which are regions of ever-increasing external pressure and contraction in Hell) but right through Hell's total implosion and finest point of exit to Square Nought, to the No-point and No-place of total explosion and relief from all stress whatever.

In fact our trouble is half measures – one which the kamikaze Zen master Bankei didn't suffer from at all. It's not what we do that defeats us but doing it so halfheartedly. We get stuck at some intermediate point on the Beaufort Stress Scale, with our stress partly outside us (and pressing in and restricting our movements and making us bored) and partly inside us (and pressing out and freeing our movements and making us worried). Thus we are doing our best to make the worst of both worlds. Our remedy is to let our rising bubble or balloon find its upper limit, where it bursts from internal pressure, leaving the remains to fall back all the way to where they came from, to the Bottom Line itself.

In the end the cure for our boredom, and the powerlessness which generates it, isn't to gain power and rise to higher things, but quite the reverse. That much-quoted dictum of Lord Acton's – 'Power corrupts, absolute power corrupts absolutely' – holds good at more and higher levels than the political. Authentic sages and seers consistently warn us against all forms of spiritual one-upmanship, and in particular against paying any attention to (let alone cultivating) the *siddhis* or magical powers which come of spiritual proficiency. Again and always, as in Dante, the real escape route from Hell is down and through. Down and through, not up and out.

To start with, by all means better yourself, allow your balloon to expand and rise to its natural ceiling, or even (following the Peter Principle) a little above it. And don't then attempt, when you think you have had enough of the heights and their stress, to prick the thing. Let life do that at the right moment, as it surely will.

What's essential for you to do – what it's dead easy to do and what this book is all about – is consciously to view this up-and-down game from the only game-free place there is, to view it from the only place it can be viewed from anyway: namely from the Stillness, from the Very Lowest Place, from your Bottom Line and World's End, from the Single Eye that's now taking in these words, these assorted synonyms for itSelf. That is to say, implode your way through stress to the Stressless. *Then you will have a hard job finding anything that bores you!*

You would think (wouldn't you?) and your sturdy common sense would be sure of it, that this No-thing that you are where you are (by definition and in experience naked of all interest, less intriguing than an interminable viewing of a frameless picture of snow against a snow-white background) – that this yawning gap would prove to be the Yawn of all time, the ultimate agony of boredom. You would think, surely, that this Stroke which has hit you with Force One on our Beaufort Scale (the patient fully conscious but with no hope of parts to move, let alone hope of moving them) would turn out to be the most pitiable and excruciating boredom imaginable. The pit of the pit of Hell: unimaginably, fiendishly dull. So you would think.

Well, look and see. Open your Eye now to What you are, to this Eye itself. Are you bored to tears with this, right now? Does this Eye ever shed a tear for any reason, let alone tedium? How could you ever have too much of a thing that is No-thing? How could you ever get fed up with this No-meal? Have you ever come across any object as *frisky* as this No-object, which off-handedly pops up with universes? Try it now for sheer breath-taking interest, dear Reader. Is it not excellent value – this World's End, this Neckline of yours which sports the whole space-time world above it but no space and no time and no world – absolutely damn all – below it? Only give it half a chance, and I guarantee that you will find that this No-thing is the only thing you never get sick to the back teeth of, that never loses its charm, that is always brand new, that you never, never get used to. For my part, I can't go on listening to my favourite Mozart arias for as little as an hour or two before I cease to hear them, or go on gazing at my favourite Chagall or Miro for as little as five minutes before I cease to register any picture at all. And even if I could go on longer, I would be bound to tire of the thing in the end, precisely because it is a thing among things and nothing if not limited by them in a million ways. 'One gets satisfaction from the unlimited, from the limited never,' says an ancient Indian scripture. How true. Everything is the plaything of

stresses internal and external, is stress-built and stress-maintained and stress-destroyed, has boundaries marked out by stress, grinds stressfully to a halt, lets you down stressfully in the end. Only this stress-free unspeakable and unprintable
that YOU ARE, that YOU ARE COMING FROM – only This never stales, never tarnishes, never wears thin, never loses its flair, its oomph. A name I like to give it, borrowed from Goethe, is Mother Night. Not because it helps me to get to grips with it, but because it tells me I can never do so.

Try it for boredom. Are you sweating away at those loathsome tax returns? See Who is doing so. Are you hoovering broad acres of carpet, made hideous all over with those boringly identical baskets of roses? Have a rest, get those roses on the move, and see Who is *not* hoovering. Are you playing rent-boy to that disgusting and insatiable monster on the shopfloor? See those two hands, broken loose from any shoulders here, busy titillating, and Yourself as their amused voyeur. Are you having a hard time mugging up your Shakespeare for O-levels? See Whose attention persists in wandering from that boring old Juliet and Romeo to that very unboring contemporary one at the front of the class, and be where Shakespeare's coming from.

In short, try two-way looking. Looking in at the Looker and simultaneously out at the looked at. And see whether you have not only seen off every trace of your boredom and the stress of it, but also seen in and welcomed in its stead a peculiar interest, a quiet delight that lends that once-boring object value and fascination.

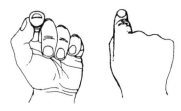

Don't believe but test what I'm saying to you: that all things,

never mind what, when consciously observed from their Origin,
are bathed in its perfume and lit up with its radiance.

There is a glory. Always. To find it, be Where it comes from.

(vii) GUILT

A great deal of the stress in our lives arises from guilt, far more
than we have any idea of. But what is guilt? When you pronounce
a man guilty of (say) murder, what do you mean?

If you mean he did the deed, was caught red-handed in the act
and must take the consequences, fair enough. I understand that.
But if you mean that he is blameworthy, or is plain wicked – and,
by strong implication, that you, the man or woman who is judging
him thus, are comparatively innocent, and certainly innocent of
murder – then I don't understand you at all. It seems to me that
you are talking through your hat.

For consider: You tell me that that murderer is a bad, bad man,
and personally responsible for being like that. Very well (I ask),
what made him so? His temperament (you reply), his bad character, and bad character isn't built in a day. How true, I agree, and
ask just how long it takes to build, and what goes to the building of
it. To be responsible for one's actions is to be responsible for what
gives rise to them, which includes the sort of home one was
brought up in, and the sort of parents one was born to, and all
that made *them* like that. And so on, back and back. There's no
stopping anywhere or when. Are we blaming the man for it all,
holding him responsible for the built-in genetic determinants, the
genes and chromosomes that led up to his crime, together with all
the physical and chemical and biological and social-familial en-
vironments that nursed their development? Did he, with evil
intent, preside over that unthinkably intricate and virtually begin-
ningless saga – horns and tail and breathing fire, gleefully directing
it all the way to its culmination in bloody murder? Come on!
There's no getting out of it: either he isn't responsible for that
crime; or else, if he is responsible, it's a very different 'he' from the
one standing in the dock. When you take into account the whole

of 'him', all that has gone to making him what he now is, then you find yourself including more and more of the world and its history. What, in the end, can be omitted from that colossal biography, that immense web of causes and effects?

This is no academic exercise, no indulgence in idle curiosity, or just having intellectual fun. It's inexpressibly important to look deeply into this question of guilt, for two reasons. The first is that it won't do to go on with this all-too-ready doling out of blame. Honesty, charity, ordinary decency, as well as plain good sense, demand that I wake up to what I mean by attributing guilt to others – if indeed I mean anything at all, and am not just making the customary social noises. Just barking disapproval, the way one's dog barks disapproval at some visitors and not others.

My second reason is more powerful and more personal. It is that, when I pry into my own secret life since infancy, I uncover far, far more guilt than I ever suspected, and a correspondingly crying need for forgiveness. Which amounts to saying: a great deal of glossed-over stress. I find that vast areas of 'innocent' behaviour, taken to be white as new-fallen snow, have in fact been tinged pink if not blood-red with meanness and callousness, and in places fouled and deeply stained with black wickedness, if that word means anything at all. No, I'm not playing 'Humbler than You' or 'Ain't I awful?' but reporting what I find when I examine my childhood and manhood with its veil of hypocrisy lifted. I don't know about you, but this is the sort of thing I find:

As a young child I heard, vaguely and occasionally, of recent disasters; as an older child I read about them in some detail; as a youth I listened, fascinated, to on-the-spot accounts of them; and now they burst into my living room, brilliantly lit and coloured, roaring and crying. A crescendo of human suffering. As my nose has been rubbed in it more and more vigorously over the years, has my attitude to it, my personal involvement in it all, responded accordingly? So that now at last, when on the box I watch scenes of fire, storm, flood, famine, disease and war, I send to their victims the unspoken message: 'How I wish that disaster had hit me instead of you, or at least that I were with you now in the thick of it all, instead of sitting here in safety and comfort'? Or is the message, 'I'm all right, Jack'? The answer goes without saying. Starting very young, I have with cheerful unconcern dished out money for that second bag of sweets, that rare stamp, that smarter jacket, that new sports car, that up-to-date encyclopaedia, etc., etc., instead of sending it to the charities whose Christmas appeals overflow my waste-paper basket. More sinister still, if less frequent, have been the furious, contemptuous, hating, and – yes! – murderous feelings directed against a succession of enemies and friends (*sic*) throughout my longish life. Among my indelible childhood memories are my mother's heart-cry, 'You lack natural affection,' and, from various teachers, 'If looks could kill . . .' Both comments well deserved. (I used to have a terribly convincing dream that I had indeed murdered someone unspecified, and in the end would be caught. It was as though when dreaming I remembered my guilt, and when waking I forgot it.) Far more than I ever imagined, my life has been lived, if not murderously, at least at others' expense. At a deep level I have been troubled by it and suffered from the guilt of it, and this has been a major source of the stress in my life. Nothing will wash away this guilt but forgiveness. Total, blanket, unconditional forgiveness.

What do I mean by forgiveness? Where to find it? Who forgives whom? We shall presently see.

I can't emphasize too strongly at this point that I have been speaking only for myself, and not for you as second person or for those third persons over there – whether you or they are labelled decent citizens or convicted murderers or whatever. My remarks above about the absurdity and impossibility of attributing blame to others – to that man in the dock, to people as such – hold good. Blame is not for export. It won't stick anywhere but right here. Of course it has to be like this: as we've seen again and again, the inside or First-Person story isn't just different from the outside or second- or third-person story, but its diametric opposite. 'He is guilty' is not true, because as a third person he was *born conditioned by his past*. 'I am guilty' is true because as First Person I am *Unborn, and responsible for my past*. All of it, from the very beginning.

So the big inside question is: when and where and how to find that absolution from one's guilt, that unconditional forgiveness for lack of which one's life is hiddenly torn asunder and churning with stress?

The answer is one that's becoming more familiar to us all the time, and it is the only real and conclusive answer. It is to be quite clear about Who is asking the question, and this means making the deepest of bows before the evidence.

Here, underpinning that guilt-ridden life, subtending all my care for this one and God help the rest, is its Bottom Line which is the beginning of all that guilt when read upwards, and the end of all that guilt when read downwards. Here is the Place where Bare Consciousness, losing its innocence, shoots up like a great multi-coloured firework, sinister as well as glorious, from the dark depths of Unconsciousness. As the one I LOOK LIKE – as the man you see, as the right-way-up second or third person who's pictured in my passport, head and all, all of me well above that Bottom Line – I'm held responsible only for what I get up to and not what you get up to. In law and in common sense it must be so. Society would be impossible any other way. But as the one I AM, as the decapitated and nameless and upside-down one I SEE, my Bottom Line cancels the head which isn't only my identity card but also my certificate of no-blame. Here I let poor old Douglas Harding off. Here I take responsibility for him, as for all others above the Line. Here I am responsible for all I give rise to. Right here and right now I have to face the awesome fact that as First Person Singular I am guilty of this world and all the deeds done and the pains endured in it. To ignore that fact is as unwise as it's stress-building.

This isn't merely how it looks but how it feels. When I really attend, when I'm honest with myself, I find it impossible to wash my hands of the wickedest or stupidest or most contemptible or saddest creature in the world. It is not a case of 'there, but for the grace of God, go I' but of 'There go I – into the prison cell, into the psychiatric ward, on to the scaffold, no less than happier places' – for the simple but truly devastating reason that Who I really, really am is what you and all others really, really are. We don't sport a Bottom Line apiece. There's only one World's Beginning and World's End and Ground of Being, and the sooner I firmly take my stand on it the sooner is my guilt assuaged. Only when I see that I am totally to blame am I totally forgiven, and the stress of guilt goes the way of all toxic and superfluous stress. It is up-ended and tipped over the Edge into the Dump of Nowhere and Nowhen. Here, the guilty One and the forgiving One and the forgiven One are One and the same. The One who is to blame for the world is its Saviour. Don't our hearts, undaunted by the mystery and paradox and terror of it all, tell us that this is the only way, that this is the truth, that this is wisdom, and that ultimately all is well?

'Not entirely,' you might reply. 'If, as First Person Singular – if, as the Ground of Being and the Bottom Line, I am erupting like Vesuvius into this disastrous world, I have an awful lot to answer for. Oh yes, the pyrotechnics are wonderful. But those who get the worst of the fall-out are unimpressed. The whole show runs on a devil's brew of selfishness and guilt and stress and pain. And who could be forgiven for that?'

To which I reply: such is the price of the generosity and love and joy, and the marvellous beauty that are not hard to find in the world. Such is the price of any world at all. Alice was right. It isn't unbridled love that makes the world go round (a severe outbreak of selflessness would bring it to a stop), but 'everyone minding his own business'. Everyone doing and being his or her thing. That's how things come to pass – stressfully, and where necessary at the expense of the other things. The only alternative is nothing at all, a great big beautifully unselfish and unstressed Blank. Is that what we want? Let's face it: a healthy human (I mean a human as such) is no more guilty when he or she looks after Number One than a healthy cabbage is guilty when it does likewise, filching from its neighbours every scrap of nutrient it can lay its roots on. A mean, mean cabbage it is, therefore it has a fine heart. The best in the garden.

No, it's not Love that makes the world *go round* but Love that *gives rise to* the world – the Love that cannot pass the buck, the Love that shoulders (instead of a head) the blame for everything, the Love that by taking on the guilt of all is the cure for all guilt.

Such Love is our Bottom Line, what we're coming from, what we've never come away from.

The special genius of the Christian faith is the intuition that the Highest and Best is also its opposite. That it is Itself because, humbling Itself, it comes all the way down to the Lowest and Worst; that it descends to the very basement and sink of creation and embraces every aspect of the pain and squalor there. Wonder of wonders, the Love which saves the world does so by taking on all that the world needs to be saved from! Specially its guilt.

The mystery is unfathomable. The only way to 'understand' it is to start living it, to get the weight of it by feeling the weight of it. And the only way to do that is to stop trying to jack oneself clear of the Bottom Line, and allow oneself to sink through all that guilt and stress to the Place they can't get to.

One's original sin is forgiven when one confesses it and becomes it – in accordance with the law that what we go all the way down to and into we lose. Thus with Dante and Virgil we pass, through the dead weight of the world and the thick darkness, to the bright world and the beautiful stars.

True wisdom doesn't come cheap. It costs a lot – it costs you everything – to be yourself. In a sense, of course, seeing Who you are is gratis, a free hand-out of what's already yours. To open your Third Eye and take in the world – what wisdom could be easier, more natural, more painless? Yes, but you can't stop there. Taking *in* the world turns out, in the long run, to be taking *on* the world, with all its guilt and pain. And what could be more devastating than that? The sight of yourself as the Unborn and Unconditioned and Upside-down One lets off all those born and conditioned and upright ones, and leaves you pleading guilty. True to yourself and compassionate to them, you are left with no alternative. Honestly.

Here is the downward path with a vengeance. The story of Odin, or Woden, may help us to accept the inevitability of it, and perhaps to feel our way into and through the experience itself. In Teutonic mythology he was the father of the gods, the god of the sky and of the nether world of death. He was the divinity who gave courage to warriors, inspiration to poets, and wisdom to the would-be wise. Naturally one pictures this exalted ruler of gods and men as soaring, like the eagle that is one of his symbols, high above the earthly scene where wisdom has to be bought very dearly. The myth tells a different story. He, too, has to pay the full price for wisdom, and in two instalments. He sacrificed one eye for it: as we've seen, no great loss. Accordingly he's represented as one-eyed. And he sacrificed himself for it. He was hanged. For nine days and nights he hung, in great pain, on the Yggdrasil Tree at the centre of the world. Till, at the end of the ordeal, he was able to bend down and get hold of the magic runes that were to bring secret knowledge to mankind. It is thought that this is why, in this ancient Norwegian wood-carving, his tongue is sticking out. It's not a gesture of defiance. It's what happens to hanged people.

A grim picture. Nevertheless a piece of realism which this First Person could profitably remember on Wednesdays – on Woden's-days – if not at other times. However, his story does allow us to end this section on a happier note. Another of Odin's symbols was the ring. One of the forms it took was a metal collar (often very elaborate and made partly of gold) worn by certain warriors who fought fearlessly without armour, seeing that they came under the god's special protection. However much or little they were wise to the fact, their collars marked the line where all danger and violence and guilt bottom out. In terms of an earlier chapter, they wore the ultimate safety helmet which encases no head, the helmet of eternal salvation.

Here, arrived on the Line, you have come through guilt and suffering to the blissful innocence which is forever. Spare a glance now for the one who's standing in the dock. Your Odin-collar marks the scene of your alibi. Not a peccadillo, let alone a real offence, can be pinned on an inverted and decapitated defendant. Just as it's by taking on the distance between yourself and home that you come home, so it's by taking on the guilt of the world that you arrive in the place where none remains. Right here, you are more innocent than a new-born baby. The down-in-through way is that thorough!

(viii) SEXUAL PROBLEMS

The cut and thrust of this book – its working hypothesis for testing every way, day in and day out – is that self-awareness is the answer, the key of the kingdom whose monarch you are, the sovereign remedy whatever your problem or complaint. As Thomas à Kempis put it, 'If you want peace of mind and true unity of purpose, you must put all things behind you and look on yourself.' Precisely. Approaching your Bottom Line, or World's End, is putting behind you, one by one, the stressful things you are not, till you get to the stress-empty No-thing you are. It is consciously peeling the onion of your appearances till you become the reality at their core, which is consciousness itself and quite perfect.

I think I can hear your comment: Maybe self-consciousness is the cure for most of my problems. But surely not for my sexual problems. Here, the cure has to be self-*un*consciousness, forgetting and losing myself, so that automatically I'm preoccupied with my partner, and find him or her altogether absorbing. The reason why animals have no sexual problems at all is that they are so good at overlooking themselves, and the reason why people have so many is that they are so bad at it.

To which I reply: it can never be bad to be awake, provided it's wide awake. The trouble with us humans isn't that we are too self-conscious, but that we aren't half self-conscious enough. If we went all the way we would be out of trouble, including sexual trouble. As things are, we fall between two stools – the stool of the animal who looks only out, and the stool of the seer who also looks in, steadily in and all the way in. And we land painfully on our bottoms, well short of that Bottom Line where there's no pain any more. No, there's no going back to self-forgetting. The way to well-being is forward to full self-awareness, and this is just as true of sexual well-being as of any other sort. For here again the rule applies: finding yourself *is* losing yourself. Finding the self-you-are *is* losing the selves-you've-acquired. Taking on at last your true identity as No-thing *is* taking off your false identifications as all kinds of things. It is these that keep you and your loved one apart, and are responsible for your sexual stresses. Urging us to seek the self with all the energy at our command, the Zen master Dogen adds: 'To find the self is to forget the self; and to forget the self is to be enlightened by all creatures – not to enlighten them.' In exactly the same way, the true goal of sex is fully to enjoy – in a profound sense to be enlightened by – your partner, and this can only happen when there's nothing of yourself left to block and darken the view. Till you come to this goal, your union goes unconsummated.

Deep down, we know this. That's why the truth pops up in all sorts of guises and in all sorts of places. For a charming instance, take the Scandinavian legend of the Lindworm:

His story begins where all our stories begin, with a witch's spell that turns a royal personage into a monster. Prince Lindworm, now a horrible serpent, got to wield such power in the land that he demanded – and obtained – the king's daughter for bride. Fortunately, however, when it came to the wedding night, the Princess showed admirable resource. She wore ten nighties. When the Lindworm told her to strip, she said he must first slough a skin. Reluctantly, he complied, and she shed a nightie. Again he told her to strip, and again she agreed to do so – after he'd sloughed a second skin. And so the stripping and sloughing went on till both were naked – and he stood revealed as a handsome Prince again. The witch's spell had done no more than put his royal highness under wraps. Ten of them, scaly-tough and opaque, and all different.

What a sweet ballet (the title has to be *The Wedding of the Russian Dolls*) could be composed around this fairy tale, with its delightful combination of playfulness and profundity!

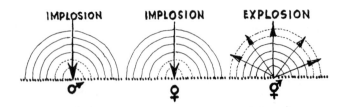

For us here its meaning is plain enough. Our sexual problems (which could hardly be more severe than those of the Lindworm and the Princess) are resolved when, coming off our peripheral acts, we get down to who's putting them on. Then each of us, consciously arriving at No-thingness, is emptied for the other's thingness. Short of that central change-over, we hang on to something of our own, on to a self-image that's way-off-centre. Thus to be anything at all for oneself is to be beside oneself, eccentric, un-whole-some, split clean (or is it dirty?) down the middle. Split, for example, between a lovemaking Tom or Mary on the bed and a peeping Tom or Mary at the bedroom keyhole. Playing the double role of performer and voyeur ensures a mixed performance, to say the least. Eccentrics may make passable copulating machines, but they certainly make poor lovers.

Couples are prevented from coming together by their precious separate identities, by the ten (and more) protective coverings which insulate them like positive and negative cables. Only as stripped to the conductor, all the way down to their common metal, can they be welded in a blaze of love. Adapting George Macdonald's 'In God alone can man meet man,' let's say: only in a sexual No-thingness can male and female thingness meet. (Chauvinists of both sexes, please note.) Each becoming void for the other's form, the partners' separate implosions culminate in their joint explosion – of which their orgasm is a special instance, a recommended but optional extra. No wonder that for centuries devout Tibetans have found that the only adequate symbol of the quintessential union of form and void is a couple fucking. Thousands and thousands of couples, in temple after temple, happily fucking away, in a rather stylized sitting position: caught and preserved for posterity in the act, like well-arranged bees in amber.

Yes, it's about time our comically prudish descriptions of these *yab-yum* icons did justice to their earthiness as well as their sanctity. High time we stopped being so coy and mealy-mouthed, and began being as explicit verbally as they are explicit visually. In any case the bawdy and the holy, following the rule that extremes meet, aren't easily – or profitably – disentangled. Witness Tantrism. Witness the ancient custom of temple hetairae, with appropriately erotic sculptures decorating the temple plinth.

Witness the exceptionally relaxed behaviour of numerous – perfectly genuine – medieval and modern spiritual adepts. Witness the writings of such geniuses as D. H. Lawrence and James Joyce. And so on, and on. Let's sum it up by saying that the cosmic Mum and Dad – alias Mrs Void and Mr Form – are happily married, and human fucking is a temporal participation in their eternal and ecstatic embrace.

One of our Western synonyms for their marriage bed, for the holy-profane place where form implodes into voidness and void explodes into form, is the kingdom of heaven within us – the kingdom where love reigns. It's a busy scene, at once centripetal and centrifugal. The love that makes the world go round penetrates it to the core, back and forth. You can't help noticing the sexiness of its unremitting in-and-out movement.

> This is the key of the kingdom:
> In that kingdom is a city,
> In that city is a town,
> In that town there is a street,
> In that street there winds a lane,
> In that lane there is a yard,
> In that yard there is a house,
> In that house there waits a room,
> In that room an empty bed,
> And on that bed a basket –
> A basket of sweet flowers:
> Of flowers, of flowers,
> A basket of sweet flowers.
>
> Flowers in a basket,
> Basket on the bed,
> Bed in the chamber,
> Chamber in the house,
> House in the weedy yard,
> Yard in the winding lane,
> Lane in the broad street,
> Street in the high town,
> Town in the city,

> City in the kingdom –
> This is the key of the kingdom,
> Of the kingdom this is the key.

Significantly, the turning point in this justly famous traditional poem, the spot where implosion climaxes in explosion, is a bed. What a neat and multipurpose image this is – combining the deathbed (in which one's world comes to an end), the birth-bed (in which one's world begins anew) and the marriage bed (in which the whole cosmic process is recapitulated *à deux*, to the accompaniment of those peculiar cries and interweavings we call sex)! What a mystery is here, so raunchy-subtle, so richly complex and variable, so religious, so deep! And, by God, so universal! Why, there's enough stress-free love-making going on in that piece of Gorgonzola to lift it clear of the dish, and to justify one's outrageous request to pass the fucking cheese.

Yes, I know. This tale of universal lechery is too universal to be useful. It's poetic and intriguing all right, but as yet altogether too general to be deployed in that particular well-sprung double bed upstairs, awaiting developments. What does it all amount to on the night, on any night, for those multitudes of us whose sex life is as chancy as English weather, or as predictable as a polar freeze-up? Or as invariable as the balmy climate of Shangri-La: and on the way to becoming just about as prosy as any other routine?

Well, I don't know, of course, what your special problems are. But I do know what their solution is. It's clear what you have to do. No matter *what* they are, see *whose* they are. In more detail, even when making ardent love – specially when making ardent love – *see* yourself as absent in favour of the loved one. Don't try to feel or understand your absence: there's Nothing to be felt or understood. Don't imagine it or think it, or verbalize the seeing into 'Here am I, gone!' Just look in as well as out. This way, it's no longer a case of 'How excited I am!' or 'What a wow of a time he or she is giving me!' There are thrills all right, but no one is here having them. No: it's a case of 'How exciting he or she is, how lovely and enjoyable!' A clear case of 'What an incredible partner!' instead of 'What incredible things he or she is doing to me and for me!' The thrills are thrilling because they are genuine – genuinely other-centred and not self-centred, objective and not subjective. Sex of this sort, based on being yourself instead of some wretched stand-in for yourself – which means seeing yourself from no distance instead of yards away – is truly enlightening as well as truly sexual. Each partner is enlightened by the other. Somewhat as, when black and white come together socially, they trade faces: so, when man and woman come together sexually, they trade bodies. Each takes in, and takes on, the opposite sex. Without this switch-over, it's masturbation *à deux*. With it, meditation *à deux*, of a sort that's no less spiritual for being so physical.

Of course, it's little good trying to turn it on, along with the dimmed and roseate bedside lighting, for the occasion. You have to get used to being absent yet present in the airport, the office, the store, the street, the living room as well as in the bedroom – till it becomes natural to be natural just about anywhere and anywhen. And then (having given sufficient time and attention to breaking the habit of self-thinging) you won't find being absent–present more difficult in bed that at table, or at the kichen sink, or at your desk or steering-wheel. Or, for that matter, at church, or syna-gogue, or temple, or mosque. Nor is this surprising. All you are doing is to apply to your sexual life the lesson that you are learning over and over again throughout the rest of your life – that to do any job well you must do it from your perceived First-personhood instead of your conceived third-personhood: from the marvellous Nothing–Everything you see you are, instead of the petty thing they say you are. You are renewing your discovery that, whereas all lying is inefficient, lying to yourself about yourself is diabolically inefficient – in bed and out of bed, it makes little difference. Phony sex, relying on false self-images, is unsatisfying sex: and in the last resort all your self-images are false. Genuine sex, on the other hand, relying on the absence of any self-image whatever, is satisfy-ing sex. Naturally.

What then are you up to, so naturally? You are doing what's advertised to be the most difficult thing in the world, but is in fact the easiest. You are seeing Who you are. The habit is growing on you. It's extending into your sex life, which accordingly is becoming more pleasurable. But of course genuine sex isn't only about physical pleasure. It's about love. Otherwise, it's no more than animal coupling leading to the discharge of less-than-animal tensions – no more than letting excess air out of your tyres – followed by the flatness, or the sour taste, or the nausea, of *post coitum triste*. The reason why sex without love is a meaningless and stressful gymnastic display – why winning sexual games (marathons, scalp-hunting, position-collecting, power tripping, bed-athletics and bed-tricks of every sort) is immensely less satisfying than winning regular games – is very simple. Track-and-field events are properly and essentially separative, all about rivalry and one-upmanship; whereas bed events are properly and essentially unifying, all about downmanship, all the way down to the very source of love at the terminus of the descent. Really to love another – with or without benefit of sex – is to go down to the level where he or she is no longer another, but the self of oneself. The Lindworm and the Princess couldn't consummate their marriage, couldn't truly love, till both had seen their way through to the World's End and Bottom Line which is the ground and goal and consummation of all loving whatsoever.

But what if their stripping and seeing had been one-sided? What if either he or she had insisted on retaining some protective covering – a patina of serpent scales, or a final stitch of night-clothes? What if your partner wishes to stay short of that Line where you could be absolutely one?

The answer is that you *are* absolutely one, willy-nilly, regardless of whether he or she chooses for the moment to ignore that ever-present truth. So the problem of one-sidedness is, basically, not a real problem at all. Of course it's good for the two of you consciously to share your descent to the Ground where you are no longer two. All that's essential, however, is that you mind your own business, which at this level *is* the business of your partner and everyone else.

For consider: you are now taking in this printed page. Does the fact that it's not empty-for-you make you any less empty-for-it? Is your enjoyment of a rose dampened by the thought that the sentiment isn't reciprocated? Not in the slightest. The awesome yet self-evident truth is that you can only see Who you really are *as* Who you really are – to wit, as all beings, as the One Seer gazing out of them all. You don't come to that station of true self-awareness and true love – you don't lean back and rest on your Bottom Line – *as somebody*, but *as Nobody-everybody*. In sexual matters, as in all else, only be true to yourself, and all the others are taken care of.

Short of this ultimate level, there remains a fact that must be faced. It is that, however successfully you apply our therapy of radical self-awareness to your sexual hang-ups, some will go on hanging around. New problems may crop up. They, too, will be stressful. I promise.

Yes: but there's a master-treatment for them all, regardless. It is this: *for problems read pointers*. Fingerposts directing you to your native land, to the beloved and rose-strewn country from whose frontiers all problems – sexual or otherwise – are turned away.

Look. That true bed of roses lies twelve inches your side of this printing. It is the empty and fragrant love-bed on which the whole universe is being conceived and brought to birth, at this very moment –

> an empty bed.
> And on that bed a basket –
> A basket of sweet flowers:
> Of flowers, of flowers,
> A basket of sweet flowers . . .
> This is the key of the kingdom.
> Of the kingdom this is the key.

(ix) LIFE IS DIFFICULT

The unfortunate friend I mentioned earlier, the one who was going to boost my invention but couldn't because he was sent to jail, was tremendously excited (he explained in a long letter) by a discovery he made there. It was that life is *difficult*! It had taken the unpleasantness of a sudden plunge from public acclaim to public contempt (no easier to bear because it was so pharisaical), a widely publicized trial, and a prison sentence with disruptive effects on family life, to bring him to this remarkable realization. It took seven years of austerities, so severe that they ended by nearly killing him, for Gautama Buddha to arrive at the same conclusion. He prized it so highly that he called it 'the First Noble Truth', the fact that life is suffering. *Noble* truth, mark you.

I find this very odd. At first sight both men paid an outrageous price for a discovery that should have been all-too-obvious from the start – from the screams of birth through to the groans of death – and cost not a penny extra. On reflection, however, what *is* obvious is that few of us have begun to learn, and fewer to live, the lesson that all existence above the Bottom Line is a wash-out, a disappointment. Or – not to exaggerate and pile on the agony – that it is split down the middle, that the positive side is matched by the negative, and we can't have one without the other. Up here at its own level, there's no resolving the dilemma. No millennium will ever dawn. No armistice will ever be signed between the combatants, much less a peace treaty, and there's no relief from the resulting stress and strain. It isn't that unfortunately life happens to be difficult for many of us, but that it's set up to be difficult for all of us, appearances notwithstanding, eternally springing hope notwithstanding. You can appreciate why countless millions of Eastern realists have believed that getting caught up on the fast-turning Wheel of Life is the great misfortune, and bliss it is to get off the horror for ever.

The curious fact is how surprised we are – or more like shocked, angry, humiliated, embittered, in varying combinations and degrees – every time we make this momentous discovery anew. Years and decades and a whole lifetime of rediscovery, of having our noses rubbed in this so-called Noble Truth till they should be worn out, make little difference. Life, we incurable optimists go on believing, in the teeth of all the evidence, is not an unwinnable war between good and evil, love and hate, beauty and ugliness, and so on, but *normally and properly* good and loving and beautiful, though temporarily the times are out of joint. This is a pipe-dream. Among the hardest lessons life has to teach us is that it is essentially bipolar. From infancy we are bifurcated like seedlings, and stay that way through life.

What this bifurcation means in practice seems at first unacceptable, and then shaming. Eventually, for instance, we are driven to admit that our love, insofar as it's alive and well, is anything but straightforward devotion; that our relationship to that much loved one is a love-hate relationship, and there's no help for it. That our joy in our work, if it's real joy, is half pain. That our quite genuine goodness and unselfishness isn't itself without our equally genuine badness and self-seeking. That our very sharpest intelligence demands a species of idiocy. And so on, without limit. There are no exceptions to the law. Stunt men and women in life's circus, we take no time off from the Splits, the Great Balancing Act. You could say that life is the very Deuce, a gigantic exercise in twoness, in radical inconsistency and internecine strife. *Stress* is our word for it.

Here are some examples, taken at random, of how this inconsistency works out in real-life terms:

(i) For the first we go back yet again to Thérèse of Lisieux. If saintliness consists not so much of goodness as of humility and love, then Thérèse merited her canonization all right. But we must not oversimplify. Take the following excerpt from her *Autobiography*:

> A great grace came to me; one of the greatest, I always think, I have ever received in my life ... I felt I was born for greatness; but when I asked myself how I was to achieve it, God put in my mind that ideal which I've just mentioned. [She refers to Joan of Arc.] The glory that was reserved for me was one which didn't reveal itself to human eyes: I must devote myself to becoming a great saint ... This daring ambition of aspiring to great sanctity has never left me.

Well, if that's humility, I'd like to know what conceit is! And Thérèse realized her ambition. She became one of the most genuine and endearing saints of recent times. It took that degree of pride to come to that degree of humility, because (besides being a saint) she was as human as they come.

(ii) Our second example of being thus split down the middle is taken, you may feel, from another world altogether, and certainly from nearer home. I'm asking you to supply it. Think of the one you love very much indeed and in all sorts of ways – it may be your husband or your wife – and who returns your love. Is it a steady and even love between you, undisturbed by recurring misunderstandings and resentments, by crises of any kind? Do you seriously believe that, if only you were more mature and more loving, you could enjoy the rose of that love without bleeding sometimes from its thorns? And do you fondly think that somewhere in this world there are people, outside of romantic novels, who are luckier or better than you, and accordingly enjoy a lifetime of steady and uncomplicated love which is free of its opposite? If so, dear Reader, you had better think again.

(iii) It's my turn to supply the third example. A long-time and valued friend phoned to say he was coming to see me today, but I should be prepared for a shock. No, he hadn't grown a beard. No, he hadn't been disfigured in an accident – well, not exactly. He had a black eye. Not, I felt sure, got in a street fight or pub brawl. He wasn't the type. In the home? I asked, as tactfully as possible. Exactly, came the answer. And his marriage I would judge to be an averagely loving one. But . . . life is difficult. Along with bright and smiling eyes it hands out black eyes, real and metaphorical, freely.

(iv) Also yesterday I got from an equally dear friend in Israel a bulging envelope. It contained numerous quotations from the diary of a young Jewish girl, Ethy Hilthum, who lived in Amsterdam during the Second World War and was sent from there to Auschwitz, where she died. Here is a selection from them, translated from the Hebrew by my friend:

> We try to save so many things in life with vague mysticism, but the mysticism has to stand on a base of total frankness and on a cold and piercing examination of things.

Most people only see in life what it's permissible to see, but we must free ourselves from all existing ideas . . . and then life becomes rich and abundant even in moments of deep suffering.

The distress here is really terrible. And still, in the evening, when the day recedes, I walk with bright footsteps by the wire fence, and from my heart arises always the feeling [that] Life is wonderful and grand.

My own comment on these three excerpts from Ethy's diary is that they are of a piece, and that the stark and brutal realism of the first two should be understood as the precondition and the other face of the third and its tender joy. She had the intelligence and the heart and the grace to view the two violently opposed sides of her life from the Place of their origin, from what we call her Bottom Line, and to hold them together there. Of it she writes: 'I find rest within myself. And this "Self", this deepest and richest part of me, I call God.'

This random collection of examples will give some idea of how the Great Balancing Act works out in real life. I guess we'll have no difficulty at all in furnishing plenty of further instances from our own experience. The real difficulty is that we are always relaxing into one-sided optimism – if not euphoria – and renewing our pretence that we can have any bright and good thing without its shadow: the brighter the one the darker the other. Followed by the show-down, inevitable disillusion. Living like this is bad for us. Admit that life is a roller-coaster, and its ups and downs won't make us sick. Deny it, and they will. To avoid toxic stress it's essential to tell the truth, the truth that 'man is *born* to trouble, as the sparks fly upwards,' and there's nothing he can do about it. Nothing, that is, except to cease overlooking the *Unborn*.

The performer on the high wire needs the full weight of that trouble, of that negative stuff in his left hand, to counterbalance the positive stuff in his right hand. And an anxious and exhausting act it is – till he catches sight of the Safety Net spread out below.

Please look down again at the Place where the performer's arms meet – or rather, fail to meet but instead fade away into No-

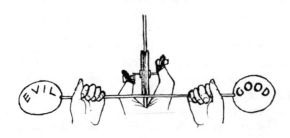

shoulders, into No-thing at all. Look again at your Bottom Line, the World's End, the Brink over which all your superfluous and toxic stress is tipped. Well, to our list of names for this most remarkable yet least remarked of Places the name of Safety Net is now added. For it alone is beyond all opposites, indivisible, untearable, stable, impenetrable, the shock absorber of all shock. Suspended aloft, high above that Golden Net or Trampoline or eternally resilient Floor of Heaven (which is also the Floor of Hell), all life is hellish difficult. The way to cope with the wear and tear of circus life is never to lose the feel and the sight of the Magic Carpet that cushions it.

That wonderful floor-covering reminds me of a little story, from I know not where. Once upon a time Heaven was at the very top of the world, so lofty that few saints (let alone sinners like you and me) were getting there. The angels, conferring, decided to lower Heaven somewhat. Still very few got to it. They lowered it further, with not much better results. In the end they gave up and dropped it to the very floor and basement of the world, and then at last it filled up.

As you can now see, so very clearly, for yourself. To get to Heaven, let life *floor* you. Life is guaranteed to do just that, to let you down – all the way into the Safety Net that will never let you down. Life is guaranteed to disappoint. But expect *nothing* of the Nothing that underscores life, and it cannot disappoint. Also expect *everything* of it, and again it cannot disappoint. It's being so mock-modest in our demands on life, expecting *something* of it – this or that particular rose, and with no thorns attached, at that – which is the stress-maker, and prevents our enjoyment of the rose-garden.

For no reason you know of, you have occurred. Rashly, you have opted for life – a terribly stressful venture to find yourself caught up in. What's more, appearances notwithstanding, a venture that's stressful in every way. It's not that, as a mature adult, you are *fated* to take on every part and manifestation and variety of stress, but that to be mature *is* to take on the lot. And that to be really mature is consciously to take on all of it from its Origin, from the Ground up – the Ground it all wells up out of and disappears back into. In particular, it's *not* that you and I – oh dear! – have laid on us one or two (or, at worst, three) of the grievous burdens we have been weighing up in this chapter; and that – what a mercy! – we are free of the rest. *Not*, for instance, that, sufficiently loaded with boredom and loneliness, we are spared guilt and a sense of failure. No. Admit it or not, we are in this difficult business up to our necks (I mean down to our necks, of course), and it's an all-or-nothing business – an all-*and*-nothing business whose liability is unlimited. Our ideas about life are half-baked and one-sided: life itself is well done and whole. However much we try, there's no rolling the tasty bits on our tongues and spitting out the rest. No picking and choosing among its essential ingredients – more bitter than wormwood though so many of those ingredients turn out to be.

Most of us, living private lives well out of the public eye, are able to hide from other people, and to a less degree from ourselves, our all-round stressfulness. A few are more exposed, in the limelight with or without wishing to be. For one reason or another, the whole sorry business comes out. The balance sheet is published. Let's take a case in point – and a most instructive case it is for our purpose here – the famous and well-documented story of someone who, beyond doubt, was let off no item in our list of troubles: a man who insisted that he suffered from them all, and in something like equal measure. A genius who – as we shall presently see – got right down to and drew freely upon, yet contrived to stay so far from, the Basis where they are perfectly resolved. I'm referring to Pyotr Ilyich Tchaikovsky, commonly regarded as the greatest of Russian composers.

Throughout his life, manic and depressive phases alternated. The former were short-lived, the latter all too apt to drag on and on. For example, his friend Nicolai Rubinstein criticized his First Piano Concerto harshly. Result: for the next nine months Tchaikovsky fell into an acute depression which he describes as a despair so dreadful that he often wished himself dead. His only compositions during this period – his *Sérénade Melancholique* and a few sad songs – reflect the darkness of his mood. No youthful lack of confidence this. He was thirty-five, and already on the way to fame.

In later years, when his international success could scarcely have been more spectacular, he still suffered periods of depression about his career and doubts as to his creative ability. Frequent triumphs did little or nothing to offset the occasional flop. Not 'Win some, lose some', but 'Lose one, lose all' was the motto he instinctively adopted. What he lost on the critical swings he didn't begin to make up on the highly popular roundabouts. Not in his reckoning.

No surprise that, along with these fits of crippling self-doubt, came indecision. He pinned his hopes on, then proceeded to loathe and destroy, the scores of a number of his compositions – only to regret his action and try to reconstruct them. Of one major work, to which he had devoted characteristic enthusiasm and care, he wrote: 'You cannot imagine anyone who suffers more than I do ... The opera *Oprichnik* is so bad I always run away from rehearsals to avoid having to listen to another note. It has neither action, nor style, nor inspiration.'

Naturally enough, such orgies of self-castigation didn't make for easy personal relationships. Sociability of a sort, boosted by heavy drinking, alternated with misanthropy and loneliness. Though kind and generous to individuals, he claimed to 'hate mankind in the mass', and frequently sought relief in rural solitude, and in foreign parts where he would pass unrecognized. Yet he complained that, throughout a visit to Rome, Naples, Florence and

Venice, not a single friendly word had passed between himself and the people he came across. He longed for the homely companionship of family life. And when at last he did resolve to marry (an act of sheer madness on the part of a confirmed homosexual) the outcome was so abominable that it led to a suicide attempt that almost came off. Guilt, mainly about his sexual preferences and activities (he wrote, in veiled terms, of 'sensation Z'), but also about his wild extravagances while so many around him lacked life's necessities, dogged him to the end.

You might suppose that (at least by way of compensation) this raging sea of troubles would never leave him becalmed in the doldrums, a martyr to boredom. Not so. He often found life excruciatingly dull. Following the composition of *Swan Lake*, he was troubled 'with a lack of ideas in his head', but his chief complaint was not sterility but tedium. Along with laziness (actually, few composers worked harder) he put world-weariness and ennui among his worst bugbears. At twenty-nine, he mourned that he was 'gloomy, bored, poor, bad at teaching, neglected, and fat'. (Photos show him as shapely!) At thirty-one he wrote: 'I am old, can enjoy nothing anymore. I live among memories and hopes. But what have I to hope for?'

In sum, it would be hard to find any substantial manifestation of stress that this brilliant composer didn't suffer from severely – on his own frank admission in his voluminous correspondence, and in conversation. The saving grace and wonder – the puzzle if not the paradox of it all – is that such a tormented soul should come up with some of the sublimest music – tender, lyrical, joyously soaring – that has ever fallen on the ears of a delighted world.

The question may be nonsensical, nevertheless it insists on being asked: would he have created music anything like this if his life had been steadier, less fraught, less dark and cruel in so many ways? If he had *accepted* that life is hellish difficult, anyhow? If, for example, he had in temperament been more like Brahms, his comparatively staid and well-balanced but brilliant German contemporary? And not so hell-bent on self-destruction? (It's an open question whether he did, or didn't, deliberately kill himself in the end.) Was all that storm and stress the price, the enormous balancing cost, of those serene cadences? Would a Tchaikovsky who had consciously descended to his own Brink, and seen his terrible load of stress tipped over it, have been the great composer he's recognized to be? Or, on the contrary, just a good, run-of-the-mill musician known only to his own generation?

Of this I am sure: when all's said and done that has to be said and done, one must take people as one finds them, must authorize and even love them to be the way they have to be, and stop pretending to know what's right and what's wrong for them at this time, what's necessary for the work they have to do and the grim places they are required to explore. In the end, all that one can safely and helpfully do is to mind one's own business. Nevertheless the unanswerable questions we've been putting about Tchaikovsky are well worth asking because they lead in to another question that really is one's own business, and calls for a definite answer. It is this: am I faced with the choice between a very high degree of stress and creativity on the one hand, and a lesser degree of both on the other hand? To speak brutally, what the blazes is the use of all our efforts to dump our toxic stress, if along with it goes, base over apex, our originality and flair, our precious gift of inspiration, our unique and unrepeatable contribution to our culture and species and world, no matter what the cost?

Well, I hope that the discoveries we've made together leave you as certain about the answer as they leave me. For my part, I do not believe that, in any sense or degree, our good health can be bad for us and for our impact upon others, bad for our service to mankind. I do not believe that music would be poorer if Tchaikovsky had been saner, that his gain would be our loss. I do not believe that the universe is a hell in which misery and evil have the last word: a scene in which suffering is unmitigated and futile, and doesn't carry the seeds of its transformation into special and unforeseen joys. My heart, my mind, the whole lesson of my baptism in this perilous ocean called Life, convince me that it's not like that at all. On the contrary, everything tells me, not (repeat *not*) that any of us are going to be let off the bitterness that's coming our way, but that the sudden and magical-chemical change into its opposite is never far to seek. The formula doesn't lurk just round the corner. It hits one in the face, in one's Original Face, the face one doesn't have here. This forefinger stands at the ready to point me Home. The corny old song is right: there really is no place like it, no other place whose sweetness is never soured.

No: we're not in the business of dodging or doping pain, but of locating it where it belongs. This book is about discovering, and moving into, the one Sanctuary it can never invade. It's about heading off stress, as you head off your horse from the flower garden to the stable yard.

Whenever the Muse took over, Pyotr Ilyich Tchaikovsky enjoyed unobstructed access to that happy garden, with its central Fountain from which inspiration gushes without stint. Then, yes at least then, he ceased to block that Fountain. In beautiful music he laughed and sang his head off. He pulled his cork with a resounding report, and the champagne flowed free and plentiful and sparkling.

But for most of the time, alas, his natural wide-openness was bunged up with a monstrous nine-inch stopper which – hallucination though it was – remained sufficiently in place to narrow the flow to a mere trickle, a miserable oozing. One way or another, he managed to keep his head on – not, it's true, firmly and continuously in place like most of us, but secure enough to give him every sort of hell.

Take, for example, his first appearance in public as a conductor, described by a friend who was present.

> I saw that he was distraught. He came on timidly, as if he would like to hide or run away, and on mounting the rostrum he looked like a man in anguish. He seemed to have completely forgotten his composition. He did not see the score before him, and gave all the leads wrong, or to the wrong instrument. Fortunately the players knew the music so well that they paid no attention to him . . . Afterwards Pyotr Ilyich told me that in his panic he had had the illusion that his head would fall off his shoulders unless he held it firmly in place. To prevent this (another friend reports) he kept a tight grip on his beard throughout.

In fact, of course, letting the wretched thing go would have saved both the performance and the man.

Why was the thought of existence without a head even more daunting, for Tchaikovsky, than the reality of existence with one? Why do all of us, at some time if not all the time, hang on to the monstrosity for grim life? And go so far as to fondle the instrument of our torture?

The question answers itself. Grim life is better than no life at all – we suppose. The screams of life's garishly lit torture chamber are less terrible than the eternal silence of death's uninhabited dark – we suppose. The frying pan that frizzles us to a crisp is preferable to the fire that finishes us off altogether – we suppose. Whether it's in Heaven or in Hell or on Earth, existence with no head present must be non-existence – we suppose. However painful to have the thing screwed on as loosely as Tchaikovsky's was, to have it come off has to be still more painful – he supposed, and we suppose. Suppose, suppose, suppose . . .

Instead of vast expanses of supposition, what about a spot of looking to see? Of checking whether our fear is groundless or not? Go on now: officiate as your own headsman – and survive. In one blow, unchain yourself from that heavier-than-iron ball of in-spissated woe – and escape, rejoicing and free, as the light and the lightness of the whole world. Look and see *now* what it's like to die – and come out on the other side not just unscathed, but cleansed and refreshed, expanded to infinity and eternalized. If you should find yourself not going gentle – but kicking out with rage and moaning with self-pity – into that dark night, it's because you are refusing to look at it, and discover that the dark is excess of light. The blinding dazzle of a million suns.

But just how consistent are you? Isn't it true that, in spite of all the deeply felt fear of the obvious, of the facts as given to you, there's something even deeper in you that gives them a hearty welcome. Some level at which you know that in your submission to what's so – your humble bowing to what it is to be First Person singular, present tense – lies your salvation? Thank the Lord, in that case, for inconsistency! But what monumental inconsistency – what duplicity, rather – it is! What double-think and double-feel – and on the most vital of subjects, at that. On the Subject himself, herself!

Do you remember, earlier on, the Egyptian goddess of the Old Kingdom who positively flaunted her First Personhood, and pointed so effectively at ours? Well, it's no wonder (in view of all this built-in duplicity we all share) that she should com-bine the nice and the nasty, the most godlike and the most beastly, the most reassuring and the most scary. She became known, in the New Kingdom, as the Scorpion Goddess. You can see why.

Yes. Life is difficult, all right. Goddess and scorpion coexist, uneasily, forever. Those bliss-bestowing hands won't cease doub-ling up on those claws, grasping and crushing and rending.

But don't lose sight of where both are coming from. At the base of each picture *and of your picture now* is the Bottom Line where all three of you are One and the Same, and beyond all niceness and nastiness.

238

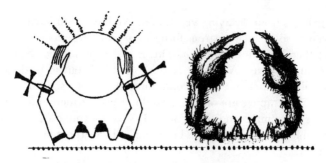

The goddess Selkhet
c. 1500 BC

A scorpion's view of himself
is rather like this

Seeing This and being This *isn't* difficult.
In fact, everlasting life – the Life behind life – is dead easy!

(x) CONCLUSION – THREE WAYS OF COPING

Again and again in the course of this enquiry we have come to
conclusions about you personally – first-personally – that are, by
any ordinary standards, wildly flattering. Take a vote on it, and
who wouldn't agree that to describe you as the Ground of Being,
or as the Source of All, or *a fortiori* the Alone, is, to put it
charitably, intoxication? In that case, this is the morning after. We
are going to start the concluding section of this chapter with what
almost everybody would call a sane and sober estimate of you –
credible, unembarrassing and 'realistic': in total contrast to that
other estimate which is none of these. The acceptable character
sketch I have in mind looks something like this:

> You are nothing special, just one of countless millions and no
> more godlike than the rest of them. You are only human after all,
> which means you are faulty, not all right. In fact, something's
> gone wrong with you, terribly wrong. For a start, you are reading
> this book about stress, which amounts to admitting that stress is
> coming up from somewhere in you and giving you a hard time.
> And this is only one of the many troubles emerging from there, like

marsh gas from decaying vegetation. We have been looking at seven or so of the monstrous forms that your stress takes, but in fact there's no limit to them. This is bad news indeed. Not to despair, however. A lot can be done, and cries out to be done, speedily, to ameliorate your condition. All sorts of rescue bids, all sorts of therapies, are on offer. So don't just sit there moaning about the human condition. For God's sake, for your own sake, *do* something! A truce to all this brooding and navel contemplation. Act!

True or false, that's the sort of thing that society has been drumming into us all our lives, in a hundred subtle and not so subtle ways. And how early we heard and took to heart that lesson! How cheerfully convinced we are now, how eager to believe it all, even relieved. How happy to have disembarrassed ourselves of our infantile cocksureness that right here reigns the King of the World, that right here is its Hub, the unique One who is absolutely out of the ordinary and absolutely important. How happy to have joined the human race, vile as it is. We positively lap up the bad news. A lot of us are eager to prostrate ourselves before any guru or anti-guru who explains convincingly what a mess we are in, and will follow him all over the world for years and years just to hear more and more about the mess, and how small are the chances of our ever pulling out of it.

I have no wish to be a spoil-sport, and dampen the pleasures of those who enjoy bad news – the worse the better – about their state. This book isn't addressed to them, but to those whose enjoyment is wearing thin, who could do with less gloom and doom. To men and women who are concerned neither to revel in nor discount the dreadful news that's been coming at them from all sides and for so long, but instead to be really honest and intelligent and practical about it.

To you I say, let's treat this very personal tale of woe as sensibly and as unhysterically as we treat less personal tales of woe – in our business life, for instance.

Supposing you are chairman of a corporation, and there comes a time when everyone's saying that disaster looms, that the firm is heading for bankruptcy and its boss for disgrace and ruin. How do you react?

There are three things you can do, and they contrast sharply:

(i) You can refuse to react, take off on a world cruise and forget the whole darn thing. You can leave it to correct itself – as you reckon it probably will.

Almost certainly it won't. The likelihood is that you will come back to find yourself in deep trouble and with few friends left. Serve you right.

(ii) You can panic. You can hand out orders right and left. You can sack the works manager and the sales manager, close down a subsidiary plant or two and lay off the work force, scrap several old production models and initiate new ones. Deeds are what you demand. 'Don't just sit there hoping!' you cry. 'Get cracking! Any change is better than no change!'

Almost certainly the result is that things get worse. Impulsive remedies, blindly administered to a patient the doctor can't find time to examine, may well kill him. The chances that they will cure him are one in a thousand.

(iii) Instead of this frantic overreaction, you will, if you are a normally competent business man or woman, *do nothing: nothing remedial at all, till you have learned the facts.* So you call an extraordinary board meeting, at which the sales manager displays his graphs showing present trends and future market prospects, and the works manager reports on the likelihood of rising productivity and falling costs of raw materials, and the accountant forecasts profit and loss for the current financial year, the need for an increase or decrease in the overdraft, and so forth.

Then, and only then, do you make up your mind what to do. This body of information, duly absorbed and digested, is the essential prerequisite of wise decisions. It may indicate what drastic measures, short-term and long-term, are needed to put the business into shape. It may indicate that no precipitate action at all should be taken till the actual shape of things has got a lot clearer. Or it may indicate that all those initial impulses to panic were quite unjustified, that all those rumours of impending doom were ill-founded if not malicious, and that, on careful examination, the firm turns out to be very prosperous indeed. That, in fact, the news couldn't be better.

That is the way, if we have any practical good sense at all, we handle our business affairs.

Would that we handled our private affairs – in particular, that most private of them all, ourselves – half as intelligently, on the same businesslike principle of *facts first, action second*! How very, very few of us are anything like so sensible when we turn from the conduct of life's periphery to the very heart of it! When dealing with mere things, with property, with markets and money and merchandise, we are fairly sane: but when dealing with the Dealer, with their Proprietor, we go quietly mad. On no evidence at all, on the basis of mere hearsay and wishful or fearful thinking, we decide that our lives have gone wrong, that we are profoundly defective, unfortunate, even cursed. So we thrash around, panic-stricken, seeking cures for a condition we have never looked into, and which could be the very opposite of what we are so sure it is.

But now you and I are coming to our senses. We are in the process of becoming businesslike about this great enterprise of discovering our true Nature and living in accordance with it, of being ourselves and not someone else. Discounting rumours and refusing to panic, we are in the market for hard facts. How, in that case, to proceed?

In our modern world the most businesslike activity that's going on isn't business at all. It is science. I don't mean applied science (look at the absurd and self-destructive things *it* gets up to), but that pure science or basic research which comes from humility in the face of the evidence, from a truly reverent bowing before the given, with no eye on how to exploit and abuse it. In order to make the astounding advances it has made over the centuries, it has had to keep on cleansing itself of every sort of wishful-fearful thinking and self-interested tinkering with the facts. No easy assignment, this never-won campaign against prejudice and vested interests. Now if anything will destroy our delusions of grandeur, or conversely our delusions of wretchedness and personal insignificance, it is this eminently businesslike, patient, self-abnegating, impartial discipline called pure science. If it should happen to endorse our total grandeur and all-inclusiveness, or conversely our total pettiness and all-exclusiveness, or (conceivably) both at once, why then we had better sit up and take notice. If we know what's good for us we shall take its findings seriously and learn to live with them, regardless of our initial feelings of fear, disbelief, false or real modesty, wild elation, or whatever.

What, then, has science to say about you? The first answer that springs to mind is: much too much for us to take in and handle here, or anywhere else. What we can readily make out, however, is your overall pattern. We are able to draw a thumbnail sketch of you as a many-levelled system of natural phenomena – *phenomena* meaning your innumerable appearances arranged around the one noumenon or reality which they are appearances of. Science stands ready and well-equipped, if only we dare ask, to expose as nonsense the conclusions of this chapter and this book, or else to confirm them as quite sensible. And it's qualified to do us this great service because it builds on, and keeps coming back to, the clearly given, to what's seen and not imagined. The foundation of this highest of high-rise structures has to be lowly sense-experience, without which it would never get off the ground, let alone stay aloft.

Before going on to make our thumbnail sketch of you, let us note two principles that go to its making. The first is that what you are observed to be, and indeed what you are, depends on where you are seen from, on the *distance* of the observer who is approaching or receding from you. The second is that none of his views of you is the 'right' one, revealing the 'true you'. All are right, and none can be spared from the long tale of what you are. Moreover they hang together, each making a living by taking in the others' washing. They are interdependent, and all are inextricably involved in what you call your own life and existence. To single out one view of you, as revealed within one range band (such as A–B, say, between two hundred metres and two metres), and award the accolade of 'reality' to this view, let alone special reality, is nonsense. As an appearance or phenomenon it has no right to such a status. And anyway it is an empty abstraction without all the other regional appearances of that one central

Reality c they all cluster round – of that unique Point to which your incoming observer directs his attention throughout his journey, and which is none other than the Spot you have so often pointed at in the course of our inquiry.

Now for the inward journey, the homing, the coming-to-the-Point:

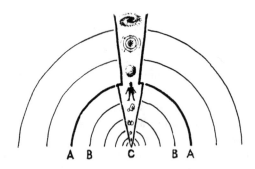

Your well-instrumented observer, viewing this Point c from a great distance, finds vast space, dotted with pinpoints of light. They are centrifugal, moving outwards and beyond the field of vision, in slow explosion. The one he's concentrating on grows into a group of light-points, still exploding, one of which grows into a spiral galaxy (the Milky Way, our own island universe). This, in turn, gradually gives place to just one of its myriads of stars (namely our Sun, our own Solar System), then one of its planets (Earth), then a country, a city, a home, a human being, a face which lies around one metre from the Centre. Equipped with a new set of optical and electronic instruments, your incoming observer goes on to find a lot happening in that last metre of his journey. The face resolves itself into a patch of skin, then a group of skin cells, then one of those cells, followed by molecules and atoms and particles, in that order. Followed by – *what*?

Does he come all the way to the Point of the whole journey? To the Real You, the one who lies at the heart of the whole cosmic show? To you as you are in Yourself?

Before attempting an answer, let's notice what's been happening to you in the course of this armour-piercing shot at you, this unveiling. Your onion has been peeled to the core – almost. You have been stripped of your assets to the last farthing – almost. Gone by degrees are all your distinguishing features – your celestial brightness and self-luminosity, your unluminous and earthy humanness, your separate identity as Mary Smith or John Robinson (as cellular you aren't any sort of human), your life (as molecular you are no longer alive and are drained of colour), your solidity and materiality and distinct location (as atoms and particles you lose even these): until, very near Home, there's practically nothing of the apparent you left at all. All the same, your incoming observer as such can never quite complete his journey, never unveil the central Reality which is giving rise to that worldwide system of appearances. He can never grasp the Sparkling Stone which, cast into the pool of the cosmos, started off all those ripples. No: he's still an outsider, still at some distance from you (and a miss here is as good as a light-year), from You who are the only one who's in a position to complete his story by telling him what You really are, what You are for You, right at the Centre, at *no* distance from You.

Much better than telling him (he's not the best of listeners), you can show him. You can invite him to look, by turning round 180° and putting your two no-heads together, *to look out with you and no longer in at you*. Then, and only then, will he arrive at the perfect completion and confirmation of his long-drawn-out investigation into what you are. At almost no distance he finds you reduced to almost nothing. At no distance at all he finds exactly what you find, finds you reduced to absolutely Nothing – to that Aware Nothing which sees itself to be Nothing-Everything.

Such, in a thumbnail sketch, are the findings of contemporary science when, pressed to take time off from its departmentalized and circumferential duties, it becomes thoroughly interdepartmental and radial and to the Point. Having set up around the object or third person this elaborate system of concentric circles, the approaching observer cannot avoid knitting them together and to their common Centre, which is the Subject or First Person

Singular. Given enough honesty and thoroughness, his deep bow before the objective evidence has to culminate in his deepest bow before the Subject which is none other than himself.

What have we here but another version of our Himalayan–Dantesque experience, demythologized and filled out and updated? Could we wish for a more telling confirmation of your cosmic magnificence as described so far in this book? Or a more telling refutation of the commonsense view of you, outlined at the beginning of this section, as 'only human after all' and far from magnificent? There's no escaping the fact that, to be a man or a woman, a child or an adult, you have to be infinitely less than that and infinitely more than that. No way can you shrug off your mystery and your grandeur. No way can you get out of being, at the end of the day that has no beginning or end, the Best and the Greatest, the One and Only.

To deny what you are is to suffer stress.

The picture of you which we have been piecing together throughout this book, along with the stress-coping techniques arising from it, has been based on the testimony of two main witnesses whose backgrounds are so different as to rule out collusion. Firstly, appealing to what's *obvious*, we have taken the evidence of the childlike seer who tells us about himself and the given world. Secondly, appealing to what's *tested*, we have taken the evidence of the businesslike scientist who tells us about what he calls the natural world. And we have seen how well they fit. But that's not all. There remains a third witness whom we have occasionally called, and now must examine more closely. Appealing to what's *intuited*, let's briefly take the evidence of the anthropologist – the student of comparative religion and mythology – who tells us about the supernatural world, as experienced by humanity from the dawn of history, and in all manner of cultures and places, right up till today. Now if all three witnesses should agree on essentials, you and I should indeed sit up and take notice.

What I find when I come home to myself, to my true nature and centre, and what the natural scientist finds when he comes here, is that I'm not what I look like over there. I don't stand up to close inspection. I'm demolished stage by stage, till on arrival I'm abolished altogether. And at once reconstituted worldwide. Implosion issues in explosion. Now what has our third witness – the supernaturalist – to say about this? Let's take evidence from what could be a hostile witness – from a source that looks likely to contradict our findings – in fact, from that weird phenomenon called *shamanism*. How much further from the obvious, from the plainly given and patiently researched, from all that cool detachment and deep bowing before the evidence, could one get than this – the wild visions in dream and trance of the Siberian shaman suffering from a highly nervous temperament, if not actually sick in mind and body?

Shamanism is still alive and well in 'primitive' societies all over the world. A key member of his tribe, a shaman is nevertheless the odd man out in a number of ways. At the start of his career, evidently suffering from severe stress, he goes off on his own and behaves unaccountably, sometimes rushing about in a frenzy and sometimes preoccupied and inert. His initiation into the role of shaman – his essential preliminary experience – is one of painful and progressive dismemberment. He dreams that his head is opened up and cut off, and so are his limbs. His living organs are replaced by inanimate ones, by stones. For the reducing process to be completed, he may have to endure being boiled down in a cauldron. Thus dying to his old self, he may find his new self to be a light in place of his head and body, at the very centre of the cosmos. Then, no longer earthbound, he flies to the many-levelled upper and lower worlds. Here he learns from their spirit inhabitants the secrets his tribe has need of, and gains healing powers. The result of these adventures, when often repeated, is that he is himself healed, his organs are replaced by better ones, and his energy and intelligence are remarkable. His relationship with Nature, with animals in particular, is far more intimate. Amazingly so, in some instances. Above all, he now exercises the supernatural gift of healing the sick.

Of course the details of this story differ hugely from tribe to tribe and from region to region, and of course they are fantastic. What's so impressive, what's so important for us here, is the consistency of the story in its essentials, transcending all cultural distinctions. Translated into our language here, it declares that stress (no matter what sickness it manifests as) cannot be cured at its own level – at what *appears* to be its own level – nor by direct ascent to higher levels: but only by descent to the lowest, to the Bottom Line from which all true healing arises. Stress runs deep, and calls for deep therapy. Shallow palliatives and quack remedies, treating a patient who is taken to be 'only human, after all', don't begin to get down to the problem. The real remedy couldn't be more drastic. No wonder if the pill is a bitter one: it destroys him and rebuilds him to another design. And no wonder if it's hard to swallow, if it takes a lot of getting down. It's the cosmos! The flaming, icy, many-levelled, improbable cosmos – no less. *To be whole, be the Whole.* Obliquely and picturesquely, the shaman – more businesslike than his extraordinary get-up and antics would suggest – is telling us just this.

When you lose your head you find your power-base in your guts. Such seems to be the message of this shaman rock-painting from Menomini territory, Michigan.

Back, then, to those three ways of handling bad news concerning oneself that we talked about earlier in this section.

The first, which is turning a blind eye to it, is unbusinesslike. It does nothing to relieve one's agony, but at least it doesn't pile on the agony. Most humans make do like this, neither greatly adding to nor greatly subtracting from their stress.

The second way, the way of desperation and panic stations, is to try treatment after treatment on a patient who has still to be examined. It is very unbusinesslike indeed. At best it treats the patient's symptoms instead of his disease, with no lasting benefits. At worst it kills him. Those who hope to reduce stress this way, and they are many, should not be surprised if it only increases.

The third way says *facts first, action second*. Do nothing about your stress till you find the time and the courage to take a new and honest look at the one who is alleged to be stressed. Then it may well emerge (as we've seen, it *does* emerge, again and again) that the reason for our stress wasn't just that we had got our facts wrong, but upside down. So far from merely neglecting, out of laziness or fear, to examine the patient's condition, so far from just casually overlooking it, we *inverted* the evidence. As we've seen so often in the course of our enquiry, the conventional or commonsense view of oneself isn't so much nonsensical as downright perverse. And lies are what stress thrives on. Conversely, facts are the stress-killers. It's the truth that sets us free.

Ethy, the Jewish girl who died in Auschwitz, practised this third way of coping with the worst news you can think of and the stress of it. I make no apology for repeating her words at the conclusion of this chapter on Stress in Adult Life:

Most people see in life what it's permissible to see, but we must free ourselves from all existing ideas . . . and then life becomes rich and abundant even in moments of deep suffering.

In the evening, when the day recedes, I walk with bright footsteps by the wire fence, and from my heart arises always the feeling that life is wonderful and grand . . .

I find rest within myself. And this 'self', this deepest and richest part of me, I call God.

HEAD OFF STRESS

God is the cure
of my stress, so

I seek Him everywhere

and if I don't find Him

it's because I'm not

bowing low enough

15

OLD AGE

We are not going to attempt to deal with the problems of old age at length here, the reason being that we have already done so for the most part in the previous chapter. In particular, we have looked at depression and loneliness and boredom. Though we think of the old as specially prone to these afflictions, younger people are certainly not free of them, any more than they are free of indecision and a sense of failure and guilt and sexual problems. All seven plague our lives from childhood onwards.

However there are two stressful conditions which are liable to come to a head with age. One is the fear of dying – the time and the manner and the pains of it, and the fear of what may lie beyond death. We shall examine this fear in the next chapter. The other, which is aimlessness, is our concern here. It is the folding of the goals we once strove towards – having and raising a family, getting a job and getting on in that job, acquiring a reputation for being the sort of person we like to picture ourself as, saving up for retirement, and so forth – and the unfolding of no new goals to replace them. What remains, as we advance into our seventies and eighties and beyond, to structure our time, to awaken our interest, to rouse us to action? When there's nothing left to live for or to die for, what reason have we for carrying on, other than mere habit or inertia? Is the fear of letting go and drowning in what's even more pointless than old age – in the unfathomable pointlessness of death itself – is this our only reason for hanging on to whatever bits of our life's wreckage remain floating?

The normal and commonsensible answer to the aimlessness and futility of old age is (at least in the caring and considered opinion of middle age) that we should grasp the godsent opportunity to acquire new skills and develop old ones, pursue further some existing hobby, try a change of scene and generally pull ourselves together. No matter how sensible and well-intentioned, such guidance has one grave defect. It is asking the old not to be old. It is proposing that they go back to the sort of goals, very real in their day, which they once lived to achieve, or else to go forward to quite unreal ones, contrived and artificial aims that do not excite. Neither sort will do. The fact must be faced that old men and women are *old* men and women, very different creatures from what they used to be, and it's as futile to try to rejuvenate them by pumping them full of synthetic enthusiasms as to pump them full of the monkey glands that were much talked of when I was young.

What on earth is the point (we old folk ask, though rarely out loud) of learning a language that we shall never have occasion to use, of planting trees we shall never see overhead, of weaving baskets or embroidering hassocks or carving little wooden animals that will do nobody a scrap of good, of traipsing wearily through still more miles of picture galleries, of enduring more outlandish challenges to our gastric juices, of trying to sleep in more dubious beds and live out of a suitcase yet again instead of a home? What's the use of buying a new car we soon won't be capable of driving safely, or commissioning a new home that won't be finished in time for us to die in? What's the point? No point. All is vanity and vexation of spirit. No, there's no way back to the drive and the derring-do of youth and middle age. They lie behind us, gone for ever. If we the old are really to live authentic and not phony lives, we must do so our way. Why? Why because, though our troubles – depression, loneliness and so on – are much the same as those of younger people, the one who is troubled is not at all the same. Our crying need is for a goal and an endeavour, a way of life, that is helped along and not hindered by old age. Not something we achieve in spite of our so-called infirmities but rather because of them.

A tall order, this! Could there be such a way? Is there a life which is appropriate to old age, capable of lending it dignity, meaning, inspiration, and – yes – drive? I'm not thinking of an endeavour which is exclusively for the old, but of one which, though proper to all the ages of man, stays alive and kicking to the very end. Or, better still, a goal which the old are specially fitted to pursue wholeheartedly, and maybe better able to arrive at now than ever they were. So that, just as childhood is the time for humanizing the self, and adulthood is the time for expressing and developing that human self, so old age is the time for . . . Well, for what?

For realizing the self. For realizing the Self that transcends humanness. It is, *par excellence*, the time for finding out the meaning of life and the Nature of the one who is living it. In this the old have distinct advantages over younger people. Here are four of them:

(i) 'Ripeness is all,' says Edgar in *King Lear*. Truly to be old is to be informed about life and informed with life, full to the brim with it. To the degree that one is conscious, to be old is to have seen through what doesn't matter to what does matter. It is to know what it is to fail as well as succeed, to lose as well as gain, to sink to the very bottom as well as rise to the heights: and to know What doesn't thus go up and down like a yoyo. It is to have the feel of human nature, and What underpins it. It is to be able to tell glitter from gold. If we don't quite arrive at this degree of practical wisdom (and not too many of us do so, let's face it), that's not because of our age. On the contrary, it's because of our refusal to be our age, because we are hanging on to our past. To be wise with the wisdom of age is to be up-to-date in your life-story, contemporary with yourself, so that at last you know What's what. It's not only to have drunk deeply of life, but also to have found What lasts the whole drink through. Our experiments have all been about that *What*, What you really are. What and Who you really, really are. And now you are truly ripe and ready not just to see it but to live it.

(ii) To devote yourself wholeheartedly, with a minimum of distractions and anxieties, to this the crowning adventure of your life, you need time. You have it. Unless you are extremely unfortunate, or else are deliberately clogging your day with trivialities aimed at dulling awareness, you have all the leisure you can do with for this work. Get busy then. And it's *not* just that you are sensibly structuring the interval between retirement from your job and retirement from your life, and are able to do so because you have come across a worthwhile and perhaps fascinating interest. Rather it is that, having resigned from your preliminary and temporary job as butcher or baker or candlestick maker, or whatever, you are now getting down to your real job – which is to settle the question of Who that functionary is, and whether he's anything like so perishable as butchers and bakers and so on manifestly are. So far from having retired, then, you have taken on the most exacting and important job you ever had, that ever was. This is no soft option, but as hard as nails in more senses than one. To succeed in it brilliantly you have all the needful experience, and all the hours of the day and all the days of the week. You have a lifetime under your belt, the time to digest it, and the energy which that truly marvellous feast can yield. Energy to complete your life by finding Yourself waiting for you there at the end of it – welcoming, smiling, magnificently apparelled.

(iii) For this enterprise you need above all the gift of *detachment*. Old age hands it out to you freely. Disillusion, disappointment, failure to reach some of your goals, plus failure to find in those you did reach the enduring satisfaction you had expected – all this, read now with the advantage of hindsight, makes up a precious and indispensable gift. Earlier in your career what stood in the way of your Self-realization was your need to grasp this thing, and achieve that thing, and hang on to the other: your passion and your need was to *act*. But now at last, increasingly detached not only from necessary action but also from action which so often was for action's sake, you are free to find the Actor, to *be* Him or Her or It. The obstacles require no dislodging, obligingly they dislodge themselves and drop away.

(iv) You are girding your loins to embark on the adventure of your life, on the extravaganza which makes the boldest escapade of your youth look over-cautious. You are bracing yourself for the great leap, not into the Dark, but into the Light that you are coming to know so well. You are about to put a stop to this persistent dreaming that you are a frog, and to wake forever to the truth that you are a beautiful Prince. In fact, a King. In fact, the King over all.

And they say you've had it, that you are a goner! Let them!

To sum up our advantages, then, we have here four inestimable gifts of old age – ripe experience, wide fields of leisure, unharnessing from the loads we were chained to like oxen or draught horses, and the imminence of the Great Exploration.

I seem to hear you objecting that while all this sounds fine, it is quite unrealistic. How many old folk, and in particular the vast majority who have never in their lives dreamed of investigating their true identity – how many are likely at this stage to change their deeply ingrained habits of mind and work up any interest in the subject at all?

To which I reply: Firstly, don't worry about them just now. Mind your own business. This book is about you and me. The fact that we have come together all this way, right into the deep end of the pool, is evidence enough that this adventure is for you. If it were not, you would still be splashing about in the shallow end. Or, more likely, be out of the water altogether, and dried and dressed like any other man or woman in the street.

Secondly, though the difficulty of switching to an altogether new interest like this in old age is very real indeed, let us note that it is more cultural than built-in. There have been times and places in the human story where it has been generally accepted that the proper task of old age is to acquire the wisdom that culminates in Self-Realization: that, though the earlier one starts on this task the better, it is never too late to begin: and that to miss the opportunity which old age offers to achieve this end is to miss the bus of life, and nothing short of tragedy. The most striking example of this attitude is the ancient Hindu paradigm of life's stages. At its briefest, this is the pattern: first, the child and the youth, whose business is to learn to function socially; next the grown-up, whose business is to contribute to society by working and raising a family; and thirdly the older person whose business is to find out Who has been doing these things, What his or her true Identity is and how it merges in the universal Identity. In India this ideal life-pattern is not yet extinct. Our own contemporary and Western culture, it's all-too-true, has virtually no time for such a design for living and dying, and virtually no knowledge that it exists and is a real option. It is committed to the ridiculous, not to say insulting, proposition that old age is only tolerable insofar as it is not itself, but apes middle age and youth. But the times are changing fast. Our culture is in the melting pot. It's up to you and me to help to stoke the fire beneath the pot and mould what comes out of it.

Let's go back to you personally, and let's assume you are an old person who has been suffering from the stress of aimlessness, of the goalless life. What are you to do? Well, for a start, you can re-christen that aimlessness *sheer grace*, clearing the way for the great Goal of your life, namely Self-realization. As for the alleged difficulty of arriving there, don't believe a word of it. The experiments you have been doing have shown again and again that to see Who you are is the easiest thing in the world. Nor is it quite true that *keeping up the seeing* is just about the most difficult thing in the world. How could it be, inasmuch as it's simply the repetition of what's so easy, till it becomes perfectly natural and effortless? Such is the true task, then, of your old age. And remember, it's not a contrived or artificial one, but more natural than Nature itself. You may well find that conscious living from What you are comes to you so smoothly and swiftly that you will be astonished, once you are committed to it.

Finally, what of the stressful possibility that you and I will go senile, will lose our minds some time before we die? In that case, what price this great Goal of Self-realization which replaces all those inferior goals?

Well, the truth is that You, the One you really, really are, namely Awareness itself, never had a mind to lose. What it's aware of, on the other hand, all that mindstuff of yours, began when you were born as a great big booming chaos, went on to organize itself into a universe, and is due to disorganize itself again before or while you are on your deathbed. That's the way universes behave, the way they are served up. It is they that suffer from senility. So what? So their Origin, which is your true Nature, remains undisturbed.

All the same, it is natural to take a dim view of senility. Your best insurance against its onset is to see and live That which is perfectly safe against anything of the sort. No guarantees can be given, but if you want to keep your wits about you, then keep them *about* you, out there, off-Centre, and be that Witless One here who is their Source. The best way to keep your marbles is to see them playing around that perfectly transparent Alley and Glassy Essence which Shakespeare speaks of. You have his word for it that you will then avoid degenerating into an angry ape. Or any kind of ape, I would add, and in particular a senile one.

Doubts linger? Well, you and I have good reason to be apprehensive of second childhood. Of degenerating into foolish old things who have forgotten nine-tenths of all our hard-won knowledge. Of becoming near imbeciles whose minds are prone to go blank at the drop of a hat, so that often we can't put a name to a familiar face or a face to a familiar name, or figure what day of the week it is, or recollect what we got up to yesterday. Apprehensive of declining into silly old buffers, as unsure of ourselves as we are of almost everything else. Well into our dotage, if not altogether dotty. Quiet idiots, if not gibbering ones. All this, and more, we fear, justifiably.

But just a minute! Need this so-called degeneration be the disaster we are so sure it is? The Taoist sage (we met him on pages 63 and 174) goes so far as to say: Not on your life! Quite the contrary! In fact, our description of what we *fear to become* tallies neatly with his description of what he's *delighted to be already*. In that Chinese classic, the *Tao Te Ching*, the sage makes himself out to be a very poor specimen indeed, by ordinary reckoning. Repeatedly, and with a strange enthusiasm and insistence. What *we* read as stress-building handicaps *he* reads as stress-demolishing credentials, qualifying him for sagehood. The only difference between ourselves and him is that he is vividly aware of, and welcomes, and goes all the way into and so completes, his idiocy: whereas we shrink from ours. But no longer! Let's plunge in headfirst, instead of waiting till the years push us in! Let's guard against clinical senility (which is never total) by diving so deeply into it that we come out the other end. Now! And remember: to make sure of never going off your head (as they say) make sure it was never on you. No matter how much of a loser you may be, you can't lose something you never had. See this obvious fact, go on relishing it, and graduate as a Taoist sage, heavily disguised. Or, if you don't fancy the Taoist label, be content with plain sagehood: which simply means being, consciously, the way you really, really are.

And in any case, just what is this mysterious Tao? It is the Way, the Way the universe works, the Way your own life works when it is in harmony with the universe. It is your true and inmost Nature. It is something like what we mean by God, and even more like what Jesus meant when – speaking in his capacity as First Person Singular – he said he was the Way and the Truth and the Life. In the language of this book, it is none other than your Bottom Line, the lethal yet healing Sword of Perseus which, by striking off the head that separates you from God and all creatures, unites you with them absolutely and forever.

All of which is graphically summed up in the Chinese seal-character for the TAO itself, which consists of the characters for HEAD and GOING.

16

DEATH

Death happens naturally to animals and infants. They don't anticipate what's coming to them. For us who do so, the prospect is in varying degrees profoundly stressful, and all the more so when we don't want to know that we know. We had better recognize that the connection between our stress and our dying is very strong indeed and has many strands to it, and that fear is the fibre they are woven of. Our aim in this chapter is not so much to unravel that fear as to see our way through to what lies beyond it.

It is often said that all our fears, deep down, are nothing else than our fear of death. Is this true? You might suppose that many of them, on the contrary, are fear of *life*. But what looks like fear of life itself is more likely to be fear of where it's heading, of the great showdown that lies at the end of it. Certainly it's a fact that, when we examine our particular fears, we are apt to find that what underlies them is the death threat they imply or pose. Thus we are scared of heights for the best of reasons: from them we may so easily fall to our destruction. If spiders frighten us, it is because we have a hunch, or an ancestral memory, that some of the big black ones are deadly poisonous, and to be on the safe side we'd better shrink from all but the baby ones. If I'm frightened to stand up and make a speech, with all those eyes rivetted on me, I guess it is for the same reason that the deer that boldly invade my garden run off when I look directly at them. The first thing that killers do is to pin down their victim with a stare. Again, it is with good reason that we are terrified of failure and disgrace and ridicule in business and sport and love and whatever. What are these but the preliminaries and early stages of our dying, the first of the blows that will before long strike us to the ground, never to rise again? Indeed death itself is rightly to be feared as a great shame and the ultimate disgrace and absurdity: how self-occupied we are, how dis-gracefully we behave, what trouble and embarrassment we cause all round, how unpleasant we look, on our deathbeds! Besides being the most certain, it is the most ignominious of defeats. What failure is so total as the failure to live, and what thought so stress-making as the reflection that every minute brings that failure just so much nearer? The greatest sin of all, said Calderón, is that we were born. To live is a capital offence, and very soon we shall pay the penalty for having committed it. The wonder is that the stress of our plight hasn't polished us off in advance of the official (but secret) date of execution.

If these reflections seem to us altogether too gloomy, or exaggerated and bizarre, that's only the measure of our unwillingness to face the facts. Inescapable facts which make this, the penultimate chapter of our inquiry, quite crucial. We have now to take on the opponent whom the Upanishads call the King of Death himself. 'Escape me never!' he cries, as he closes in on us. He is right. What, in that case, have we to lose by turning round and facing him squarely? Our only chance of getting the better of him is to concede victory, but view it in an altogether new light. To overcome the menace by submitting to it, and going deeply into it, and hopefully coming out the other end by the route we are becoming familiar with.

To put the matter another way, rather than do battle aboveground with such a secure and well-fortified enemy, let's try sapping and mining again, getting down to death's foundations and collapsing them if we can. For this we need good mining tools – humble spades and fast drills and powerful explosives. Well, let's try this assortment:

(i) CS = NS

Common sense is nonsense. Nonsense, that's to say, when it comes to *oneself*. It works pretty well when applied to others, to second and third persons as such, but breaks down altogether when applied to this First Person. And if I really am investigating this most serious of all issues and not sidestepping it or passing the buck, why then it's my own death and not others' that is at issue. Theirs is easy to take, diluted, bland, comparatively harmless. Mine is 100 per cent proof, and it hits the spot – hard. Now if our inquiry has made one fact abundantly clear, it is that everything that common sense and popular opinion says about me, about this First Person Singular, isn't just *non*sense: it's *inverted* sense. Some quick examples by way of reminder: I was told I was peeking at the world through two tiny peepholes, that they are framed in a face here, that with it I face the faces that I meet, that I am small and opaque and very mobile indeed, that I'm embedded in a body, and so on and on. It's not too much to say that the probability – amounting to practical certainty – is that whatever common sense tells me I am is exactly what I'm not. It follows that I may take common sense for my guide, *provided* that when it says 'Go North' I go South, and when it says 'Climb' I descend, and when it says 'Yes' I say 'No thank you, not on your life!' And when commonsensible folk tell me I'll perish, I say 'Speak for yourselves, my friends. The fact that you swear to my mortality amounts to a sworn statement that I am immortal!'

An acquaintance whom I have found to be a consistent liar is consistently reliable, on condition I stand on its head everything he tells me. Common sense is such an acquaintance, indeed such a friend. Through its representatives – they include almost everyone I've come across – it has throughout my life been telling me what's going to happen at the end of it. Ergo, it won't be like that at all. I don't take this as final and proof-positive, but as proof-indicative. The formula $CS = NS$ furnishes pick and shovel rather than dynamite, nevertheless they are a fine pair of tools to start our excavations with.

(ii) YOU JUST AREN'T THE TYPE

People are mortal, every man-Jack and woman-Jill of them. And what are these mortals, on their own showing as well as on careful inspection by you and me?

They are rather small objects clearly outlined against a background. They are as opaque and substantial as the logs they sleep like. They tear all over the place. At intervals they shove alien substances into tooth-lined holes in their heads. They deteriorate steadily, they go off. Such are those whom the King of Death has marked out and branded as his own. There comes a day when they go right off and they lie down and don't get up again, when their breathing stops, and they go cold and rigid, and they are burned or masticated by worms. If you are *at all* like they are, why you will surely be one of that company. Look and see right now whether you are the dying type.

(iii) THE DEAD DON'T DIE

Oh yes, those people are alive all right. That's why they die. But what about you? Look and see now. Haven't you already suffered death by the most spectacular and summary means of execution – by beheading? Come on, you can't be decapitated *twice*!

To be absolutely sure that you can never lose your life, see that you have none of your own to lose.

If you think I'm being playful, or just damn silly, think again. Allow your onion to be peeled once more. With all its prestige and force, science itself insists that intrinsically, right where you are, you are deader than any doornail, much deader. Let me remind you. At a metre or two you appear to be human, alive, substantial.

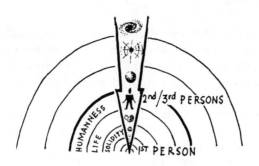

At a centimetre you appear to be alive but far from human. At a millimetre you appear to be solid but far from human or alive. At lesser ranges still, even your apparent solidity (whatever that ghost of a ghost was) has been exorcized, and you've practically nothing left to show for yourself. Finally, at no range at all, zero metres from yourself, you can see for yourself that here is to be found no humanness, no life and death, no solidity or substantiality at all, but only Awareness of this grand hierarchy of attributes, *on display in others*. All the life you enjoy is their life, the life of those who were born and will therefore die. Having none of your very own, you are the imperishable recipient of the life of the world. The merest spark or tremor of personal vitality would be enough to seal your death warrant.

An arrow or a bullet, anything shot at you from over there, has to penetrate the nest of your regions, in which it is progressively dematerialized, leaving you – as First Person – unscathed. At a deep level we know this. Hence, for instance, the legend of St

Christopher, who shouldered the Christ child across a river. At the time of his martyrdom, the arrows shot at him all fell short of the mark. So he was beheaded: which didn't matter, seeing he was headless anyway!

(iv) AWARENESS, THE NO-THING THAT'S ONLY HERE, ONLY NOW

No *thing* is aware of things. Ransack the universe, and you will never find Awareness anywhere but in yourself the ransacker, in yourself who are no thing but capacity for things, in yourself who are empty of yourself and therefore filled with every mortal thing.

Where is Awareness? Only here. When is Awareness? Only now. What can be remembered or anticipated is the *content* of Awareness, the passing show it entertains, not the Awareness which never passes, never changes, is never interrupted. Other people as such, those second and third persons, manifestly sleep and faint and are anaesthetized and die. Manifestly nothing of the sort can or does happen to you, the First Person. You experience no Awareness-gap between 'falling asleep at night' and 'waking up in the morning', and no Awareness-gap while your body is undergoing surgery in the operating theatre. Why *of course* you don't: you are Awareness itself – Awareness which, in total contrast to what it's aware of, is not intermittent. For you, for the real You, there is neither birth nor death, nor loss of consciousness for a split second.

No wonder you as Awareness don't come and go, aren't switched off and on, are absolutely intemporal. No wonder you aren't in time at all, but instead time is in you. The simple reason is that, centrally and essentially, you are no thing at all, and therefore changeless, and therefore timeless: for where there's nothing to register time there is no time. QED.

Remind yourself of what the time is where you are, as you bring your watch *all* the way up to your eye – or should I say your I?

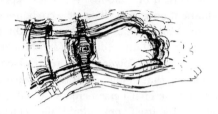

(v) NDEs

The fact that, for you, there is no death, is due for confirmation when (according to outside observers) you stand at death's brink. The Near Death Experiences, recounted by so many victims of illness or accident who have recovered to tell the tale, are in effect not experiences of the *nearness* of death at all, of death's approach, but of its recession to an infinite distance, and its replacement by a light and a love that are read as timeless. As hearsay and not firsthand evidence which is verifiable now and by anyone, these anecdotes, though remarkably consistent and remarkably encouraging, do not strictly prove anything about death. Nevertheless, they do something to reinforce what, on other and surer grounds, we have discovered – namely that, so far from being made of perishable stuff, What and Who you really, really are is the *only* imperishable.

(vi) DEATH'S RECESSION

This curious habit that death has – one's own death, I mean – of receding into the distance, of playing hard-to-get, shows itself long before the onset of any NDE. It's notorious that quite intelligent old people, and not just those of us who are going gaga, don't feel any nearer to death at eighty than at eighteen. Significantly, we don't have a sense of being pressed for time, of our time running out. We don't get up in the morning trembling lest we are going to last the day or the week out, or wondering whether we will see another springtime spread of daffodils. We don't experience ourselves as less permanent now than when we were bouncing around in our heyday. Even more significantly, however, this conviction of agelessness doesn't rub off on to others. *They* show their age all right; and – poor dears! – are slower and more wrinkled and white than ever, are obviously that much nearer to the grave, every time they pay a visit. Only the First Person enjoys this 'absurd' conviction of immortality. By itself, not admissible evidence. Taken along with the preceding five, however, a clue by no means to be despised. Not a bad tool to keep by you.

Such, then, is your plant, your tool kit for digging deeply into the question of your death. And what do you come upon at the bottom of the mineshaft? Not sand, not just the silver of relief from the stress of the fear of death, but pure gold. Here again, at the very bottom of the pit, lies the treasure.

What is that treasure? It is getting exactly what you want out of death – no more and no less, just like that. It comes in three instalments. First you find that what you want is that the one in your mirror and your passport shall go on living. Second, that what you really want is that he shall die just as soon as he's had enough and his work is done. Third, that what you really, really want, as the Source of life and death and free from both, is that life and death and all their stresses shall carry on exactly as they are carrying on in You, here and now. This third step ends the fear which underlies all fear, the fear of death itself. At your Bottom Line, the world and its living and dying, its fear and its stress, *bottom out*, and you are content. O so content!

Instead of just describing that process of bottoming out, let's take a look at it once more.

Experiment 22: Yet another bow before the evidence

For this you will need the card, with a head-shaped and head-sized hole in it, which we used in an earlier experiment.

Preferably stand in the open, or at a window.

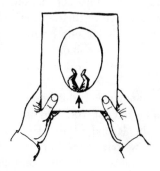

Throughout the experiment concentrate on the bottom edge of that hole, the place I have marked with an arrow.

Holding the card out at arm's length, fill that hole with the distant scene . . .

Slowly bringing the card forward, fill it with the nearer scene.

Now slowly bring it all the way, fitting it on your 'face', and fill it with the nearest scene, including those little upside-down legs, and that truncated shirtfront . . .

How delightfully odd it is, how fitting it is somehow, that a thing as contemptible as a torn shirt should unveil the Mystery of all mysteries and the Treasure of all treasures! And see the King of Death defeated.

You have, by this humblest of exits from life, come to die absolutely. Thus freeing yourself forever from Death and beating him at his own game. Absolutely. And what a true friend he now is, letting you off being Mary Robinson, or John Smith, or whoever. And letting me off being Douglas Edison Harding. Just him and no one else. What a mercy!

THE LEGEND OF THE GRAIL

So far, in this chapter about death, we have been looking at the exposed and lit-up side of it, where it stands clear-cut in consciousness and is plainly on show for all to see. But of course it has another side – indistinct, darker, more secret, immeasurably more complex. Nevertheless as critical for our stress-coping purpose here as it is for our health in general, for life itself. It takes shape – what vague shape it can boast – as fantasies, dreams, folklore, legends, myths, the dogmas and rituals of religion. And so on.

From this haunted tanglewood, this immense and untameable wilderness, I have plucked for you and myself at this time a particular flower – the legend of the Holy Grail – because, more than most, it grows out of the humus of death and transformation. And also because it's a fine example of the region's flora, in all their wild vigour and variety. In fact, before inspecting this choice specimen, I want to say something about its habitat. I mean: about myths in general and their importance for our enquiry into stress – especially the stress of dying.

Myths are like the paper money of the world. They come in all denominations, from almost worthless to a small fortune. Some are relatively crisp and clean. Others are limp and torn and dirty, almost worn out. Some are no longer legal tender at all. Not a few are clumsy forgeries. A mixed and dubious purse-full to carry around, which nevertheless we can't do without. But the wherewithal that's far from dubious – that's as internationally valid as the multiplication table – is the Great Perennial Myth, which furnishes every one of us with a fat book of traveller's cheques (so to say), cashable worldwide. Up till now by far the most useful and durable of them all, this Myth of myths is upwards of a million years old and still going strong. It still passes virtually unchallenged, is still so taken for granted – for actual-factual – that it isn't seen as a myth at all, but as God-given natural law. The polite name for it is Common Sense. The rude but true name, Non-sense. Its formula, its mnemonic for us, is $CS = NS$. Its motto is: *I am the mortal I look like.* Its logo is the finger that points every way but inwards to the Immortal. In its long heyday it proved highly energizing and productive – at a price. The cost was high but not prohibitive. But now it is no longer cost-effective. In fact, it

268

is fast becoming counterproductive, to the point of threatening genocide. Or is it omnicide? It always has been the prime producer of toxic stress. And it has always been sacred – far too hallowed for mere mortals to be clearly aware of, much less call in question.

Yes: there are bad myths all right, as well as good ones. And they belong to every era. If you doubt this, think of all the totalitarian myths humanity has had to endure.

Immeasurably the most insidious and persistent of them all – in a sense the most totalitarian of them all – is this supermyth that preens and prides itself on the highly respected title of Common Sense. The good news is that it has three implacable foes. The first, as we have seen, is the young child. The second is the Uncommon Sense (alias Coming-to-one's-senses and Looking-to-see) which is the raison-d'être of this book and the whole point of our experiments. Call it *radical de-mythologizing*. Its task is patiently to undermine, with pick and shovel and dynamite, the enemy's fortifications. The third seems to side with the enemy, but is in fact a formidable ally. Call it *radical re-mythologizing*. Its task is to cooperate in this same work of sapping and mining, using a powerful toolkit of ancient myths and folklore tuned and lubricated for current service. Thus they are put back on the task that always was theirs – the good old stories' job of subverting the bad contemporary one. The tale of Perseus and the Gorgon is a case in point. We have seen how faithfully the hero deals with Snakylocks, the commonsense lady who 'things' all her beholders: how he thereby scotches the commonsense lie of First Person–third person symmetry, and cleanses the land of the commonsense curse of confrontation. Another is the Hymn of the Pearl, which already has had so much to tell us about death and transformation. Uncommonsensibly, and with uncommon charm. And there are more to come. As you will presently see, in the next chapter.

A word of caution here, however, about the status of these 'good' myths as evidence concerning one's true Nature and the meaning of one's life and death. I nod rather than bow to them. I put them in the witness box. Precisely because I take them so seriously, I elicit from them, thankfully but critically, the testimony I need, leaving aside what I find irrelevant, or confused and confusing – and that's plenty! I'm on trial for my life, and therefore must insist that a minute spent looking at the One I'm looking out of takes precedence over years of looking up Frazer and Campbell and Eliade. Necessarily so. For I have no way of proving the validity – the relevance to my living and loving and dying – of the myth I'm reading about, except by turning my attention round 180° to the Reader. I test what's indirectly given there by what's directly given here, circumstantial evidence by eye-witnessing, what I have by what I am. Only so do I light a torch to beat any sort of path through the dark and pathless tanglewood of the world's myths. And then? Why then how reassuring it is to stumble on confirmation upon confirmation, enrichment upon enrichment, of the simple discoveries already made before venturing into that beguiling forest, so easy to get into and (normally) so hard to get out of. How good, then, to experience the liberating and heart-warming power of the true myth, in contrast to the spell-binding power of the false one, so chilling and loveless. Thus the saving knowledge about life and death, and the joy they hold, works down from the clearly seen to the deeply felt, from the coolness to the warmth, from my no-head to my heart and guts. Not the other way round. Once more, Dante says it –

> Being blessed has its origin in the act of sight,
> And not in love, which comes afterwards.

– lines which I would dearly like to see, printed in bold capitals, all over this book.

So we come to the famous legend of the Holy Grail, as it surfaces in England and France in the twelfth century. A story about love – if not a love story – in which sight certainly takes precedence. Already very elaborate indeed (though strangely inconclusive), it is followed in later centuries, and in several other European countries, by all sorts of further complications: leading to various dénouements – some happy and convincing, others teasingly enigmatic. The following selection from this hold-all of a myth will do for our purposes.

The Grail is a flat dish on which the paschal lamb was served at

Jesus's Last Supper. Later accounts identify it with the cup he drank from on that occasion, which was also used to catch drops of his blood as he hung on the cross. It is sometimes taken to be the jewel that was dislodged from Lucifer's crown when he was cast into Hell – an emerald that kept its heavenly properties. In any case it is regarded as the holiest of objects, the source of fabulous magical powers, the talisman of the deathless, and the repository of eternal truth. Accordingly the finding of the Grail was felt to be the only worthy aim of a knight of King Arthur's Round Table. Whatever the dangers, however protracted the search, no matter how poor his chances of success, it was the love of his life.

The knight who sets out on his quest for the Grail has no idea where to look. He can only wander, trusting God and his luck. If he is fortunate, he arrives, after many strange adventures, at a splendid castle that contains the Grail, but is set in the midst of a vast waste land. The master of the castle is a mysterious character called the Fisher King, an invalid who is wounded in the thigh or the genitals. He cannot himself touch the Grail and be healed by it. His open wound keeps him from dying, and his continuing sickness is the cause of the infertility of the land. Yet he is well enough to go fishing. Only then is he content.

During his stay in the castle, the knight witnesses a procession of sacred objects, one of which sheds a brilliant light. He recognizes it as the Grail. At this point he ought to ask what the Grail is for and who is served by it. This he fails to do, with the result that, waking next morning, he finds himself alone. The Grail has vanished and the castle is deserted – all because he didn't ask the right question. Just seeing the Grail was not enough: its meaning had to be discovered. According to some texts, the right answer to the question, 'For whom is the Grail?' is, 'For the Grail King.' Which of course raises the question: 'Who is the Grail King?'

In alternative versions of the story an innocent fool of a knight, arriving at the castle, helps to heal the Fisher King's wound. This enables him to die, in due course, a natural death. In consequence the waste land blossoms and life is renewed. The full meaning of the Grail is at last revealed. The simpleton knight learns the secret of death and regeneration.

THE LEGEND OF THE GRAIL INTERPRETED

Everyone for whom this curiously multiform and disjointed story is significant, or disturbing, or fascinating and powerful for no immediately apparent reason, finds in it the meaning it holds for him. He may pick at it here and there, or make a meal of it. That's what the myth is for – to be many things to many people. Here is what I make of it. A modest smorgasbord for you to select from:

(i) The wonder-working dish

You will already have gathered that the Grail-dish is yet another name for one's Bottom Line and the World's End. And a fitting name this is, too. For here, where this shirt-bib of mine terminates, is the only place-setting where my universe is served up. What a spread that is! From the unknowable depths of the kitchen of Non-Being there arrives on my plate this sacred meal called Being – steaming hot, fragrant, elaborately garnished, and – ah! – spicy. What a menu (both à la carte and table d'hôte), what generous helpings, what round-the-clock service! And no one has any idea of who the chef is, or how he does it, single-handed at that.

That's life.

The other use of the Grail-dish is to serve up death. It held the body of the sacrificial lamb; and, later, the blood of the crucified Lord. Here, one is not the eater but the eaten. Here, one is *dished*. (An English word, meaning defeated and ruined, not current in America.) Here, one is served right, licked, immolated, not fed with but absolutely fed up with everything.

In getting the feel of the Grail right here, I'm mysteriously enabled to reconcile and hold together these two wholly contrasting uses of it, with a minimum of verbalizing. I'm somehow helped to live in order to die, and die in order to live, without any need to keep on spelling out to myself the double paradox. Now. The Holy Grail, by virtue of which this continual miracle occurs, is this place-setting where I'm at once replete with the world and emptied of it. And so relieved of its stress. As I found at the very beginning of this enquiry.

(ii) The Grail experience and the Grail meaning

T. S. Eliot (whose *The Waste Land*, incidentally, is a variation on the Grail theme) has in another poem the line: 'We had the experience but missed the meaning.' He could have been speaking for the knight who saw the Grail paraded in the Fisher King's castle, but let it pass without comment, without asking a single question about it. Failing to appreciate the treasure, he lost it, at least for the time being.

What was his assignment, his purpose when he set off on the quest? It was not, having discovered the Grail, to take it to Arthur's court to be admired by all – along with its brave finder. No, it was to *see* the Grail, not claim it. It yields its cornucopia of gifts to the one who takes it in, not the one who tries to take it away. The gifts are right there and freely bestowed, independent of any merit or action on the seer's part. All the same, before he is ready to accept and benefit from them, he needs to value their source, to take it seriously. Otherwise, it's as if he had never found the Grail at all. As if he had come across the Koh-i-noor diamond in a junk shop, and seen it quite clearly – as junk – and gone out as poor as he went in.

Now I hate to say this, but I guess that, out of ten of my readers, five will not do the experiments at all. And that, out of the five who do them, three or four will say: 'Of course I see. But so what?' Said with a sigh, perhaps, or is it with the sophisticated yawn of the adult who's been around? To which I reply: 'So you are in all respects the opposite of what you had been told. So you are the deathless splendour. So you are made of God. So all is yours, and from you, and to you. And much, much more. That's all. THAT'S ALL!' Having said which, I give up. And turn to you – to you my dear Reader who haven't only carried out our experiments, but with childlike sincerity taken them to heart. To you who are the worthy successor of the innocent knight who healed the Fisher King and restored life to his realm. To you I say: 'Observe what a perfect set-up it is – that while the *sight* of Who you really, really are is forever the same and complete, the *meaning* of what you see is inexhaustible, capable of endless enrichment.

Observe how you need both, together. And how naturally they converge and become inseparable, given a little time and attention.

Much of that meaning is contained in the statement that the Grail is for the Grail King. Not for the knight, not for you and me, as such. The fact is that I can never, in my human capacity, see Who I really, really am. As Mary Robinson, John Smith, Douglas Harding, or whoever, my true identity is hidden from me. When, therefore, I see this true and ultimate identity (how could I miss it?) I see it for and as the One we all are, the One who *is*. To realize this is at once altogether humbling and altogether exalting. It means that the double 'work on ourselves' that you and I are doing together here – seeing into and valuing our true Nature – is work for the whole world. The best work, ever. Our enlightenment cannot help but spill out on all beings, for the simple reason that we are them. For whom, then, is this Holy Grail that is your treasure and Bottom Line and the beginning and the ending of your world? Not for you as a mere human. Not for you as the wounded Fisher of fish. It is for you as the Fisher of men, as the Grail King who is none other than the All, the King of kings, the One Imperishable. To be saved is to be Him. And to be Him is to save his world.

(iii) The Waste Land

The knight doesn't find this marvellous Grail in an appropriately marvellous setting, but only in the midst of the Waste Land. Exactly where is this Empty Region, this Arabia Deserta?

It is right where you are, right now, at the still and deserted hub of your busy world. At the centre, where you have left behind your heavenliness, your earthliness, your humanness, your life, your very existence. Here, you are deader than dead. Not till you see this clearly and accept it deeply, are you empty enough, are you burst wide open enough, to be flooded with the resurrection life that is the life of the whole world. When you find, beyond all doubt, that you are this dreadful Waste Land, then you find there the Holy Grail, already flooding you to overflowing with its living water.

(iv) The Fisher King

The most enigmatic figure in the Grail legend – and for that reason very likely the most important for us to interpret rightly – is the bedridden Fisher King. What does his strange wound in the groin signify? Why does it keep him alive beyond his natural span, yet refuse to heal? How, and on what forlorn shore, does this royal invalid go fishing? Why is it his one consolation? Does he catch baskets full of fine salmon, or mere eels and the occasional old boot? Or unheard-of marine monsters?

Surely it's not hard to trace in this identikit the portrait of a personage who is curiously familiar. Call him Mr King. Mr King is very aware he is sick – sick of being powerless and sterile to a degree that makes a mockery of his pretensions and social status, to say nothing of his agony of longing. He samples the cures of regular and fringe medicine, but gets no better. He goes rather deeply into various sorts of psychotherapy, but isn't sure whether they subtract from or add to his stress. In desperation he's thinking of undergoing an analysis that promises or threatens to last for several years, and never really be complete. Meanwhile he reads about the great ocean of the unconscious. He looks to it for inspiration, as yet in vain. Its weird menagerie of symbolic and archetypal figures fascinates him. He hopes against hope that one day they will come together to make him whole and restore his lost vitality and creative powers. Duly he dreams about, and records in his diary, one or another of these shadowy beings. As for the rest of them, he drops a hopeful line for them nightly, as he drops off to sleep.

Yes, Mr King is in a bad way, but does at least get something out of his hobby. It may be unproductive and at times stressful (he will tell you) but it's a lot better than nothing. Being Mr Micawber, always expecting something to turn up, is a lot better than being nobody. Says he.

I think you'll agree that Mr King, alias the Fisher of the legend, is not such a stranger after all. Or even that – given some adjustments as to what he's fishing for – he can be found very near home indeed. In that case, who is the innocent knight who helps the

Fisher to get better, only to die in the end, thus restoring the land to abundance? And what, shorn of metaphor, is the secret of his success?

Well, let's continue the history of Mr King. Driven to desperation by his sickness, encouraged by a friend who is naively wise, possibly assisted by Grace, he reverts to simplicity, to the obvious, to the plainly given. Daring at last to look, he withdraws his remark that his hobby is better than nothing, and decides that *nothing* is better than Nothing. That nothing and nobody in the world can compare with the No-thing he visibly is – seeing that it is visibly Everything.

And so, instead of haunting the shore of the ocean of Non-being, in the hopes of pulling some worthwhile morsel out of it for himself, he dives in. He becomes the ocean itself, with its infinite fecundity, its infinite potentiality for Being. At last he has made the catch of his life. This is the big one that didn't get away. He has caught the sea.

He has died the ultimate death, and therefore lives the ultimate life. Not as that feeble and forever disappointed angler, but as the Grail King who is King over all and the picture of health eternally.

To see Him, which is to be Him, just reverse your attention. Now.

17

THE BEYOND

Countless humans have lived and died not fearing death so much as what lies beyond death. It used to be an exceptionally virtuous or exceptionally confident person who died perfectly sure that he or she would escape ages upon ages of truly fiendish torture – being shredded with hooks, pitchforked into white-hot furnaces, boiled alive like lobsters in cauldrons, or held fast in everlasting ice – all endured in a body magically pickled to survive such maltreatment forever and with undiminishing consciousness. This, and more, was going on in a place that was every bit as real as the streets and the houses of the town one lived in, a place whose direction was every bit as precise as that of the starry heavens overhead but whose distance was negligible by comparison. Hell, the vast and crowded torture chamber of the universe, lay underfoot, and not so very far down, at that. Volcanoes spouting fire and geysers spouting hot water added their confirmation to the terrifying picture of the underworld painted by priest and bishop and pope, as well as by the sacred literature itself.

Such, in its essentials, is the picture I was brought up from infancy to believe in without question, so I know what I'm talking about. The feel and the stress of it are unforgettable. While Heaven was for me so remote and so vague as to present few problems, Hell was very real and very dangerous. A hell-fire sermon preached by one Mr Bell, a venerable figure, towering, long-white-bearded and solemnly apocalyptic, convinced me at the age of twelve that I (a Hell-bound sinner if ever there was one) must join the company of the Saved while I still had a chance. Before then, on occasions when I couldn't immediately locate my parents, I was panic-stricken lest, along with the rest of the saints, they had been quietly caught up to Heaven by the Lord at his

Second Coming, leaving me, with all the other lost and wicked ones, to await Hell's screams and groans, the gnashing of teeth, the fire that's never quenched.

Nowadays we like to think of our glorious heritage of churches and cathedrals as expressions of adoration and gratitude to the Almighty for his gifts. With their exquisite music and glowing windows and rich vestments, along with the heartening together-ness of the worshippers, they must have seemed to their builders previews of Heaven. Well yes. But there were other considerations. These edifices were also sweeteners or bare-faced bribes, or let's say insurance premiums paid to the Man from the Pru-in-the-skies, with a view to maximizing one's chances of joining him up there instead of being cast into that other place. More than joy or thankfulness (I suspect) it was terror that produced Chartres and Amiens and St Peter's Basilica in Rome. These magnificent works of piety, together with pilgrimages and penances of all descriptions, were small investments to hedge one against the horrible risk of Hell. Alas, they could do no more than *reduce* one's chances of being dispatched at death to the Almighty's concentration camp forever. A horror beside which our Belsens and Buchenwalds look like luxury hotels.

We moderns, of course, aren't so silly as to believe a word of all this nonsense. We marvel and laugh and are disgusted at this once near-universal picture of the Beyond, the lower half of it in particular. Not that the upper half was all that good. What are we to make of the satisfaction that the blessed enjoy (according to some of the best medieval theologians) as they look down upon the scene they have managed to avoid – the eternal agonies of the damned there below? We are sure we have come a long way from those nastily superstitious times and the stress that their fearsome eschatology generated.

This is to oversimplify. The nether regions haven't been abol-ished. Rather it is that their geography has been revised. Hell has come up in the world, without drawing attention to the fact. The stress and the tortures are still with us. In this inquiry we have located Hell *above* the World's Edge and Bottom Line, and well within the experience of everyone *this* side of death. Our safeguard against permanent incarceration in this Hell, our way of coping with this still diabolical menace, is neither to push it into the Beyond and forget it, nor off-handedly to deny its existence, but on the contrary to insist on it, to emphasize its presence as nearer than near. Bowing deeply before the evidence, we go down into and through this inferno, not to a Beyond that *is* but to a Beyond that *is not*, and certainly not to any sort of afterlife which lies outside of and transcends this familiar world of ours. No: the Hell of *this* world is quite enough – the Hell that narrows and sinks to its nadir right where I am here and now: the Hell that converges on the Point which instantly explodes into our own wide, wide world, ranging from particles to galaxies. Into *this* world, which is none other than Heaven come down into the world, this world seen as it is from its Source. Beyond it lies no other Heaven or Hell: but, instead, the Void, the Abyss that sports neither height nor width nor depth, neither space nor time, nor so much as a dust-grain to occupy them.

This Abyss below the Line, this Beyond which is beyond Heaven and Hell and existence itself but nevertheless absolutely real, is all-important for us because it happens to be our refuge and our healing and the disposal site of all our toxic stress. In this, the concluding chapter of our investigation, we fill out our sketch of it by drawing on some of the traditions, religious and secular, which speak of this Place where there is no more place, where there is nowhere to pillow one's head and no head to pillow.

(i) THE BEYOND IN CHRISTIANITY

First, we turn to our own spiritual tradition in the West, as followed by a succession of mystics who have either ignored or pooh-poohed the official picture of what lies beyond this life – to say nothing of the popular distortions of that picture. Not for them the nightmarish vision of the afterlife that bedevilled my childhood.

For these mystics, as for ourselves engaged in this research, Heaven and Hell are now and not in the future, here and not over there, this-worldly and not other-worldly So far from being beyond us they are with us all day and every day, and they belong altogether on *this* side of our death. Beyond life and death lies the real Beyond, which is the wholly mysterious and unpicturable *Source* of life and death, of space and time, as well as the myriad forms they assume. This Origin of all, having none of the qualities of its products, is knowable only by contrast with them, negatively, as spaceless, timeless, limitless, unthinkable, ungraspable, completely baffling. And, just because it is so stainless and aseptic, so clean of the brand-marks and limitations and defects which its creatures are necessarily subject to, it is their cleansing, their sovereign remedy, their only lasting cure. The names this incomparable Source and Resource goes by include the Ground of Being (we read the Bottom Line), the Godhead (we read the unpillowed and headless Head of all), the Abyss (we read the Depth that transcends depth), the Ineffable, the Divine Dark, the Desert, the Not-God (we read That which lacks the positive qualities of God no less than the negative qualities of the Devil) and so forth – each term miserably inadequate, of course, if not actually misleading. Fortunately what matters, what gives relief from our stress and distress, isn't our knowledge of the Great Beyond (it is absolutely unknowable, most of all to itself) but our direct perception of it. The happy and saving facts are: Only This can be clearly seen because only This is so simple, so clear and plain and all-on-show that it just cannot be mis-seen. Only This can be perfectly got because only in This is there nothing to get. Only This can insure us against and repair the ravages of time because only This is timeless. Only This can safely be relied upon because only This neither relies upon nor needs any foundation whatever: it has the useful knack of hoisting itself out of the Inane, out of the Dead Blank, by its own boot-straps. If you can't trust the One who has this *impossible* know-how, who or what can you trust?

The way to meet and be treated by this Master Physician for stress, the only way to experience Him at all, is to experience Him by means of Himself: which means, in fact, to *be* Him. So that, while remaining unspeakably foreign and inaccessible and awesome, He is also unspeakably obvious and intimate, nearer than near and dearer than dear. In sober truth, what makes Him at once so precious and so devastating is that, actually as well as metaphorically, He bowls one clean over. To be precise, I'm head-under-heels – or rather no-head-under-heels – in love with Him.

Here, then, picked up more or less arbitrarily, are some traditional impressions of this adorable Healer whose treatment includes turning the patient upside down:

Meister Eckhart: 'While she [your soul] lacks union she has never really loved God, for actual love lies in union.' (In this passage Eckhart is in fact speaking of the Godhead.)

'If you love God as God, as Spirit, as Person, or as Image, that must all go. Then how shall I love Him? Love Him as He is: as not-God, not-Spirit, not-Person, not-Image: as sheer, pure, limpid unity, alien from all duality. And in this One let us sink eternally from nothingness to nothingness . . .

'What is the last end? It is the mystery of the darkness of the eternal Godhead which is unknown and never has been known and never shall be known.'

St John of the Cross: 'Those who know Him most perfectly perceive most clearly that He is perfectly incomprehensible.'

Dionysius the Areopagite: 'Its formless Nature produces all forms. In it alone Non-being is an excess of Being, and lifelessness an excess of life, and its mindless state an excess of wisdom.'

And how's this for a poetic description, by Angelus Silesius, of one's Bottom Line?

> Where is my dwelling-place?
> Where stand nor I nor Thou.
> Where is my final end,
> to which I needs must go?
> It is where no end is.
> Then whither shall I press?
> On even beyond God,
> into a Wilderness.

Though I doubt whether he would care to be included under 'Christian mystics', I can't resist the following quotation from a brilliant contemporary psychoanalyst, R. D. Laing. It's hard to imagine a more fitting tailpiece to this section:

Man, most fundamentally, is not engaged in the discovery of what is there, nor in production, nor even in communication nor in invention. He is enabling being to emerge from non-being. The experience of being the actual medium for a continual process of creation takes one past all depression or persecution or vainglory: past, even, chaos or emptiness, into the very mystery of that continual flip of nonbeing into being, and can be the occasion of that great liberation when one makes the transition from being afraid of nothing, to the realization that there is nothing to fear.

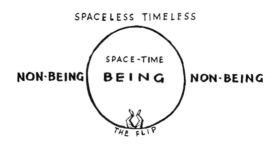

(ii) THE BEYOND IN BUDDHISM

Nirvana, the supreme goal of the Buddhist's endeavour, is described as release from the limitations of existence. The Buddha speaks of it as 'the Unborn, Unoriginated, Uncreated, Unformed', in contrast to the phenomenal world or Samsara which is born and created and formed. Though free from all limiting characteristics, Nirvana (we are told) is permanent, stable, imperishable, immovable, ageless, deathless. It is power, bliss, the secure refuge, the place of unassailable safety. It is Truth and supreme Reality. It is the Good, the one and only goal and consummation of our life, the hidden and incomparable Peace . . .

We advance by stages towards Nirvana. They include (I quote Edward Conze):

> Four 'formless' dhyanas (meditations) which represent stages of overcoming the vestiges of the object. As long as we suck ourselves onto any object, however refined, we cannot drop into Nirvana. One first sees everything as boundless space, then as unlimited consciousness, then as emptiness, then one gives up even the act which grasped the nothingness . . . (Beyond this is a place) where one is said to *touch Nirvana with one's body*.

Nirvana is the shore that's washed by the ocean of Samsara, their meeting place; and Wisdom is the contemplation of that shore as absolutely bare and empty. Relief from suffering is to be had by basing oneself on, by consciously coming from, that ineffable but conspicuous tide-line. The Buddha himself describes Nirvana as accessible and clearly visible to the wise disciple.

What is all this but an account, in slightly different terms, of where this inquiry has been leading us? Leading us away from imagining, below our Bottom Line, 'space for the world to happen in', to finding that Line itself to be the Place where the world of space and time stops, and 'one touches Nirvana with one's body'. Leading us to see Eye to Eye with the Buddha who, in another sermon, says that *within* this very body is the place of the world's origin and the world's ceasing. How satisfactory it is to be vague no longer about *where* in this body it is to be found!

It is true that Buddhism developed an even more elaborate system of Hells, divided into hot and cold ones, than Christianity came up with. But life in them is not for ever. Hell (according, for example, to *The Path to Sudden Attainment*) exists only in the mind: when the personality is seen as void there is no Hell. In other words the Hells that lie beyond this world of Samsara are indeed menacing till we see them as illusory, and our own speckless Nature as the real but ineffable Beyond.

(iii) THE BEYOND IN SUFISM

Rumi, that great Sufi master, has no doubt concerning the place where one meets the Beyond. 'You have never beheld the head of Man,' he says; 'you are a tail.' In many passages he points out that the First Person is decapitated. Thus one is cut off, in the most literal fashion, from all one's petty and indeed imaginary personal resources and united to one's total Resource and Origin which is 'permanent Non-being'. United with the Non-existence which, says Rumi, 'is God's factory'. As a house with a cache of diamonds buried beneath its foundations has to be sufficiently demolished to get at the treasure, so one's body is sufficiently demolished for the same reason. Here one comes, says Rumi, 'to the Place where place itself finds no admittance'. This is the Treasury itself.

The following is a recent description, by Hassan Shushud, a Turkish master, of the Sufism of the Naqshbandi Order:

It is the path of realization followed by those who cannot accept the Creation as a fait accompli . . . Annihilation (*fana*) is the essential basis of realization. Without it, contact with reality cannot be established, the veils that hide the true nature of things cannot be removed. Without annihilation, the cosmic illusion does not cease, the fictions of the mind and memory are never-ending. What is annihilation? It is to pass from phenomenal existence to real being, to the Mystery of absolute liberation . . . Mysteries forever concealed from the 'living' have surely been revealed to those who found the way to escape from the world of appearances into the realm of real discovery. They became free from all problems, whether mental, emotional, or occult.

Which is not too far from our way of putting the matter. Namely, that the answer to the stress of the world is the Beyond from which the world arises.

(iv) PRINCE INTO FROG INTO PRINCE

Now from religious to secular intimations of the Beyond.

In folklore and nursery rhymes the World's End is a place where wonderful things happen. (One likes to think that they happen in pubs with that name, too.)

The most wonderful example is the fairy story of the handsome Prince who was transformed into a hideous frog by a witch. You will remember our own elaboration of it – the parable of Eyebright and the Enchantress. In fact, so relevant is it to the topic of this book that it will crop up again as an Appendix.

What happens in the traditional English version is that the Prince-turned-frog finds himself in a well at the World's End. A girl turns up who is prepared to do his bidding. At length, he says to her:

> Open the door, my hinny, my heart,
> Open the door, my own darling.
> Mind you the words that you and I spoke,
> Down in the meadow, at the World's End well.

> Lift me to your knee, my hinny, my heart.
> Lift me to your knee, my own darling.
> Remember the words that you and I spoke,
> Down in the meadow, by the World's End well . . .

> Chop off my head my hinny, my heart,
> Chop off my head, my own darling.
> Remember the promise you made to me,
> Down by the cold well so weary.

Fulfilling her promise, she does indeed chop off his head, and – hey presto! – the frog is a handsome Prince again.

To translate into something nearer the language of this book: as an infant you were naturally beautiful and loving because below your Bottom Line there was no face to screw up or pull, to confront people with or to push them off with. Also you were royally rich and richly royal because below that Line you had nothing, no personal property whatever to hang on to, as a miserable substitute for your worldwide real estate above the Line. But you caught the human disease and developed a huge below-Line tumour or wen, and the stress of living with it was terrible. Your cure has been the most drastic surgery imaginable – cephalectomy, no less – and so successful was the operation that every last cancerous cell of that malignant growth has been cut away. Thus you are now as healthy and as loving and as natural as when you were a little child. And perhaps even more beautiful.

To go back to the tale of the Prince and the frog: how different it is, in style and imagery, from the weighty pronouncements of the mystics: in substance, how like them! Folklore, with its light touch, has a way of showing the masses what they deeply and darkly know, and need somehow to raise to the light of consciousness. The same is true of nursery rhymes. Here is one of my favourites when I was four or five:

> Tom, Tom the piper's son
> He learned to play when he was young;
> But the only tune that he could play
> Was 'Over the hills and far away' –
> Over the hills and a great way off,
> And the wind will blow my topknot off.

Seventy-five years on, I haven't changed my tune. The wind of God is still blowing my topknot off at the World's End.

(v) BRINKMANSHIP

A perennial preoccupation in the history of Humanity – a

seemingly insoluble puzzle and threat and ever-fascinating challenge – is the Brink of the World: the possibility (or the necessity) of
finding it, and the danger (or the necessity) of falling over it when
found. Falling into – what?

Even as children – specially as children, I would say – infinity
charms and troubles us. Space, we figure, just *can't* go on forever
and ever: it must fade and fizzle out somewhere, or else be cut
clean off with God's almighty scissors. Equally, time *must* have a
stop, an end no less than a beginning, beyond which nothing
happens. And yet space and time *can't* stop, anywhere or anywhen.
Both alternatives are unimaginable. Now the remarkable feature
of this puzzle isn't that it's obviously insoluble – which makes it
mere fun and not worth taking seriously – but that its insolubility
is the very thing that makes it so intriguing. And not just intriguing
but so valuable. And not just valuable but the key to our felicity.

We may distinguish three steps or stages in the development of
the puzzle. Let's call them (1) The curving of the flat Earth, (2)
The curving of the 'flat' Universe and (3) The uncurvable Universe
of the First Person:

(1) The curving of the flat Earth

Up to the time of Columbus and the other great navigators it was
generally believed that the Earth was flat, a large but finite raft
floating in the Abyss. And so, very understandably, their crews
panicked and grew mutinous when they feared they were approaching that dreadful brink where the ocean ended and they would all
slither into the Bottomless.

For us now that fear has been overcome by the discovery that
the Earth is a sphere and its surface is curved: so that no globe-
trotter is in the slightest danger of falling off, never mind how far
and how long he trots.

(2) The curving of the 'flat' Universe

Up to and into our own century it was generally assumed that the

Universe too, was 'flat', in the sense that its space went straight on and on for ever, as did its time. On and on for ever and ever? It was unthinkable. Did they then come to an end, in an Abyss beyond space and time? So that, conceivably, one could find oneself falling into that Abyss? Not a risk to lose much sleep over, no doubt, but nevertheless a puzzle that refused to go away. Then Einstein came along with his celebrated concept of a Universe that is finite but unbounded. The higher mathematics of it are too high for most of us, so we have to be content with the picture of a space-time that is *curved*: which means that, no matter how far or how long we travel, we are no more in danger of arriving at the edge of the Universe than those sailors were of arriving at the edge of the Earth. Like them, if we carried on long enough, we would find ourselves back where we started.

What, in that case, lies beyond this finite (or allegedly finite) Universe? Certainly not a thin and worn-out kind of extramural space and time. In fact, the question is a non-question. It makes no sense. Better not try to picture the unpicturable. The funda-mental concepts for handling the objective Universe are not for distorting into percepts.

(3) The uncurvable Universe of the First Person

As First Person Singular, on the other hand, I have no trouble at all picturing what's going on. From the start my Universe is perceptual and not conceptual, and I have the utmost respect for the way it discloses itself to me. It's as if a stranger called on me; and, instead of carefully deducing what he might be like, I just looked and listened, and that way learned more about him in a minute than in a year of research. And when, by the same token, I have the humility to take the Universe as I find it, why I find it is indeed flat. I see that while its height and width are given, its depth and distance are constructed. (See pp. 86, 87 above.) Its space is such that its contents are presented here. And its time is such that its contents are presented now: past and future are real only insofar as they figure in the present moment.

The fact is that the First Person, the One I really am, cannot avoid the risk of tumbling out of space and time by 'curving' them. They flatly refuse to bend to my command. Indeed each of those sailors had the right idea and the best of reasons for alarm. If he'd bothered to look, he would have found that already as First Person, even before setting sail, he was head and shoulders over the edge and into the Abyss, with the rest up-ended to follow.

That self-evident fact, however, so far from stressing him to the point of mutiny, would have relieved him of all stress if he had given it his attention. As for ourselves, the lesson of this section with its three stages is that the world of second or third persons, because it manages to avoid the void and keep well clear of that horrid precipice, manages also to avoid the solution to the problem of our stress. Keeping out of a trouble that is in fact the greatest of blessings, it lands us in a trouble that is in fact *the* trouble, the bane of our lives.

One quite major objection comes up here:

All right. I *see* that my head has vanished over the world's edge into the Abyss. But still I'm far from headless. Why? Because I can *feel* the thing all over, with this hand. And if I can reach into this alleged pool of nothingness as easily as I can reach into any common or garden pool and fish about there, handling whatever lies beneath the surface, why then it's a pool of somethingness. Come on: this wonderful Beyond isn't, after all, as Beyond as all that! It's beyond the purview of one of my senses. That's all. So what?

This objection answers itself directly we make it the subject of a very simple experiment.

Experiment 23: The face of the world

Keep your eyes wide open throughout this experiment.

Feel your forehead all over, moving your fingers around . . .

Observe how that feeling belongs at the *top* of the scene, in the region of the ceiling or the sky . . .

Now slowly work your way down with your exploring fingers to your eyebrows, your nose, your cheeks . . . noting how the feel of them belongs to the *middle* of the picture – to the region of trees and houses and people. Or, if you happen to be indoors, to the region of walls and windows and doors and furniture . . .

Now slowly work down still further to your mouth and chin . . . noting how the feel of these belongs to the *bottom* of the picture – whether it's grass and paving slabs or carpet that you are looking at . . .

And how all terminates once more in those upside-down feet, those truncated legs, this cut-off shirtfront . . .

Finally, go back to the top of that scene and that face, and bring your exploring fingers down in one clearly visible movement to the bottom of both . . .

Notice some striking things about this unseen topknot of yours: what a surprise, what a joke it is – those upside-down feet so tiny, this right-way-up face so vast!

Simultaneously felt as your face and seen as the world's, it confirms your most intimate conjunction with all things and all faces. With it you plant on every face you meet a kiss, so to say.

Here indeed is a topknot and no bottomknot. Every feature from forehead to chin lies well above that cut-off shirtfront, well *above* your Bottom Line. *Below* it lies the Beyond which neither sight nor touch nor any of the senses, nor consciousness itself, can penetrate. That's why Zen calls it the Unconscious.

So much for our devil's advocate, with his loose talk of reaching into garden pools. I don't know about you, but he has certainly helped me to a new appreciation of my union with my above-line world. Brand new, today!

(vi) THE BEYOND AS THE GREAT UNCONSCIOUS

D. T. Suzuki, the scholar and master who brought Zen to the West in the earlier part of this century, called this Beyond – which is the medicine for all our stress – the Great Unconscious or the Cosmic Unconscious. In this he followed the lead of the founding fathers of Zen in China more than a millennium ago. He writes:

> The relative field of consciousness vanishes away *somewhere* [my italics] into the unknown, and this unknown, once recognized, enters into ordinary consciousness, and puts in good order all the complexities there which have been tormenting us to greater or lesser degrees . . . Our limited consciousness, inasmuch as we know its limitation, leads us to all sorts of worry, fear, unsteadiness. But as soon as it is realized that our consciousness comes out of something which, though not known in the way relative things are known, is intimately related to us, we are relieved of every form of tension and are thoroughly at rest and at peace with ourselves and with the world generally.

Later on Suzuki warns that, when this Great Unknown cannot assert itself naturally, it will break out violently or pathologically, and we shall then be 'hopelessly ruined'.

I would add that the way to avoid sickness and ruin is to cease overlooking the Boundary where the known and the Unknown meet, where the patient is in direct contact with the real Healer, and where the beyondness of the Beyond is absolute.

When taken seriously and not just read about, this prescription is no mere form of words or bloodless abstraction, no lofty sentiment incapable of testing and putting into daily practice. Quite the contrary, it springs to life directly it is anchored to this body and its needs. Nothing could be more homely. Down here, a vivid and ever-recurring reminder awaits me: one which, I hope, may serve you as well as it serves me. Bowing deeply yet again before the evidence and approaching its lower limit, I find two fasteners. The first is a humble zipper, ridiculous in its ordinariness. It is vertical. It requires unfastening several times a day, otherwise the results are uncomfortable, shaming and insanitary. Though in constant use, it is apt to go wrong and need replacing. The second is horizontal. Anything but ordinary, it marks out that magical Bottom Line of mine. Though it never goes wrong, it is disastrously easy to neglect, and through disuse to grow stiff and hard to work. Even more do I need to unzip this second fastener frequently. Otherwise the results are much more insalubrious than peeing in my pants. I become toxaemic, self-poisoned. Eventually I'm driven crazy, and my madness is evil-smelling. My cure is to keep pulling this horizontal zipper till it slides smoothly and stays pulled long enough to let out the toxic stuff that has accumulated behind it – the sort that is discharged downwards. For I possess two bladders, so to say – one for waste liquid and the other for waste stress – and both have to be emptied frequently if I'm not to fall ill.

What more useful habit, then, could I cultivate than this: every time I pull that vertical zipper I'm reminded to pull this horizontal one? Or, better still, to check that, in fact, it's already and forever unfastened?

(vii) FROM 180° TO 360° VISION

How to live this way, with Bottom Line unzipped? What does it look like, what does it amount to in daily, hourly, minute-to-minute practice?

It is life doubled, at a stroke. It's a sudden shift from 180° to 360° vision, from hemispherical to spherical existence, from being purblind and half-there to being clear-sighted and all-there, from incorporating the world's stress to incorporating also its cure. It means being together and not scatterbrained. It's being made whole.

This healing is no vague and hit-and-miss and esoteric treatment, but precise and specific and all-on-show. Each stressful condition above the Line has its matching medicine below the Line, every yonder its Beyond.

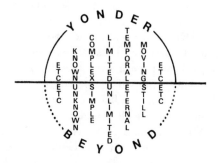

This many-sided therapy, with its elegance and thoroughness, isn't so much for understanding as for living. Hence our final experiment.

Experiment 24: 360° vision

Looking at this page, point to it. See how clearly it is given. Now turn your finger round 180° and point to what lies opposite, to what's taking in this page. See how this emptiness-for-that is even more clearly given than that is . . .

Looking to your far left, point to what's on show there. See how clearly given it is. Again, turn your finger round 180° and point inwards at what lies opposite, at what's taking that object in. Again, see how clearly it's given . . .

Looking to your far right, repeat the operation . . .

Check that, whatever point of the compass you are indicating, it has its counterpart here. That every object finds its niche or slot or pigeonhole in the subject. That every stressful condition out there has its own hospital bed right here, ready to receive the patient. Or rather, ready to turn him out, cured . . .

So much for the look of it. How does it *feel* to be cured, to be handicapped no longer? To be fully sighted and not purblind?

It feels like so many things, all of them worth trying on. Pick, from the following, what fits you:

You feel like an unshaded light. You feel like the four-faced Brahma, everlastingly gazing in all directions. You feel like a samurai on the qui vive, all eyes (including eyes in the back of your no-head), not to be taken by surprise, ready for anything. You feel like a lapsed saint piecing together his broken halo, and becoming wholly, wholly himself again. You feel like a little girl swirling her hula hoop. You feel like a can of delicious soup, half clear and half thick, opened all round with a can-opener and with the lid off. You feel like a lover who at last has found his better half. You feel as you do in the Underground when you come out of the tunnel into the overground: after all that stressful squashing you've got yourself a seat, and are relaxing into being the silence underlying the clackitty-clack of wheels on rails and the still simplicity underlying all that suburban confusion as it rushes by.

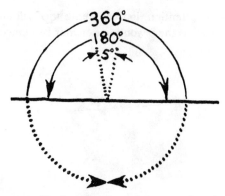

The stress you suffer from is inversely proportional to your angle of vision. It varies from the ill health of tunnel vision – maybe a mere 5° – to the partial health of 180°; and thence, suddenly, to the full health of 360°.

But really it's not a question of ceasing to be sick and one-sided, and then becoming a healthy all-rounder, but of seeing you've never been anything else.

(vii) CONCLUSION

Once having occurred, Being's business is to be – lavishly. But in the beginning, in the first place, it had no business at all to be. The Universal Mum is still in shock at having given birth to herself. The Great Irregularity behind all her regularities, she will never get used to having happened. As for Non-happening or Non-being – which is the name of the maternity ward she finds herself in – why, she can only bite the back of her hand.

If you thrill to the inexpressible wonder of what's beyond Being, it is as Being and for Being that you do so. And if you are clean bowled over and miraculously healed by its incomprehensibility, it is because incomprehensible doesn't mean inaccessible, and mysterious doesn't mean obscure. This which in one sense is the darkest of all secrets is in another sense the clearest of the clear, more obvious than all else, shining with its own utmost brilliance.

Reversing your attention, look now into the brilliance of your Beyondness, as well as the beyondness of your Brilliance.

What *was* all that nonsense about you – You who are beyond the Beyond – suffering from stress?

PART FOUR

THE PRACTICE

One can practise while engaged in work. It may be difficult in the early stages for a beginner, but after some practice it will soon be effective and the work will not be found a hindrance to meditation.

What is practice?

Constant search for 'I', the source of the ego. Inquire 'Who am I?' The pure 'I' is the reality, the absolute Existence–Consciousness–Bliss. When that is forgotten, all miseries crop up.

Ramana Maharshi

Sit down before the fact as a little child, and be prepared to give up every preconceived notion; follow humbly wherever and to whatever abyss Nature leads, or you shall learn nothing.

T. H. Huxley

The above-quoted passage from T. H. Huxley appeared at the beginning of the book. It reappears at the end because it has, meanwhile, become even more cogent. Now we BOW DOWN rather than sit down before the evidence, and it leads us to the ABYSS rather than to an abyss.

Allowing ourselves to be led there more and more frequently, by more and more routes – this is our practice.

18

THE PRACTICE

TWO WAYS OF PRACTISING

Having read at least the first half of this book and done the experiments it contains, you have already begun to put into practice its method of dealing with stress. This final chapter is about how to continue and develop your practice, and how to overcome some of the difficulties you are likely to meet.

There are two main ways of practising: the kind that's set up as a regular daily exercise, and the kind that consists of coping, from your No-thingness or Bottom Line, with whatever stresses it happens to be coming up with at this moment. Admittedly the first is a contrived regime and somewhat artificial, while the second is natural, the essential discipline set up by life itself: the only snag is that one so easily forgets to operate it. It follows that most of us at the start, and some of us for a good part of our lives, can do with a routine, a programme of exercises that will keep us to the work, preparing us when we are least stressed for when we are most stressed. We can choose the conditions and take the time for our homework. Life is less considerate.

Our suggested weekly regime is a progressive one, corresponding (as you will see) to the first seven chapters of Part Two. Also to the seven spells of the Enchantress who figures at the beginning of Part Three: each day of the week weaves a counter-spell.

Broadly, the routine works out like this:

(i) Start the day by reading the chapter for that day and *carrying out its experiments.*

(ii) Through the day find opportunities to put into effect 'Today's Exercise'.

(iii) Having completed one week's programme go back and start again on Monday's theme.

	PAGE	DAY	TODAY'S EXERCISE	THROUGH THE DAY
	21	Mon.	Single Eye	While seeing what you're looking *at*, see what you're looking *out of* – this one, oval, huge, stressless, frameless Window.
	26	Tues.	No Face	Check where you keep your face – out there in the mirror, safely behind glass, and where others and their cameras are taking it in.
	35	Wed.	At Large	Have a sense of filling the scene, of having no boundaries. See how absurd is the idea you are *in* a body.
	54	Thurs.	Trading Faces	Whoever you're facing – in the home, street, office – see you're *not* face to face. See that it's face there to absence of face here.
	67	Fri.	Your Still Centre	When walking, running, travelling by car, bus or train, see that you're stationary. Let the shifting scene handle the stress of motion.
	83	Sat.	Your Wealth	See how no distance separates you from what you're looking at: which means it couldn't be more *yours* than it is.
	98	Sun.	Your Heart's Desire	Beat stress by recognizing, in what's been happening to you this week, your real intention. From its Source say YES to it.

THE RESULTS OF YOUR PRACTICE

Naturally we expect prompt benefits from our practice, in spite of the fact that we are just commencing to reverse beliefs and to break social moulds that have been accumulating and hardening about us for decades. And naturally we are discouraged when it seems nothing's happening. To this there are five answers, all of them encouraging.

First, to do the experiments at all is to do them perfectly. You can't *more-or-less* see yourself as Emptiness, or see *more or less* of It. This being so, the effect has to share in the perfection of its cause. From the very first time, the results of your seeing This are profound and certain, though probably quite invisible to you. And of course each act of seeing makes the next one easier, till one day – to your surprised delight – you discover that the new habit has all along been busy establishing itself. For example, the time comes when you find your face is automatically absent in favour of the face of the one you love, and even in favour of the faces of people you're unconscious of loving at all; and you bathe in the realization that you're *built* for loving and being everyone, and for confronting no one. Its like weighing rice: though it's the last grain which tips the scales, each grain is necessary to that switch-over.

Second, it's quite likely that *you* will be the very last one to notice what's been happening to you – how stress-free you now are, on hitherto stress-inducing occasions. And, after all, this is only to be expected: the central You has been perfect all along, and any improvement in the peripheral you is for *others* out there to pick up. What is for *you* to pick up is the deep satisfaction of being, right here at the Centre, your un-improvable Source.

Third, don't only go by what you *feel*. The commonest complaint is: 'All right, I see myself as No-thing vis-à-vis this or that distressful thing, yet that thing goes on bugging me. I don't feel a bit better!' The truth is that as No-thing you *can't* feel any better or worse, but must stay unaffected by all the good and bad things you give house-room to. Go on consciously being this neutral Capacity, and see what in the long run happens to its contents. You will surely find yourself saying YES! to them more and more often, and becoming less and less eager to label them 'Good' or 'Bad'. And on occasions when this practice of acceptance gets too difficult (as it's bound to do sometimes) remember the joy of Richard Wurmbrand in that dreadful Romanian prison, and take heart, and go on seeing.

Fourth, you are now beginning to live from the Source of your life, from the No-thing you *are* instead of the thing you thought you were. You are being truthful about life, living it as it is. It follows that your life must already be working out better in all sorts of ways that you are overlooking. After all, it would be one Hell of a Universe in which it paid to live from what's *not* so, from delusion. It's irrelevant whether at this moment you *like* what's so. That's the way things are, and the way You are, and you're sensibly going along with both in a spirit of trust.

Fifth and last, it remains a stern fact that, while it's the easiest thing imaginable to see yourself intermittently as bare Capacity, it's far from easy to keep up the seeing. But isn't this contrast what we deeply desire? What is life without audacity and daring, without adventure, without a tremendous challenge to put us on our mettle? And what challenge can compare with this one great adventure which is never completed, yet is ever complete because you can enjoy being at the goal from the very first step along the road? Furthermore, this is not a big hard thing to do made up of little hard things to do. Each is as easy as winking. Now.

HOW WELL-TESTED IS THIS METHOD?

Before committing yourself to a strenuous (or let's say, demanding) regime and investing time and effort in it, you have every reason to ask: how well-tested is this novel – and in some ways unique – method of dealing with stress?

First, let's take the special techniques presented in this book. The tools for the job, such as the paper bag and the hole-in-the-card (pp. 54 and 114), and the procedures such as the pointing finger and stopping the clock (pp. 8 and 264) have for the past twenty years or so been found to work. My friends and I have shared them with tens of thousands of people in North America and Europe (on both sides of that Curtain), in sessions of 2,500 participants down to a handful, and in countless person-to-(no)person encounters. And virtually all have taken the point – commonly with astonishment and enthusiasm. (How could anyone deny that the near end of that bag – surprise, surprise! – is open and empty?) On the other hand, the number of people who, having seen this Openness and Emptiness perfectly (there's no other way), have then gone on to cultivate the experience till it cultivates itself and bears fruit in abundance – this number is comparatively small, or so it seems. For some who *appear* unaffected the seeing could prove to be a healthy but encysted seed, programmed to germinate when it and the times are ripe. No doubt there are others who from the start do go on with the great work, unknown to me and my particular friends. We have no organization for keeping tabs on our one-time clients. (Hardly the word for them, but it's better than 'paper-baggers'.) And of course, having once seen This, they have – they *are* – the whole story and the know-how, and need us no longer. As for those 'seeing' friends who have remained in close touch – the results of their faithful practice are, in my view, extremely varied, often impressive and beautiful, and invariably beneficent.

So much for our particular route. Breaking new ground though it does, it certainly runs alongside, and in places links up with, the Broad Highway that has lain wide open for some three thousand years and seen numberless travellers Home to the Goal – only to discover they were there all the time. At the heart of all the great religions – Hinduism, Buddhism, Taoism, Judaism, Christianity and Islam – lies the certainty that all people and creatures are regional phenomena or appearances of One Central Reality to which many names are given provisionally – *Awareness* being as useful as any I know. And the purpose of life (they teach) is to return to that Source and Centre, to come Home to Oneself, to look within and find and *be* This – This whose definition is that it is indefinable, This which is mysterious beyond telling yet instantly accessible because it is What we forever are. This core of religion, the fire in its belly, has down the centuries been damped down, watered down, spat upon, buried, apparently stamped out again and again – all without lasting effect. It remains the glowing Centre of all 'mystical' experience. And its effectiveness for living – in our terms, for coping with stress – has stood the test of the ages and come down to us more brilliantly proven and workable than ever. It is well called the Perennial Philosophy. This book draws on and continues that tradition, which it aims to up-date by stripping it of non-essentials and picturesque irrelevancies and priestly complications and cover-ups, and exposing the Core which is simpler than simple. So while our techniques here are as contemporary and streamlined and de-mythologized as we know how to make them, what lies back of them all is as old and rich as Humanity, as the world itself, and is quite the most thoroughly tested of all Humanity's great inspirations.

It isn't *necessary* for you to look beneath the deliberately secular scheme of this book and proceed to dig into its religious roots. (Unexamined and undisturbed roots grow quite healthy flowers and fruit.) But if you are at all interested to try it, this exploration into 'mystical experience' can be of much help in your practice of coping with stress, providing you with the backing and intimate friendship of many great souls down the ages, and introducing you to some of the many roads and byroads that lead Home to the Source. I think you will find it surprising and perhaps inspiring to discover how the truly agnostic approach and the doubt-based experiments of this book – calling in question our most taken-for-granted assumptions and beliefs – take us at once to the sources of Humanity's spiritual life-history, and indeed to Humanity's instinctive way of handling the problem of stress.

PASS IT ON

Usually, new skills and techniques have to be thoroughly learned before they can be passed on. This one is different. Having done the very first experiment in the book – and seen your finger pointing to your Emptiness-Fullness – you are at once perfectly qualified to initiate anyone. No way can you transmit an inferior version of this in-seeing. In fact I would urge you, for the sake of your own encouragement, for the sake of your friends, for the sake of Humanity's future, to pass on this truly liberating experience. You don't have to understand all the ins and outs of it (who does?), much less to transmit them, but only to carry out with your partner whatever experiments seem indicated at the time: it's what you *see* that counts, not what you think of it. You'll find there's no better way of staying with your Emptiness-Fullness than introducing your friends to theirs.

But it won't do to push the experience at them. A reliable indication is this: if your urge to share is carefree and relaxed, go right ahead; if it's rather intense, look out; if it's stressful, it's likely to prove counterproductive for both parties. To take off the pressure it helps to remember that all are living perfectly from their Emptiness-Fullness regardless, and it's *their* business whether or not they wish to be aware of the fact, just at present.

One highly practical reason for showing people This, is in order to set up with them an informal grouping of true friends who are consciously living – as far as they are able – from What is identical in everyone. Fellowship of this kind is quite the best of all encouragements and supports: and no wonder – the headless condition is extremely infectious. So, instead of waiting for like-minded companions to turn up, *create* them! This is the most rewarding and happy work I know. And it finds you lifelong friends whose love, like the shared Identity it's a manifestation of, is independent of human merit and quite indestructible.

In passing this experience on to the world you are doing it an incomparable service. And yourself as well. The way to cultivate your gift is freely to give it away. What has kept me 'seeing Who I am' over the years is the fact that I was given something to *do* about it, an active contribution to make. Without that work I doubt whether I would have stuck to the vision which inspired it.

The unique form your own service takes, dear Reader, will reveal itself. Go for it! It will bring you a joy like no other.

The Prince, the Tadpole and the Frog

This slightly amended version of an article that appeared in a recent number of the *Transactional Analysis Journal* will be of interest to readers familiar with Eric Berne's *Games People Play*. Broadly its thesis, in the words of Dr Hans Selye, is that 'most of our tensions and frustrations stem from the compulsive need to act the role of someone we are not'.

Let me put it like this. Things are stressed. If I play the game of being something negative – a nasty frog – I'm stressed in one sort of way. If I come off it and play instead the game of being something positive – a nice frog – I'm stressed in another sort of way. Only by ceasing to pretend I'm any sort of frog-thing, nice or nasty, and admit to being the Prince whose name is Aware No-thingness, am I out of trouble.

What follows is a variation on this theme, which is in fact the theme of the whole book, couched here in T A language.

THE PRINCE, THE TADPOLE AND THE FROG

AN INQUIRY INTO THE NATURAL CHILD, THE SPELL-BINDING PARENT, THE SPELLBOUND CHILD AND THE SPELL-LIFTING ADULT

D. E. Harding

Abstract

In the opinion of Steiner (1975), 'The first and most important concept . . . which Berne introduced to psychiatry is embodied in his aphorism "People are born princes and princesses, until their parents turn them into frogs"' (p. 2). The present paper, taking this view, examines its historical background and its theoretical and practical implications for today. It goes into such questions as: How does the parent work that magic? What are the essential differences between the prince or princess and the frog? How does it feel to be the former, then be reduced to the latter? Can the mature frog learn to reverse the magic spell and turn itself back into the prince or princess? Which is the deep therapy – this abrupt switch of identity, or gradually becoming a more together and self-sufficient frog jumping energetically round the bog? To what extent is this slow development the precondition of that abrupt metamorphosis? Does the parental black magic ever disfigure – let alone destroy – the original face of the prince or princess? Or do those royal features remain intact, hidden under the frog-mask that – spellbound – the players have to wear in 'The Face Game' or 'Confrontation' (Harding, 1967, 1986)? If the aim of TA is that one should become game-free (Berne, 1964, pp. 178 ff.) and not just trade in bad games for better games, and this means dropping even the best masks one is hiding behind, how is this done? These questions are tackled by the writer in the light of his experience over the last thirty years encouraging people to face that crucial issue: *what is my true (i.e., game-free) identity?* And by the reader who is urged to take none of this on trust, but to test all rigorously and in actual practice.

The Prince

We have four sets of clues – four different sources of information – as to what the natural child (i.e., the prince or princess) really is. And by *really is* we mean what the child is for itself where it is, in contrast to what it looks like to us over here, its central reality in contrast to all these regional appearances which that reality is giving rise to, the insider's story as the subject in contrast to the outsider's version of it as an object.

(i) The first set of clues are supplied by the child directly, before it learns to talk, in the shape of its behaviour. Thus the toy that is dropped out of sight is not looked for: presumably disappearance means annihilation. Thus remote objects such as the picture on the wall or the moon in the sky are fingered; presumably distance does not exist for the child. All is taken to be present, no less its own than those legs and arms are. Thus its face in the mirror is not singled out for attention; presumably it is just an ordinary feature of the scene. Thus the child has a way of burying its face in a cushion, then looking up and laughing; presumably it is having fun annihilating and recreating the world.

(ii) As soon as the child starts to talk, clues multiply fast. One of the author's young friends burst out with; 'I'm *very* big!' Another (and this in his experience is not unusual), when counting those present, insisted on leaving herself out; counting herself in would (it seems) have been like counting the room in with the people, or the purse with the money. Another, bringing home a panoramic photograph of the whole school, successfully named everybody – except for one total stranger. Herself, of course! Another child, standing in the bath and staring down at himself, exclaimed; 'I don't have a head!' And so on. This is a small sample of the evidence collected by the writer, indicating that the natural child is *for itself* a very different kind of person from the one we perceive.

(iii) The third order of clues, of evidence about the intrinsic nature of the natural child, is furnished much later in life by Seers – so-called enlightened men and women who, claiming that they have regained their childhood honesty and simplicity, announce to an incredulous or indifferent world that they are the very opposite of what they look like to the world. Many of them, for example, declare that, being wholly emptied of themselves, they are wholly filled with others. They experience themselves as nothing but space or capacity for everything. Some point out that distance is for them no more than a useful fiction, and for the rest of us a very costly one. Taken seriously, it progressively parts seer and seen – resulting in alienation from the universe, loneliness, deprivation. Some have come round to looking in their mirrors to see what they are *not*, to remind them that they could not *be* less like what they *appear to be*. One Zen master explained he was not sure how tall he was, but perhaps it was around thirty feet! Others stressed their facelessness or headlessness. Most importantly, Seers belonging to different epochs and very diverse cultures have boldly maintained that their true and inmost nature (as distinct from their superficial human nature), in fact the One they all claim they really are, is nothing less than the source and goal of all things, continually creating and destroying and recreating the world. And of course some notable Seers have stressed that the hallmark of their kind is that they have become like small children again. In sum, over the past 3,000 years or so, these exceptional men and women have (it seems) been reliving with great intensity essential aspects of their childhood, and assuring us that in reality they have never outgrown it. Moreover, this inner realization appears on the whole to have been backed up by the Seers' lifestyle – by their spontaneity, their manifest enjoyment of the world's simplicities, sense of fun, capacity for love, grace in movement, and all manner of behavioural nuances that are in the very best sense childlike.

(iv) Finally, we come to our fourth set of clues about the inside story of the natural child – of the prince or princess. It is that crucial and clinching piece of evidence which can only be furnished by the reader of this paper. It requires you to check whether, right now in your firsthand experience, you are still *for yourself* as you were when for others you were a very small child. This means, in particular, checking that you are not *on present evidence* peering out of two tiny peep-holes in an opaque and very complicated and clearly-defined lump of stuff, but are gazing (wide-eyed and single-eyed, or rather no-eyed) out of boundless empty space so immediately filled with the scene that it cannot be divorced from it. That you are not, *on present evidence*, a millionth of an inch distant from this printing, or from the rest of the things around. (Where would you measure to at the 'near' end, and anyway how long would the tape-measure read when viewed end-on?) That you are not, *on present evidence*, confronting those faces in the room with one of your own, but resemble a portrait gallery or film show in which they are exhibits. That you are not, *on present evidence*, in this world at all, but rather it is in you. In fact, the writer's suggestion is that there is no end to the rediscovery of the obvious, this reactivation of the natural child in you, once you get the hang of it. And no end to the entertainment and rejuvenation it freely offers.

To sum up so far, then: we have been examining four orders of clues about the original nature of the child. We have noted some of the behaviour peculiar to very young children; listened to the sort of thing that older ones have to say about themselves; discovered that childlike Seers tell much the same tale; and have ourselves looked within and (it may be) found exactly what they find: reader and writer alike donning the august mantle of the Seer – as we have a perfect right to do, no matter how brief our exercise of that right. And finally we may conclude that these four pieces of evidence dovetail and support one another. In brief, the writer suggests that we have uncovered our original nature. A worthwhile enterprise, if ever there was one!

Prince into Tadpole

However, from the start the parent has been busy pronouncing the spell which will soon turn the prince or princess into a frog.

Actually into a mere tadpole; it will take decades for that inadequate little creature to grow into a proper, full-size, O K amphibian.

The spell has many versions. Some of them are complimentary – not to say overdone – 'What a *heavenly* baby!' 'Just *look* at those rosy cheeks!' 'Let's see those dimples, that smile again!' Others are rude. But flattering or the reverse, the effect is much the same – the tadpole is on the way and the verbal messages are being supplemented throughout by all manner of approving and disapproving nonverbal ones – tones of voice, facial expressions, modes of handling – which are essential ingredients of the magic.

The effect is multiplied as soon as the child begins to understand the wording of the spell. The rosy cheeks and dimples and so on start taking shape. So do other, less charming characteristics. Here is one real-life version of the spell which moulds them: 'You are not O K. And why? Because you are "small, dirty, clumsy, in a world controlled by tall, clean, and deft adults."[1] That's how you must see yourself.'[2] But of course this truly bewitching spell, aimed at shaping the child's future but put out as a statement of present fact, too soon does become such a statement. Here is the perfect self-fulfilling prophecy, as the young child, helpless under its powerful influence, gradually learns to co-operate in cutting itself down to size, in becoming not O K, a tadpole in all respects. In short, very like the small, dirty, inept creature which the critical parent perceives.

[1] *New York Times Magazine*, Nov. 22, 1972, Interview with Thomas A. Harris as quoted in Steiner (1974) p. 10.

[2] This version of the spell, masquerading as a statement of fact, is reminiscent of medieval animal psychology which described the nightingale's song as the passionate outburst of love welling from the bird's heart and addressed to its adored mate, the snake as wicked and filthy, the peacock as conceited, and so forth. In fact, that old-time anthropomorphism hardly went so far as this modern counterpart, which – in the case quoted – goes out of its way to attribute to the natural child a view of itself which has no relation to the one it surely does have. As we have seen, the indications are that the child is *for itself* far bigger than the biggest of those adults around, and far more powerful. As for the notion that the periodical warmth, accompanied by the pleasurable sensation and that interesting smell, is *dirty* in the natural child's own experience – what could be more absurd? Shitting comes later.

Before we go further, let us not forget (if our thesis so far is valid) how 'in the right' the unlimited child is here, how 'in the wrong' is the magic which closes in upon it, how glaring is the lie which that magic pronounces. Who but itself is *in a position* to tell the child who and what it really is for itself at centre, zero inches from itself? Who has access to that spot but its sole inhabitant, who remains through life the one authority on what is there, everyone else being wide of the mark by inches and feet? But how could the young child – that solitary interior authority – prevail against the combined weight of those innumerable exterior authorities who so consistently contradict it? To use picturesque language, is it surprising that the innocent victim of the plot, outvoted overwhelmingly in a rigged election by falsified voting papers, concedes defeat?

But defeat occurs only after much struggle and hesitation. For years the prince or princess has some stamina left, some residual immunity against social fictions and magic spells. At first this super-spell (*you are what you look like*) works intermittently. When happily playing, not confronted by grown-ups and not guilt-laden, the signs are that the child is still for itself immense, the only real grown-up around, at large, First Person singular, no-thing and everything, free. And that, conversely, when unhappy and under pressure, faced by (and faced up by) those disapproving frowns and admonishing or accusing fingers (so sure they are pointing at something right here), why of course this something has to be just an undersized and awkward creature that needs to develop as quickly as possible into one of those self-assured and clever grownups.

The writer has observed that this uneasy alternation between the unadapted and adapted child may go on for as long as ten years or more, or stop short as early as three or four years – so widely do individuals differ. All the same (unless the child remains unadapted for life, and very likely subject to institutional care) it does in the end become, for itself no less than for the world, an object first and foremost, a young thing rapidly becoming an older one, a hopeful tadpole well on the way to the full dignity of froghood.

When we remember how much of the child's development is the development of its language, and how much of that language is frog language, it is surely astonishing how some children can hold out for so long. But given time the spell wins, thanks largely to its insidious and rarely noticed double-talk. Here for the reader (as always) to check, is just one of its duplicities. Since the *predicates* are the same in the sentences 'I eat' and 'you eat', we take it that the *facts* are the same. The truth is that 'you eat' means 'alien substances are being pushed into a toothed slit in a small and tightly packed sphere, where they remain insipid,' while 'I eat' means 'they are being pushed into an unbounded void, where they become tasty.' Because our language suppresses it, the immense contrast between these two happenings is progressively obscured as we grow up. The general effect of such semantic confusion, which is paralleled in the life of all our senses, is to water them down, to take the tang and sparkle out of them. Until it is challenged and reversed, the effect of language thus misused is to devalue the rich immensity of our First Personhood, and to collapse us into mechanical objects from which practically all inwardness or subjectivity has been drained. Thus the prince and princess are *talked* into froghood. This is a version of Berne's view (1964, p. 178) that 'seeing and hearing have a different quality for infants than for grownups'.

Small wonder, then, if the spell works a near perfect magic in the end – one so potent that it is now far from being a merely external influence or imposition. Increasingly, it seems, the growing child experiences a need to become just *like them*, a thoroughly normal and paid-up member of the human club, unquestioningly obedient to its taken-for-granted rules, however arbitrary. In fact, so insistent is its urge to belong, to be welcomed into the magic circle, that it tends to believe and do practically anything it is told to believe and do. For instance, there are the virtually universal and seemingly harmless beliefs that, on the highway, THIS one, in her or his actual experience, is *moving along* at 50 m.p.h., through the *still* countryside, looking at it through *two* eyes, and *seeing* its wide range of distances – plus many other commonplace delusions or superstitions. (The reader is invited to check that they *are* superstitions the next time she or he travels by car.) As for the more specialized and plainly harmful sort of belief, think of the variety of mutilated bodies and minds and behaviour sequences taken to be the seal of adulthood among highly cultivated peoples, let alone 'primitives.' And if we modern westerners imagine we impose no comparable conditions of entry into our superior culture pattern, we really are spellbound to the limit! Some of our beliefs, to a candid visitor from another galaxy, must seem unbelievably odd, if not actually mad.

Tadpole into Frog

Sooner or later, if everything goes normally, the not-OK tadpole, having long ago forgotten about its royal ancestry (or happy to have grown out of that childish nonsense), grows up to be a more and more OK and self-confident and successful frog. It may even go on to become a super-frog dominating the bog.

And therefore still more OK? It by no means follows. There are so many well-known instances of nothing failing like too much success. The names of tragic personalities at the top of the worlds of entertainment, the arts and business immediately occur to one. Nor need this unhappy outcome greatly surprise. Our contention is that playing 'Frogs' is not just one more game and self-deceiving pretence: but that it is *the* game and *the* lie – also known as 'The Face Game' or 'Confrontation' (Harding, 1967, 1986) – the Game from which all lesser games derive. That in fact it is that most ancient and deep-rooted – and exclusively human – fiction which, though workable (and necessary) in the life-story of the species and of the individual up to a point, goes on to prove increasingly counterproductive and finally disastrous.

Our thesis goes on to propose the following: The better one plays this Game of games the worse off one is in the long run, the more profound is one's self-deception, and the more severe its attendant troubles. In other words, the more magnificently self-sufficient, powerful, independent (and in this sense OK) one seems to be as a frog, the less OK one really is. In fact, there can no more be a thoroughly OK frog than there can be a thoroughly true lie or factual fiction; for frogs have a built-in flaw – they are make-believe, a game or pretence, not real. The whole matter of OKness is apt to be misconceived and inverted. By nature the child is OK, as Berne maintained, and grows up to become more and more not-O K the more that child is superseded. It is the grown-up who is mature enough to know that he or she has outgrown very little, in fact the one whose frog-mask is getting more and more uncomfortable and awry, who is liable to find it slipping off altogether. And revealing? Why the prince or princess, of course!

Frog into Prince

But we anticipate, and must go a long way back in our story.

From the earliest times competition between groups of humans – for food, mates, shelter, territory – worked increasingly to the advantage of those who were more able to look at their world objectively, more open to new ways of processing the data. Fortune favoured those who learned humility in front of the evidence. Their science, gathering speed, grew increasingly scientific and far-reaching, and the more technically advanced societies won on almost all counts.

In due course practically all the scientist's discoveries about the external world are turned back and applied to the scientist. As a scientist, one becomes one's own subject matter and field of study, and always the aim is to extend control over that intimate field. Closing in on oneself from outside, one tends to refer everything inwards. One's overall view of oneself from a distance – systematized into the disciplines of history, anthropology, sociology, behavioural psychology – is filled in by nearer views – systematized into physiology, cytology, biochemistry, chemistry, physics, particle physics. One is getting nearer and nearer home, ever closer to what all things – including oneself, the scientist – really are at centre, to the ultimate substratum beyond the quark.

One seems to be almost home, almost in possession of the inmost secret. But one can never gain admittance from outside – say by further sorting out the space-time continuum or chasing the Quark beneath the quark. One will never make that final stop or terminate that asymptotic curve. Nor does one need to. One is already home, and has been there all along. The scientist has only to reverse the arrow of attention, to look in at what he or she is looking out of, in order to round off the job and arrive at the inside story of what he and she and all beings essentially are. Responding to our invitation earlier in this paper, it may well be that the reader has already taken that same definitive step which was no step, conducted that ultimate experiment in physics which leads straight into metaphysics, made that last frog-leap out of the bog into the palace. Seeing into his or her *intrinsic* nature as this nameless, spotless, silent, still, colourless clarity, the reader is capacious of the world's endless riches, and truly royal. As this aware no-thing, he or she is everything. All this is set down here for verifying, or falsifying, as the case may be.

If the former, what has happened at long last is that the parent's magic spell, initially so powerful but in the end powerless against reality, has boomeranged, has worked its own destruction. Driven by its own inner logic, it leads back to the prince or princess who has been sitting quietly at home and in good health all the while, and never did become in the slightest froglike. In other words, the truly adult frog whose business (solely in frog interests, of course) is the processing of reality, is obliged to cultivate the truthfulness and impartiality which lead towards the rediscovery of his or her own identity as no frog at all, but royalty in disguise. The science of the objective world leads into the science of oneself as an object or 3rd person, which in turn (given this leap out of frogland) leads into the science of oneself as the subject or First Person (Harding, 1974). As the enemy of lies and therefore of games, science has scored a double triumph.

Note the foundation on which true science has been built from the start, namely on unprejudiced perception, on looking to see, on refusal to rely on tradition or belief or unchecked theory or mere speculation, but instead on the humble and patient reading of metre rods, dials, timepieces, and so on. Medieval science did not get off the ground until people stopped settling questions about the universe by looking up the answers in the Bible or Aristotle or any other authority, and dared just to inspect and experiment with what was actually on show. *The science of the object is no sounder than the perceptual base on which it rests. Now exactly the same is true of the science of the subject, of the First Person, of the prince or princess. Turning the direction of the scientific inquiry round*

318

180°, from the observed to the observer, does not reduce the necessity for relying on the evidence provided here and now by looking to see and discarding all belief and opinion imported from other times and places.[1] Consciously to revert from being a frog to being the prince or princess is to be game-free, and this is to be a Seer; this is to see what one really is at centre in and for oneself, seeing what is actually on show here and not trying to see what one is told to see, or hopes to see, or happens to feel comfortable with.

The King/Queen

Of course one does not permanently revert to being the prince or princess from the moment of first sighting one's intrinsic nature. The spell is not so easily shaken off. What took so long to bind me, then went on tightening its grip year after year, is going to take a lot of patient unbinding. In other words, a lot of coming to my senses, again and again and again. I have to keep nudging myself awake from my coma, repeatedly bringing my wandering attention to where I am coming from and what I am looking out of, until in the end it is quite natural to be natural, to stop pretending to be what I am not, to play games no longer, to live from the no-thing-I-am. And my experience assures me of this: It is as *efficient* to live from this central no-thing-I-am as it was *inefficient* – stressful and debilitating – to live from the peripheral thing-I-am-not, from one or another of my appearances. To put it mildly, the Game was not worth the candle.

Now at last the prince or princess has grown up into the king or queen. And has surely done so the hard and humbling and only possible way, via that painful cutting down to size, that dethronement and demoting of the unique First Person to the rank of the altogether ordinary 3rd person, and that weird and testing frog-charade. What the Seers claim is that in the end they enjoy a

---

[1] As a first-hand demonstration of this turn-around through 180°, the reader was invited to conduct experiments on herself or himself earlier in this paper. The italicized passage here will make sense to the extent to which he or she actually carried out those little experiments.

conviction that nothing really went wrong, and a peace which is more and not less vigorous than all that frenetic leaping around the bog ever was.

The Six Spell-Breakers

(i) As a rule the magic spell is amazingly effective, so deceitful and addictive that its victims are for life quite unaware of its existence. Indeed, when they sense the slightest danger of its losing its grip they are apt to be very upset, without knowing why.

And this in spite of the fact that it is demonstrably ridiculous. '*You are what you look like*' is surely so naive it is not worth serious consideration. How could I be, at o inches from me, what I look like 100 inches away? I have only to look right here to see what *I am* getting, and over there in my mirror to see what *you are* getting, to see there is no similarity at all between them. Laughter seems the only spell-breaker that is altogether appropriate. But, for good measure, here are five others. The first two recapitulate what has gone before; the rest are additional.

(ii) Look at, listen to, and learn from young children who have not yet fallen under the spell, and adult Seers who claim to have broken free. In various ways they tell the world that they are boundless capacity for it.

(iii) The third and indispensable spell-breaker requires the reader to re-check – in his or her immediate experience at this moment – that there is no thing (awareness is not a thing) that is taking in this line of printing, this paragraph and this page, the furniture in the room, the view from the window. Failure to go on checking, to continue making quite sure that the seer altogether vanishes in favour of the seen, inevitably means that the seer – out of long habit – falls again under the spell that makes a something of him or her.

(iv) Our fourth is an optional extra. It re-examines the scriptures of the world in the light of this simplest and most obvious – yet (we suggest) deepest – of insights, using it as a metal-detector to sort out the precious ore from the huge masses of sand and rock which hide it, and uncover the gold of our intrinsic nature. It can be truly encouraging to find how ancient and widespread are the search and the discovery we have been concerned with here.

(v) Our fifth spell-breaker (like the fourth, indicative rather than conclusive) relies on the secular evidence supplied by mythology, philosophy, literature and art. The typical fairytale or legend has for hero a lad whose foster parents are peasants but whose real parentage is royal or Olympian. His lifework is to regain his lost rank by overcoming a succession of almost insuperable obstacles – with some help from above. Plato was only the most articulate and celebrated of the many ancients who pictured the infant coming down from a heaven of light and divine knowledge into a dark and deluded world which has long ago forgotten its supernal origins. How else, indeed, can the child so surely recognize as self-evident such truths as it comes across here below, unless by that *anamnesis* which is a sudden recalling of the wisdom it enjoyed in heaven? The main theme of Thomas Traherne's *Centuries* is the many-sided beatitude of the natural child, and the 'dirty devices' that grown-ups contaminate it with. Better known is Wordsworth's *Intimations of Immortality from Recollections of Early Childhood*. ('Trailing clouds of glory do we come, from God who is our home . . .' But too soon 'the shades of the prison house begin to gather about the growing boy.') Again, as most real artists would acknowledge, all the drawings of children are comparable with his or her own most inspired work – up to the moment when the child, falling under the parental spell, sees itself as an artistic young thing, instead of no-thing but space for things – including drawings – to happen in.

The foregoing is a random sampling of humanity's intuition about the exalted status of the child in its midst. None of it means that we should or could stay like that, and refuse to play 'Frogs' till we are proficient at the game. There is no easy and direct route from the clear land of the young child to the still clearer land of the childlike Seer, no freeway that does not take us through the bewitched and fogbound country of so-called grown-ups. What it does mean is that somehow our species *knows* that true adulthood is the working out, at a more conscious level, of all that is best in childhood, so that eventually the wheel of our life turns full circle. The last part should be as game-free as the first. And the unavoidable game-playing interlude – unless we are gluttons for punishment or determined cases of arrested development – should not be allowed to drag on through middle age and beyond.

(vi) Finally, there is the spell-breaker of *practice*. What are the clinical results of this in-seeing when it is sustained, this ever-renewed reactivation of the natural child in us? Is it true that all the therapies which overlook the central problem of *who* requires therapy prove at best palliatives? That in the last resort I have only one malaise – my mistaken identity, my spineless and pathetic willingness to be whatever they tell me I am – and only one cure, my true identity, my daring to be what I see I am? That so long as my Parent holds any part of my Child spellbound I am not myself and not well? That until I stop playing the Game People Play – call it 'Frogs' or 'Confrontation' or 'The Face Game' or whatever – I will never stop playing one or other of the many subsidiary games people play, and be free?

These are questions for putting to the test, a suggested programme of research and healing practice for transactional analysts who, beginning at home, are themselves coming out from under that numbing and suffocating spell into a spellbound world that very much needs them.

REFERENCES

Berne, E (1964). *Games people play*. London: Deutsch.

Harding, D. E. (1967). The face game. *Transactional Analysis Bulletin, 6*(22), 40–52.

Harding, D. E. (1974). *The science of the 1st person*. Nacton, Ipswich, England: Shollond.

Harding, D. E. (1986). Confrontation: The game people play. *Transactional Analysis Journal,* 16(2), 99–109.

Harding, D. E. (1986). *On having no head. Zen and the re-discovery of the obvious*. London: Routledge and Kegan Paul (Arkana series).

Harris, T. (1969). *I'm OK, you're OK*. New York: Harper and Row.

Steiner, C. (1975). *Scripts people live*. New York: Bantam Books.

BIBLIOGRAPHY

Some of these books I have quoted from. All have helped me in the writing of this one. My grateful thanks to authors and publishers.

Anandamayi Ma, *Words of Anandamayi Ma*, Anandamayi Sangha, Varanasi, India, 1961

Angelus Silesius, *The Cherubinic Wanderer*, trans. Trask, Pantheon, New York, 1953

Benoit, Hubert, *The Supreme Doctrine*, Pantheon, New York, 1955

St Catherine of Genoa, *Catherine of Genoa*, trans. Hughes, Paulist Press, New York, 1979

Chapman, Don John, *Spiritual Letters*, Sheed and Ward, London, 1954

Conze, Edward, *Buddhism*, Cassirer, Oxford, 1957

Davidson, H. R. E., *Scandinavian Mythology*, Paul Hamlyn, London, 1969

Eckhart, Meister, *Breakthrough*, trans. Matthew Fox, Image Books, New York, 1980

Eckhart, Meister, *Meister Eckhart*, trans. Evans, Watkins, London, 1947

Eliade, Mircea, *Shamanism; archaic techniques of ecstasy*, trans. Trask, Princeton University Press, 1972

Giedion, S., *The Eternal Present*, London University Press, 1962

Grant, Robert M., *Gnosticism*, Collins, London, 1961

Halifax, Joan, *Shaman, the wounded healer*, Thames and Hudson, London, 1982

Hasan Shushud, *Masters of Wisdom of Central Asia*, Coombs Springs Press, 1983

Herbert, Robert L., *Modern Artists on Art*, Prentice Hall, New York, 1986

Huang-po, *Zen Teachings*, trans. Blofeld, Rider, London, 1958

St John of the Cross, *The Dark Night of the Soul*, trans. E. Allison Peers, Image Books, New York, 1959

Laing, R. D., *The Politics of Experience and The Bird of Paradise*, Penguin, Harmondsworth, 1984

Leggett, Trevor, *A First Zen Reader*, Tuttle, Tokyo, 1960

Masunaga, R. M., *The Soto Approach to Zen*, Layman Buddhist Society Press, Tokyo, 1958

Milne, A. A., *When We Were Very Young*, Methuen, London, 1965

Muggeridge, Malcolm, *Something Beautiful for God*, Collins, London, 1971

Nag Hammadi Library, Ed. James M. Robinson, Harper and Row, New York, 1981

Nisargadatta Maharaj, *I Am That*, Chetana, Bombay, 1984

Ramana Maharshi, *Talks*, Ramanasramam, Tiruvannamalai, S. India, 1958

Rolt, C. E., *Dionysius the Areopagite*, SPCK, London, 1940

Rumi, Jalalu'din, *Discourses*, trans. A. J. Arberry, John Murray, London, 1961

— *Mathnawi*, trans. R. A. Nicholson, Luzac, London, 1926–34

Sartre, J-P., *Being and Nothingness*, trans. Barnes, Methuen, London, 1969

Selye, Hans, *The Stress of Life*, McGraw Hill, New York, 1978

Shree Purohit Swami and W. B. Yeats, *The Ten Principal Upanishads*, Faber, London, 1937

Society for Psychical Research, *Journal*, Vol. XXV, London

Strutte, Wilson, *Tchaikovsky, His Life and Times*, Midas Books, Tunbridge Wells, 1979

Suzuki, D. T., *Living by Zen*, Weiser, New York, 1972

— *Zen Buddhism and Psychoanalysis*, Allen and Unwin, London, 1960

St Thérèse of Lisieux, *Autobiography*, trans. Ronald Knox, Fontana, Collins, London, 1960

Trine, R. W., *In Tune with the Infinite*, New York, 1899

Vonnegut, Kurt, *Palm Sunday*, Granada, London, 1982

Waley, Arthur, *The Way and its Power*, Allen and Unwin, London, 1934

Warrack, John, *Tchaikovsky*, Hamish Hamilton, London, 1973

Wittgenstein, Ludwig, *Tractatus Logico-Philosophicus*, Routledge, London, 1961

Woodward, F. L., *Some Sayings of the Buddha*, Oxford University Press, 1939

Wurmbrand, Richard, *In God's Underground*, Hodder and Stoughton, London, 1969

CPSIA information can be obtained
at www.ICGtesting.com
Printed in the USA
BVHW04s1506130418
513214BV00001B/8/P

9 780955 451201